The Pursuit
of Happiness

The Pursuit of Happiness

The Lives of
Sudbury Valley Alumni

Daniel Greenberg, Mimsy Sadofsky,
and Jason Lempka

The Sudbury Valley School Press

ISBN#1-888947-25-X

Contents

Introduction

Why should the lives of the alumni of Sudbury Valley School be of any interest? To answer this question, it is necessary to understand the unique feature that characterizes the school.

The overriding concept that imbues every aspect of the school, and of other schools that operate on the same principles, is trust. To put it very simply, the school trusts, and asks parents to trust, that children are constantly working to understand the world they are in. We feel that a child's world expands enormously from year to year and that, if allowed to do so, every child will explore the parts of their world that are important to them. We are also convinced that, when they internalize the fact that they are truly free, all human beings endeavor to function at their highest levels. Because we are secure in the truth of these statements, we have always felt secure as a school to leave every decision about how to use and process the world around them to the people involved.[1]

That means that Sudbury Valley is a school that has never had any curriculum – not a "core" curriculum, not a "fun" curriculum, but no curriculum at all. Because we trust each individual to take

---

[1] The publications of the Sudbury Valley School Press provide extensive information about the workings of this model of education as well as its philosophical underpinnings. They are available from the school, or online at www.sudval.org.

responsibility for their own education, it is also a school that never imposes evaluations of any kind on its students, but trusts that students find ways to evaluate the way they do things, and the way they spend their time, on an ongoing basis and in a manner most appropriate for them.

Every four year old, every fourteen year old, and every forty year old who walks into the school notices immediately the trust that allows individuals of all ages to lead their lives in ways that are purposeful and intense. To be trusted means that you are free to go about your day in whatever way you wish, to choose values as well as activities in whatever way your wish, and to pursue your education and your happiness, whether in ways that look traditional or in ways that look decidedly different. Because so many decisions go into utilizing such complete freedom each day, every person learns, first and foremost, to trust themselves and their own methods of learning and growing.

At Sudbury Valley on any day you can observe students pursuing dozens of different kinds of interests. They are serious, and yet joyful at the same time. Serious, because anything is serious to you if you have chosen to do it of your own free choice. Joyful, because students who are fully trusted and completely respected are able to go about their day with happiness.

Part and parcel of the principle of complete trust and mutual respect is the idea that the people in a community should be the ones who manage that community. Therefore, each student at the school is a full voting member of the body that manages the school (the School Meeting), the body that makes policy for the school (the Assembly), and (when drawn by lot) the body that works to deal with disciplinary problems in a way that is fair and open (the Judicial Committee). To be trusted with these responsibilities brings home the seriousness with which the school takes its mission, as well as the seriousness of the burden on each person.

We feel that this way of treating students, which avoids patronizing them by treating each student and adult as full-fledged thinking and deciding members of the community, promotes an extraordinary flowering of self-motivation, of initiative, of creativity, and of leadership. We believe that the school provides an environment that trains each individual to think for themselves, and to lead an examined life that is fulfilling, meaningful, and fun. We are confident that the school produces leaders – most particularly, people who are unafraid to lead their own lives, and in the course of building that life often end up leading others.

The school first opened its doors in July of 1968, and since then close to a thousand students have attended. Over the years, they have talked to us about the ease of communication that they epxerienced at school, the respect they were accorded, and the way they learned, through exercising freedom, to develop judgment and take responsibility for their lives. From the beginning, the question most often asked about the school has been: "What kind of adults develop from children who have been trusted to determine the course of their own education?" This book answers that question.

About This Book

"It's impractical to settle for less than a life that we love."

> *What Should I Do With My Life?*, Po Bronson
> (Random House; New York, 2003) p.364

"Freedom gives us a chance to realize our human and individual uniqueness."

> *Between the Devil and the Dragon*, Eric Hoffer
> (New York, 1982) p.388

Overview

A huge chasm separates the educational goals and practices of Sudbury Valley School from those prevailing in most schools throughout the world today.

This alone has led many parents to wonder whether the decision to allow their children to attend Sudbury Valley might put them at a disadvantage relative to children who attend traditional schools. To be sure, Sudbury Valley claims to be an ideal environment in which children can develop into effective adults in the modern world. But is that claim justified?

More to the point, in the complex conditions that prevail in the post-industrial era, can children be trusted with the responsibility for planning and carrying out their own education?

With over three and a half decades of experience to call on, we feel that we can give unequivocal re-assurance to those who wonder whether attending the school prepares children adequately for life as adults. We have never been able to do so as well as we can now because, after tracking our alumni on four earlier occasions[2], we are finally able to present the results of an extensive, in-depth study of a large number

---

[2] *Legacy of Trust*, Daniel Greenberg and Mimsy Sadofsky (The Sudbury Valley School Press; Framingham, 1992). The book also contains the results of the three earlier studies.

of former students of all ages, in all walks of life, who were enrolled at the school during every period of its existence.

This book presents a comprehensive report of the results of that study. It contains a large amount of statistical data and, perhaps more important, it enables the reader to get acquainted with the alumni as human beings, by encountering what they have to say on a wide variety of subjects, in their own words, quoted extensively throughout the book. Reading this material, one cannot help but come away with the feeling that these people are an interesting, thoughtful, articulate, and varied group, who lead purposeful lives filled with challenge, hard work, excitement, and meaning – and who are comfortable with themselves and with the rapidly changing world in which they live.

The Aim of this Book

What kind of people are Sudbury Valley School's alumni?

We wanted to know all of the usual things one asks about people: what kind of work they do; what kind of families they have; what passions consume their lives now; whether they pursued any formal study after Sudbury Valley and, if so, what was its nature.

But there was a great deal more that we wanted to know. We were interested in finding out as much as we could about the character of our former students, their quality of life, and more generally, to the extent possible, their world views. To this end, we included a number of broader questions in our interviews, to give the alumni an opportunity to provide expansive replies.

The responses we sought were the personal, subjective views of the respondents as they talked about their own lives. What was important to us was how the respondents feel about their lives, how they evaluate their situations, without reference to external criteria. We proceeded from the point of view that in the last analysis each person determines his own set of values and sets his own goals, and each person must decide for herself whether her life is fulfilled and her goals are being realized.

There were several things we wanted to find out about our alumni. We wanted to see if people whose education had included many years in a setting such as Sudbury Valley were comfortable in their own skins and in their own communities, and whether they felt able to choose the lives they wished for and then lead the lives they had chosen. We also wanted to get a sense of the character of the community of former students as a whole – for, dispersed as they are, and as diverse in age, they are in a very real sense a community, recognizing in each other a common bond that stems from their unique educational experience.

We had another reason to do this study. Critics of the school have often claimed that placing a child in such an unorthodox educational environment restricts their ability to fulfill their potential and to lead satisfying lives. The claim is often heard that allowing children to be responsible for their own education and growth narrows the options they will have as adults and risks being a formula for failure. It was important to us to know whether our alumni felt constricted in their life choices. We felt this study was an adequate venue to determine the answer to this question because enough years had passed since the founding of the school to provide an alumni population that extended well into middle age.

We understand that neither this study nor any retrospective study of any school's alumni can prove a direct link between the program offered by the school and the adult lives of former students. There are far too many parameters influencing the life outcome of any individual to be able to single out with confidence a particular one, or set, as the determining factors. In addition, for any given school there is always a self-selection factor that governs its population and that underlies all future outcomes. Thus, we are not claiming in this study that a Sudbury Valley education will create adults who have the characteristics and lifestyles that reveal themselves in this book.

Nevertheless, as we will see throughout the book, former students had a great deal to say about the influence that they felt the school had on their lives. Even though these self-reported influences cannot bear the stamp of objective truth, they serve as a strong witness to the high value that most former students ascribe to their Sudbury Valley School experience.

We hope that, as readers progress through the material, the alumni will increasingly come to life and their personalities will emerge with ever greater clarity.

Who the Alumni Are

The target population of this study was former students who were enrolled at the school for at least three years, entered before the age of seventeen, were at least sixteen[3] when they left the school and left before 1998. We wanted to talk to people who had significant exposure to the school and who were old enough to be ready to go out into the world at the time that they left. The interviews took place in the years 2002 and 2003; the 1998 cutoff date was chosen to allow for several years of life experience after leaving Sudbury Valley.

The total number of former students in the target population was 199. Of these, we managed to locate and interview 119, or 60% of the total. Sixty-two of the people interviewed were males; fifty-seven females.

The following set of graphs display key features of the demographic range of the respondents.

---

[3] Two students were included who left the school shortly before their sixteenth birthday.

Figure 1 shows the ages of the respondents at the time of their interview. The median age of the interviewees was thirty.

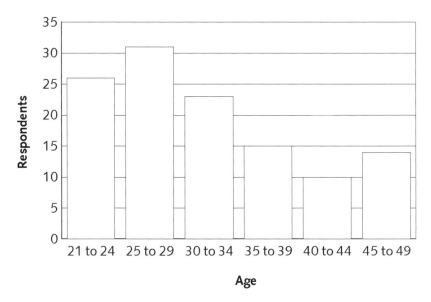

Figure 1 Age distribution of the respondents at the time of their interviews.

Figure 2 shows the distribution of entry years for the interviewees; the figure following it, Figure 3, displays the years their enrollment ended.

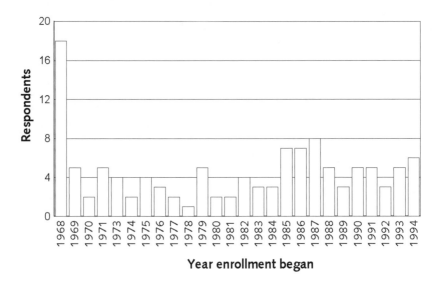

Figure 2 Distribution of years enrollment began.

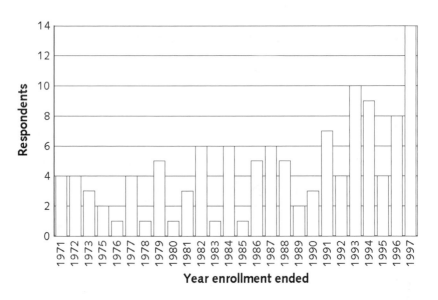

Figure 3 Distribution of years enrollment ended.

Figure 4 shows the distribution of ages of the interviewees when they first enrolled at school, and the figure following that, Figure 5, displays the distribution of their ages when they left school.

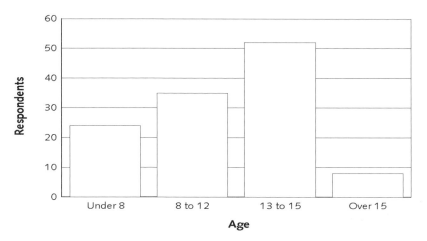

Figure 4 Distribution of age at enrollment.

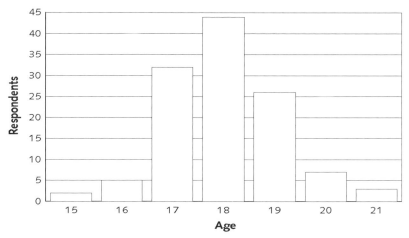

Figure 5 Distribution of age upon leaving school.

Finally, Figure 6 shows how many years the respondents were enrolled at school. The median number of years enrolled is five. A total of fifty-six of the interviewees, almost half, were enrolled six or more years and thus attended Sudbury Valley during what, in a traditional setting, would have been their middle school and high school years.

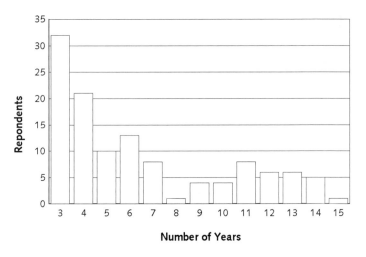

Figure 6 Number of years the respondents were enrolled at school.

The figures show that the group of alumni interviewed in this study represent a broad range of ages, life experience, and exposure to the Sudbury Valley environment. We were satisfied that they formed a broadly representative cross-section of our former students.

A word about the graphs in this study. Often, the total number of respondents displayed in a particular figure either exceeds or falls short of the total number of interviewees (119). The number exceeds 119 when some of the respondents fall into more than one category being graphed. The number falls short of 119 when some of the respondents did not provide information relevant to the categories being graphed. The number will be exactly equal to 119 when the categories are mutually exclusive and relevant information was received from each respondent.

About Their Jobs

"When I look around, people who went to Sudbury Valley are doing much more of a variety of things than people with more traditional backgrounds. They are not all just in college, or something like that. A lot of them are teaching dancing, or they're photographers, or they're living out in the wilderness – they're pursuing all different kinds of interests, being very individual."

Finding Jobs

Sudbury Valley School alumni go about finding work in pretty much the same ways as everyone else. Figure 7 groups the responses we got when we asked people how they got their jobs. The largest group of responses, "Just fell into. . .", refers to people who didn't specifically go after the position they ended up with, and includes those who were promoted within a company without actively seeking that promotion.

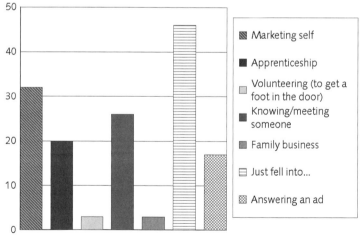

Figure 7 How respondents got jobs.

The comments some of the respondents made in the course of their replies were often colorful and conveyed the effect their SVS experience had on their job quest. Here is how a graduate described his effort at marketing himself as a chef with, one might say, sketchy qualifications. He had the job he wanted clearly in mind; his problem was getting to it without a long detour.

I remembered back to Sudbury Valley School days. One thing that I always enjoyed doing besides making music was hanging around with Margaret Parra, a great staff member who was a real good cook. She had taught me to bake when I was a kid. My mother didn't like to cook that much, but Margaret loved it. Over the years, to wind down I would bake some things that Margaret had shown me. So I just thought to myself, hmm, maybe I should open a restaurant. I talked to my friend who had become a restaurateur and I said, "Hey, I'm thinking of opening a restaurant." He said, "Well, if you want to open a restaurant, the first thing you should do is work as a cook. Learn how to be a chef, because the whole gig is, you can own all the restaurants you want, but your chef really has you over a barrel if you don't know how to do it yourself. That's where it's at." I said, "I know how to cook." He said, "Not just cooking pie in your kitchen, but learn how to cook food service style and how to manage guys in a kitchen." I knew a girl who worked at the Back Bay Hilton and she gave me a recommendation to the chef there. I kind of padded my resume, made up a thing or two. He hired me as a cook and I worked there for a couple of months.

Then I moved out to L.A. I went straight to L'Hermitage Hotel with this big story of how I was this fabulous chef from the Hilton in Boston, and I was able to get a job there. After a few months I moved over to the Beverly Hills Hotel. I was the lunch chef at the Polo Lounge for two years, and then moved back to Boston, and with my years at the Beverly Hills Hotel I got a good position as a chef at the Boston Harbor Hotel. By then I'd really learned what was going on. They had some great French chefs there. I was really good at never letting them know how little I knew. I was good at just keeping my mouth shut and doing what I did understand and then I would stroke them by saying, "Well, yeah, I do know how to do that, but I'd really like to see how you do it." I worked there for six years, so by then I'd had ten years as a hotel chef, which was fantastic.

Another graduate used the apprenticeship route to get to the same place:

I went to the best French restaurant in Boston and said, "Hire me," and they did. They hired me to cut vegetables, and they pretty much hired me on the spot. I had done some cooking training, but it was pretty useless. In a French restaurant, there's a pretty strong apprenticeship tradition, so they put you in and you suffer and work your way up. I went in as a vegetable-prep person and then they put me on as pastry chef and then they put me on the line and I sort of moved up. When I left I was a sous-chef.

Apprenticeship can work in many environments: "The fact is I've been assisting and teaching martial arts, and I learned this in an old-world apprentice style. This is my journeyman phase, if you will. I've been doing it for over a decade but professionally just for a year."

Volunteering can also be useful in getting your foot in the door. A graphic designer found a full-time job with a non-profit organization because "I had done volunteer work for them and then offered to do a little bit of work on the side, and after that they hired me." The apprentice chef we just encountered took the volunteer route in order to break into a completely different line of work:

I was working at the Art Institute. I started as a projectionist for them, projecting their shows and setting up their technical equipment, and then there was an administrative program coordinator type job that opened up. I asked if they would hire me. I'd done a certain amount of volunteer work for this organization, so they knew me. I guess volunteering is a good thing if you want to get ahead.

It doesn't hurt to know somebody when you are looking for a job, especially if that person gets a bounty for finding new hires:

> *I decided I really wanted to move back to the East Coast. A friend of mine had just gotten a job at Booz Allen and she was going to get a referral fee for everyone that she recommended who they ended up hiring. So I mentioned to her that I was looking to move back to the East Coast and she said, "Well, why don't you give me your resume. I'll give it to Booz Allen and maybe that'll work out." So I gave her my resume and a couple of months later they flew me out, interviewed me, and made me an offer.*

Sometimes a personal connection can be unexpected, as in the following case, where both apprenticing and volunteering played important roles:

> *I was always sewing at school. My parents weren't going to support me or pay for college, so Joanie sat me down and said, "What are you going to do?" and I said, "Oh, gee, I don't know. I mean, what do I like to do all day long? I'm in the sewing room all the time so I guess that would be good." I had no ideas what kind of jobs were available, or if I would make any money, or what there was. I knew I didn't want to be a designer because I wanted to design for myself but not for a job, so that I wouldn't be under that kind of pressure. Anyway, I didn't want to sell my creativity. Joanie's hairdresser's wife had been a designer and had a little business she was running out of her home, and I got a school apprenticeship where I went one or two days a week and trailed around after her and worked for her, you know, for free, for experience.*
> *When I was about to finish school and I needed a job she called up one of the brothers who owned Puritan (which became Calvin Klein Jeans). It was a very, very big company. Their factory was in Waltham, and he hired me. All this from Joanie's hairdresser!*

If your connection is a family business it can provide a healthy kick-start for a career:

I worked for my father's company. I helped him turn a computer that he had programed for his business purposes into a multi-user system and learned about how to do record-locking, and file-locking, and so forth, so that multiple users could access the same information, because his business was growing. From there I was able to get another position after leaving college with a small networking company, kind of friends of the family. I think they just hired me out of – I don't want to say pity, because I think the proprietor saw a little bit of skill in me, so he thought he'd take me on and see what I could do. Kind of a break here, a break there, and then the rest was learning and absorbing and making good decisions, I think.

There are many ways to "just fall into" a job. Here are just three examples from our alumni:

I got my job though a temp agency. I never had any formal computer training, so I couldn't really get a job the direct route, but this temp agency put me through a series of tests on computer ability and I just aced it.

I was living in Massachusetts and working part-time as a farmer, and then this farm came up for sale up here, and we just jumped at the opportunity. The farm sort of suggested that it was time to do it full-time – the availability of this beautiful farm made us leap into it.[4]

I went to Smith, had a great time, really enjoyed being a student and a scholar and planned to go on from there to get my Ph.D. in English Lit. and be a student and a scholar all my life. I went on to graduate school and kind of hit a wall. I wasn't really happy there; it wasn't what I wanted to do after all. So, I took a year off to kind of

[4] For the sake of clarity, when consecutive quotes emanate from different respondents, we have alternated between regular and lighter type faces.

say, "Well, what now?" and just process it and think about it. I spent that interim year working in a library in Boston.

I was the circulation clerk. It was a small library and I had a fair amount of responsibility and spent a lot of time working with students. I thought, "Hey, this is something I could enjoy, still within the world of education and scholarship. There's a lot of interesting things going on here." And so, from that time to this, I've been working in libraries, gaining experience, learning new things. That year gave me the impetus to get a Masters in Library Science.

Of course, there is always the looking-for-an-advertised-opening approach. This respondent was surprised at how well it worked for him:

Actually through an ad, believe it or not, because you can never get a job this way, but somehow I did. When I was still living in Maryland and I knew we wanted to move up to Massachusetts, I subscribed to an environmental jobs newsletter which listed jobs from all across the country. I saw this particular job advertised. I applied for it, and somehow I got it. I mean, it's really rare to get a job that way because whenever something's advertised nationally there's usually a very large number of people who apply. Somehow I managed to be the one who got it.

Alumni are clearly adept at using all of the avenues available to people in our society when looking for that perfect job. What those jobs are, and how the respondents relate to them, are the subjects of the following chapters.

Occupations

What kinds of occupations do former students pursue? In the interviews we inquired about what they are doing at present, and also what particular lines of work had been important to them since they left school. It turns out that their occupations run the full gamut of possibilities, from traditional to exceptional.

We classified the answers according to the system of standard occupational categories developed and used by the United States Department of Labor. Figure 8 shows the national breakdown of major job categories by percentage for the population in general. Figure 9 shows the breakdown of major job categories for our study population for all significant jobs held since the respondents left school.

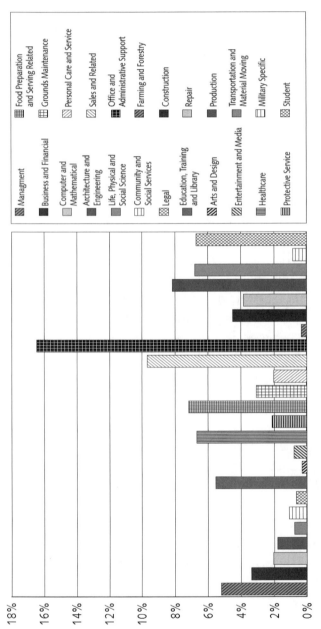

Figure 8 National breakdown of job categories for population in general. The ordinate represents the percentage of the population holding jobs in each category.

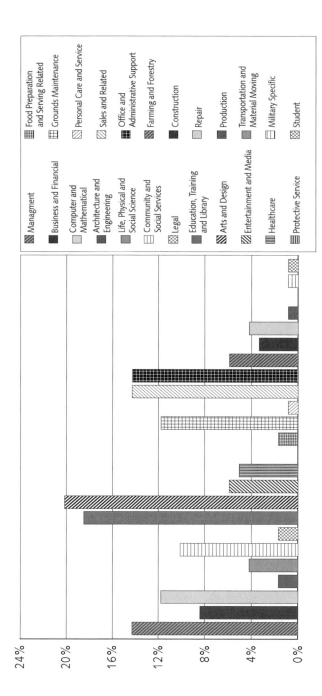

Figure 9 Breakdown of job categories for the respondents for jobs they felt were significant in their lives. Many respondents held jobs in more than one category. The ordinate represents the percentage of our study population holding jobs in each category.

We would not expect the national breakdown to correlate with that for Sudbury Valley alumni, because there are some demographic differences: our former students are somewhat skewed towards being more middle-class, more suburban, more New England, and more educated than the population at large. On the other hand, the distributions are more disparate than we expected. For example, a much higher percentage of alumni than the general population were in fields such as Management; Business and Financial; Computer and Mathematical; Education, Training and Library; Arts and Design; and Entertainment and Media. By contrast, far fewer (or none) of our alumni were involved in the areas of Office and Administrative Support; Production; and Transportation and Material Moving.

The following Table displays a list of the various jobs held by alumni after they left school. We organized them into loose categories in order to make the table easier to use. Most alumni held more than one type of job, and many of the jobs listed were performed by more than one of the respondents. The Table does not display every single job ever held by the respondents because, as we mentioned, we only asked them to tell us about jobs that they felt had been important to them. For some respondents, all the jobs they had ever held were significant; as one person put it, "I don't consider any of the jobs I have had to be completely unimportant." But for most of the respondents it was clear that they had held many more jobs than they mentioned in the interview, with the unmentioned ones being considered basically irrelevant to their main life goals.

It is also worth recalling that the median age of the respondents was 30 [see Figure 1, p, 17], so that there is a great variation in the spans of time during which alumni actually held jobs. Remember that the oldest respondents were not yet 50 and the youngest were still students. and that it was certain that the work history of virtually all of the respondents was still in the process of unfolding.

Table 1 Jobs Held by Alumni

Arts, Design and Entertainment
artist
art institute director
sculptor
art photographer
photographer
photo editor
graphic designer
jewelry creator
catalog designer
fashion pattern maker
novelist
musician
opera singer
actor
dancer
circus performer
theater director
television producer
video producer
documentary film maker
event planner
golf circuit tour guide

Business Related
management consultant
business analyst
accountant
business manager
marketing instructor
office manager
video business owner

research assistant
administrative assistant
bank teller
restaurant manager
cabaret owner/manager
regional manager, supermarket
    chain
food store manager
retail store manager
New Age store owner/manager
yoga studio manager
e-commerce manager
designer clothing shop manager
retail clerk
real estate agent
auctioneer
appraiser

Education
staff member Sudbury Model
    school
school founder
congressional advisor for science
    and technology
mathematics professor
geochemist
physicist
historian
librarian
assistant director of gymnastics
    school

Table 1 (Cont.)

assistant dean of students
university residence hall director
music history teacher
special education teacher
martial arts instructor
dance instructor
horseback riding instructor
student counselor
textbook editor

Health-Related
doctor
psychotherapist
nurse
social worker
EMT
Reiki practitioner
Shiatsu practitioner
massage therapist
patient care giver
recreation aide, nursing home
nanny
undertaker

Outdoor-Related
animal trainer
farmer
ecologist
arborist
self-styled "peasant"
backwoods guide
landscaper

Public and Government
lawyer
humanitarian aid worker
air force officer
coast guard officer
political candidate
political campaign manager
political activist

Technical
inventor
IT director
facilities supervisor, bio-tech
    company
software quality assurance
    engineer
software designer
database administrator
AI researcher
web designer
programmer
sound engineer
design engineer
data analyst
CAD developer
draftsman

Trades
chef
hair stylist
electrologist
seamstress

Table 1 (Cont.)

carpenter	industrial demolition worker
auto mechanic	house painter
bicycle repair technician	trucker
machinist	stage hand
solar energy installer	waitperson
building construction worker	bartender

Here is a sampling of the way the respondents describe some of their more colorful job situations. The samples offer a glimpse into the way they view their work worlds:

> *I did medical lab work which was my original intention when I joined the military, but it only lasted for a couple of years because right away the commander of the wing, the big guy on base, knew of me and knew that I did good work, and he needed someone to become a wing historian. Each unit has a historian, a sort of corporate historian. It's not public affairs; it's meant to be someone who captures the data about what we do, how we spend the taxpayers' money, what things work, what things don't, and it was a pretty big job for a very junior person in rank because a lot of it involves secret material and a lot of it involves sensitive stuff. You're not always going to get the straight skinny. It involves a lot of politics, but you sort of jump in there. I learned to write a little bit, and I learned to go after data.*

> *When I was in East Timor, I started out doing grants for the first few months. We were setting up our operations there and trying to put together some proposals to get funded so we could actually work. I was working for a nonprofit. And then I was put in charge of the shelter program, so it was a matter of going into communities, identifying beneficiaries, working with staff, training staff, and then doing distribution of shelter materials so that people could build homes. About 70% of the houses in Timor had been destroyed when the*

Indonesians left, so people were basically living under nothing or under blue tarps.

In Sierra Leone the work was more administrative in nature, because I was overseeing one of our field offices that had a number of programs. Some of the programs involved reunification of children with their families who were separated because of the war – for instance, some of them were abducted and forced to be soldiers.

Now I work on the Africa team and I'm the main contact between our office and our heads of staff in the field. Right now we have offices in Sierra Leone, Liberia, and we're opening an office in the Democratic Republic of Congo. I'm sort of the main person. If a policy issue comes up, if a procurement issue comes up, if somebody needs a truck, I'll do that. If they need to discuss how to liaise with the Ministry of Health I might support them on that. I'm basically a sounding board and a support person. My role is to make sure that they can do what they're there to do. I must say, I think I enjoy the field work more.

I was a chef for a while which was what I wanted to do when I left school. I got a job in a good restaurant and worked my way up. I did that in Boston for a while and then I moved to San Francisco and did it, but I got burned out and I got bored. It's a pretty high burnout profession. And then things sort of dovetailed: I started studying art and film at the same time that I was cooking. After that I worked for a non-profit art organization in San Francisco for about three years. That's where I got my first computer experience, which is important now because it's so much of what I do. The way media technology has changed, you can't really do what I do without being pretty computer literate.

When I moved to New York I was doing film and video editing, which I actually wouldn't define as important, in terms of work that I really love, but right now what I'm doing is working as a director/producer/camera person for documentaries and that's what I hope to continue doing. I think that the piece that I'm working on now will create opportunities for other pieces. I'm hoping that the work I'm doing now will build my reputation in the independent documentary field.

I'm working in the arts management field. I'm a director for an arts facility, which is a printmaking institute on an Indian reservation. I administer the facility and, because we don't have a program director right now, I do a lot of program development. I write grants, I do public relations and marketing, I do all of the graphic design and computer work, I operate a database, I do the budgeting, I schedule all the workshops and classes, and do facility maintenance, board development and lots of administrative things that have to do with operating a nonprofit.

Through this facility, people of high caliber are brought to this tiny little community to work with Native American artists and give them an opportunity to network and get a different perspective on what's out there and what's available to them. There's a high percentage of artists in the Native American community. We also work to preserve the traditional plateau arts – basketry, weaving, beading, things like that – that were dying out because nobody took the time to do them anymore. So we do workshops in that – cradle boards, shawls, dance regalia, all that kind of stuff. It's a really exciting and creative environment to work in and it's perfect for me. I collaborate with the Art Museum and the universities in the area, and so I've got a pretty good network.

I was a physics researcher; I worked at the National Academy of Sciences as a program officer; I was a science and technology advisor for a Senator, and then the founding executive director of a forum on technology innovation which provided a series of briefings for Congress on technology issues.

I have just started as the staff director of the Environment, Technology, and Standards Subcommittee at the House Science Committee. I'm responsible for a group of about eight professional staff who are experts in their fields. Each of them has a portfolio that covers certain federal agencies, and my job is to manage the whole process. I have to track issues but I don't know things in the same detail that the professional staff do. Our main function is legislative, so we're evaluating legislation proposed by others, we're proposing legislation, we're responding to issues that come up, we're responding to things that the administration does. We do a lot non-legislatively to push people in the direction that we want them to go by threatening to introduce something, that sort of thing.

The work that I do here and that I've done for years has little to do directly with physics or science, but it helps that I understand technical issues and understand how science and technology are accomplished.

Changing Careers

We saw in the figures in the last chapter that quite a few of our respondents have worked in more than one field. During the interviews, we asked people whether they are in the process of contemplating a change of jobs. Also, as they were talking about the jobs that they had held since leaving school which were significant to them, many respondents commented about their motivations for changing jobs in the past.

For some, it was a matter of looking for more meaning in their lives. One person, who felt he could not continue to pursue his primary passion, music, because of the compromises he would have to make in order to become financially viable, settled into a successful career in information technology, but found himself seeking something more.

> I don't think that this will be the job that I will do forever. I would like to combine this job with something more meaningful to me. Maybe I could be helping people who aren't as fortunate as me. I'd love to combine the technology that I get to work with now, with an end result that would further a cause that I cared about. That's not really happening now. My company makes money and the stock goes up. Well, it's great, but it's not my lifelong goal.

Another, equally successful at what she was doing – public relations for a major designer – did not feel she would be fulfilled until she found a consuming passion in her career.

> *I've actually always enjoyed working, so pretty much being engaged in any kind of a job has its benefits for me. But I wouldn't say I've had a job that's been the love of my life, which is the reason that I'm back in school and considering the options for the future. I haven't had that one job that leads me down the path that I love.*

An entrepreneur who owns a store that deals in "New Age" products, and has also enjoyed working as a photographer, was hoping to expand her business so that it could include a more comprehensive array of the passions that inform her life.

> *I'd love to expand into having an organic tearoom and coffeehouse, having a studio and having all my interests in one place, but I have to be realistic. I've realized that you have to start small and work up towards that. The nice thing about the property we're on is that there's enough room for expansion.*

Quite a few alumni who were doing work that was quite successful, in that they had lucrative and respectable jobs, nevertheless sought career change because they wanted more intellectual challenge. Here is a sample of three who were working in quite contrasting fields:

> *I hated psychology. For me, it is a fascinating topic theoretically, but to do it in practice just bored me to tears. It wasn't the clients; I really liked them, but it was just the whole practice of it – I couldn't stand it. It was just not stimulating at all. I find the practice of law much more stimulating.*

> *At the beginning I thought working in bicycle repair was quite nice. I had a chance to get out and work. I was making money,*

which allowed me to do stuff with people around me, allowed me to occasionally go out to dinner, occasionally buy a nice gift for someone I cared about. I got to buy a decent car. It was nice to be making a steady paycheck. I felt I was getting somewhere in life, but it got tiring after a little while because I was doing the same thing over and over again, and there really wasn't any better option for me within the company. That tended to make me tired of the company as a whole, because there wasn't anywhere else I could go within the company that would offer me the level of pay and benefits that I was getting and at the same time also be a better type of work for me.

When I was in college I had summer jobs programming computers, and those were essentially to make money, although they were also really interesting. I was working at Kodak in an internal computer programming department. Somebody would come and say, "We need some programs to run the computers in our warehouses to go and fetch merchandise when we order it"; or, "We need computer programs to keep track of inventory"; or, "We need programs to keep track of how long operators are spending at their terminal and what they're doing." So they would come ask this little department to write the software for them.

It was kind of an interesting look into the big business world, and it was also a really interesting job to have, because I'd always done a little bit of computer programming, and it's something that I'm reasonably good at because the skills required are sort of things that come naturally to me. One of the things I learned at this job is that the hard part of doing this kind of thing is not writing a computer program, but actually figuring out what the client wants. The difficult part isn't actually writing the software; the difficult part is figuring out how to make the application easy to use and make it do what people are going to want it to do. The difficult part is the design process, as opposed to the code-writing process.

So although this was a job primarily to make money, it was an interesting job too. When I was finishing college I was thinking, "Okay, what should I do now?" One thing I could do was work as *a computer programmer. That would be an easy job to get, it would pay well, and it was clear to me that I could also get promoted pretty quickly because I was good at the sort of human interaction required to determine what's needed in software design. On the other hand, it was also a boring job and I thought, well, it's not going to be interesting for very many years.*

So I ended up going to graduate school.

Occasionally changing careers was a matter of sheer burnout, as it was for the alumnus who worked as an undertaker:

I did that for about 20 years. Most people don't last that long due to burn-out. I was on-call 24 hours a day. I didn't have to go out and do anything in the middle of the night, but people would phone because somebody had died, and I had to make arrangements with our livery people to move the person, and phone coroners, and this and that. And being a manager was hard. I've had 15 to 18 employees in one place, and yet if something went wrong and somebody couldn't show up and they couldn't get anybody else, I had to appear and do it. That was my responsibility, to make sure things were covered, as well as running a business and seeing the clients.

Other times it was a matter of reassessing priorities, as when one former student began to realize that he wanted a fundamental change of lifestyle:

I got to a point in my mid-30s where I had kind of a crisis. I'd been living what was a really fantastic life, but I had a need for some normalcy and some balance in my life. It was a little bit frightening at that age to realize that I didn't have a lot of things that a lot of other people my age did. I was so out of touch with the idea of working a 40 hour week. I couldn't remember ever working a 40-hour week. I guess I did for a year or two when I was 18, but I was totally out of touch with having a 401K or having a dental plan or doing a lot of just normal things – having a wife or having a home or having a family or any of that. I was so much into being a rock 'n roll gypsy. Because although I did travel a lot and record a lot and get to meet tons of famous people and do a lot of limousine rides, it wasn't like I was a rich rock star. I was just parlaying one thing into the next. There were times when I had a little bit of money in the bank, but it would usually go to leather pants and hotel bills and whatever, you know? I suddenly looked in my closet and that's what it was: piles of leather pants and cowboy boots and all this stuff, but I had nothing that I could wear to a wedding or to a job interview and I didn't even know what kind of job I would interview for. And that was quite a hard thing.

So I faced it and said, "I'm going to go cold turkey. I'm going to work a regular job. I'm going to start at the bottom. I'm not going to work a straight job and play in a band at night." Because I knew, for me, my music was much more than a job. It was a lifestyle, it was the whole deal. It was very hard for me to just get together with some guys and play a song without saying, "Hey, let's learn a few more songs. Hey, this sounds good. Let's put this on the road." And once you're on the road you can't hold down a steady job. And plus, when you're 35, 36, it's a lot harder to be up all night with the young guys.

I got a job as a cook. I really enjoyed it. I learned a lot about cooking, I worked on a lot of big jobs, cooked for presidents and kings and rock stars, and got to get back into a real hard work schedule in a real world setting and got the things in order that I was talking about – my health plans and my 401ks and all that stuff, all got set up and started. And I felt a lot better about myself. It was a really good balance to my rock star days.

Of course, lots of alumni haven't felt the need for career change. As one put it:

Naah. Why change? You know, you don't whistle backstage. Do you know what I mean? You don't screw with what works.

Taking Charge of Their Work Life

Sudbury Valley places enormous emphasis on personal responsibility and independence. We were not surprised to find references to these traits popping up frequently as the correspondents discussed their experiences in the work world.

We saw above (in the Chapter "Occupations," p. 29) that a number of graduates hold, or had held, management positions. These generally imply promotions from lower level positions based upon the ability to perform satisfactorily. Here is how one person described his experience with this process:

> I was hired as a production control analyst. The job was basically 24/7 monitoring of the systems. They had a running read-out of how things were going. When the big red light went off, I had to try and fix it, and then try to call someone if I couldn't fix it. Anybody could have done it. I told them that at the interview. They laughed. That's what they were looking for. It was an entry level position. I moved out of it in three months.
>
> I had a lot of experience. I mean, I've been using computers since I was five years old. And I had been doing a lot of computer programming stuff as part of my degree. They knew from the interview that I was a smart person who could figure things out. So, they hired me sort of on spec, and it worked out.

I moved into a second level support position, which was basically who those people would call if they couldn't fix it themselves. That was not just support; we also released new versions of software, did testing, quality assurance, built procedures, all those upper level operational sort of tests.

Others describe the process more succinctly: "I started out doing work-study, and now I manage the whole place. I seem to do that in all of my jobs. I become the manager somehow." Or: "I was hired as an assistant to the catalogue creative person. Actually, four days into my job she decided that she was going to quit. So two weeks into the job, I went from being the assistant to the only person producing a nationally recognized, number two in the country, catalogue. It was 132 pages at the time." Or: "I've had four or five promotions since I have been here, so it has been a gradual ride up the corporate ladder." One person started as a temp, and "they very quickly said, 'We want you to stay,' and offered me a lot of money. Six months later they promoted me, and I said, 'Well, I wasn't really . . . okay.'"

Then there was the following tale:

My first job in the genetics company was washing pipettes, changing animal cages, and stuff like that. There were some people who let me do some scientific stuff, which was kind of cool. And I just sort of worked my way up from there, taking care of cell banks and incubators and other equipment.

Because I didn't have a degree, of course I had to work my way up. The job I'm in now started out as lab manager, and I moved from there to senior manager and then director.

Sometimes working your way up involved changing companies and attaining a graduate degree. In the following case, a jump start in a family company fueled an ambition for broader horizons, and ultimately for more meaningful work.

Every job I've had has been important to me. I haven't had very many of them. I worked for my father first. He had a factory and I worked for him for seven years helping run the factory. When I left I was the plant manager. We had 400 people working there, so that was a really great experience, to actually learn how to be a manager. Then I went to business school. After that I worked for the world's largest management consulting firm, McKinsey and Company, for eight years. Since I left there, I've been mainly doing consulting work, including a job in the not-for-profit world. I was doing the same kind of work I used to do in the corporate world, strategic consulting, but doing it for not-for-profit organizations. Now I'm in the process of negotiating a new job back in the corporate world in a start-up company doing marketing and management.

Several people introduced the "take charge" philosophy into the fabric of their work, figuring out ways in unusual settings to empower others. A university professor, working in an environment where students are often passive recipients of instruction, manages to do things a little differently:

In college, people aren't compelled to be there. They decide to come to college, they decide what they want to major in, and they decide what courses to take. My attitude toward my students is, "You guys have, out of your own free will, come and asked me to teach you this material which I'm an expert in. So that's what I'm going to do, and you can leave if you don't like what I'm doing." So, you know, I guess my attitude toward it isn't that different from the attitude I would have if I was working at Sudbury Valley and some student said, "I want to learn algebra." I would answer, "I know algebra. I can teach you algebra. Here are the rules for how I want to teach it, and if those are acceptable to you then let's set it up."

Now I realize there's a way in which I'm being slightly disingenuous when I say this, but what I'm explaining is my attitude toward my teaching. This doesn't necessarily follow for the students' attitude toward what they're doing. It is the attitude of some of the students.

The place where it's the least of a conflict is working with PhD students,
because these are students who have decided that what they really
want to do in life is learn pure mathematics really well.

A social worker found that trusting children in a difficult setting
can bring satisfying rewards:

> *I was the house manager for a residential facility. I happened*
> *to go into one of the most difficult, dysfunctional locations that the*
> *organization had. It contained girls from 12 to 17, that crucial*
> *adolescent age where they try to decide whether to go the wrong way*
> *or the right way. I think one of my biggest achievements was to bring*
> *them around and really create a culture there that was empowering*
> *to the kids who lived there while setting appropriate limits without it*
> *being so strict. I just applied Sudbury Valley principles and said, "This*
> *is how we're going to do things. It's going to be a democratic system,*
> *and everybody's going to have a say."*
>
> *At first they were just, "Oh, this is great, we're going to run right*
> *up and down the backside of this woman." But it was fabulous. What*
> *we created there was terrific. For example, kids were participating*
> *in creating dinner for everybody. It was a time that they sat down to*
> *eat their meals and everybody knew what their roles were, because*
> *they chose their roles. It wasn't enforced. As long as I was there, that*
> *was the smoothest running facility out of all of them. I was pretty*
> *proud of that.*

The most obvious way to take charge of your work life is to be
your own boss. Out of the 119 former students in our database, nine
were students at the time of the interviews who either had held no jobs
yet, or had taken jobs for the primary purpose of supplementing their
income while they were getting their education. Of the 110 remaining
respondents, over half (57) had worked in situations that did not have
rigid schedules beyond their control, and of these 49 had either been
self-employed or been the owners of small businesses. These figures

are remarkable when considered in light of the working population in this country at the end of the twentieth century, and more in line with predictions about the work world of the future.

Some respondents talked about their lives as entrepreneurs. One started her own business when "all of a sudden we had this opportunity and we secured the funds necessary and we just dove into it." A photographer is now "starting my own photography business. I'm in the preparatory stages, kind of laying the groundwork. I'm really excited about it. It's something that I didn't necessarily plan, but it all kind of came together and it made sense to do it."

A piece of luck gave another a kick start:

> My grandfather died and left me some money. So I took what I had and I bought a computer and I just started to get on the internet, etc. etc. One thing led to another. I started taking orders through a catalogue and that led to a mailing list and the mailing list wound up making a lot of money. The first year I just opened up a PO Box and I couldn't believe the amount of money that came through. It was just like hand over fist. It really worked out well. We wound up taking some of the money and investing it in small things like leasing a copier. I started to build up my credit and I just rolled things over. Just kept rolling it back over. What ever I took in, I'd put back into the business. And it just grew.

The hard work involved in keeping a business going didn't faze these entrepreneurs. A massage therapist talks about how she worked to build a private practice: "I marketed myself. That was how I did it. I walked up and down the streets and put pamphlets in people's doors. I kept calling the doctors and I kept repeatedly sending doctors information about myself." A jewelry designer admitted:

> Ninety percent of what I do for my jewelry is marketing. I love that aspect of it, but I don't like the front lines of selling. I don't like the face-to-face selling of my work to people on the showroom floor. I can

do it, and I do have to do it, but it's probably not one of my strongest points, and that's why I'm much more comfortable with wholesaling. I have a Web site. Up until this point, it's been focused on retail, but I'm switching it over to be more focused on wholesale.

One alumnus, who had already begun a successful business in art photography, and was becoming more involved with music, was driven to create his own venue:

I was a musician, and I hated all the places that I played because they were not designed with any kind of appreciation of art in mind. They're all designed to make money for the club owners. If you're an artist, then what you want is a place where you can do some focused work, where it's set up so that people can listen in comfort, and where the artist is set up to be supported with a good sound system, and where it is set up so that you can get to play very quietly or be very loud and the audience is quiet enough and impressed enough that when you're very quiet, you don't lose them. Not like a bar, where there's a din going on and where you can't get below a certain level or the din drowns you out.

Success brings the challenge of knowing where to draw the line, as an entrepreneur and inventor has discovered:

There are many reasons to take on a project. One is to be a good friend to someone who really needs help. Another is that it could be a job that looks like it's going to bring you into an interesting or different group of people. Sometimes, some other machine shop will really need something and I've always looked up to that machine shop and thought it was a really neat big shop, and it's really impressive that they're calling me. Then there's the consideration, "Well, this is what I'm all set up to do, and it will pay really well – it's an awful boring job but jeepers, it pays." And then there's, "This is really fun. I don't know if it will pay anything at all, but boy, I've always wanted to build one of those." Whole bunches of things go through your mind and cause you to over-book yourself!

But he never loses sight of the preciousness of his independence:

> *I only work now because I want to. I don't owe the bank a doggone penny. I don't owe anybody anything. Everything I have is paid for, and I do what I want.*

Traits They Display at Work

F̲ormer students had a lot to say about how they saw themselves in the work place. In Figure 10 we grouped their responses under broad categories.

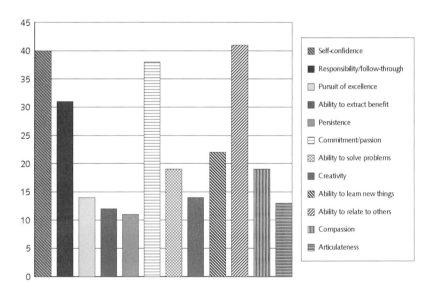

Figure 10 Respondents' self-perceived traits as workers.

We will encounter a lot of their perceptions in the next two sections. Here we would like to give a few examples of the way they articulated the characteristics they mentioned in their interviews. The figure clearly points to four traits as being particularly predominant in the minds of the respondents: the ability to relate to others; self-confidence; commitment/passion; and responsibility/follow through. Not surprisingly, for people educated at Sudbury Valley, social skills are mentioned most. For a librarian, it is the heart of the matter:

> I seem to intuitively get along with small children. I love books and I think I'm just a service-oriented person. I have the right mix of being introverted and extroverted. Also, I strongly believe in the concept of having a place with free information and the importance of the physical community and the physical books for children. I think I'm a great community programmer. Maybe that's really my calling, community programming.

For the musician who manages a café in an urban music school, his desire to nurture people through creating a sense of community has the highest priority:

> The real reason I'm excited when I'm at work ties into the café as part of the community. I know that I'm making the experience richer for all the people who are there fundamentally to do music, but who find the food and the gathering point a big part of that whole experience of sharing ideas and playing music for each other and jamming. I feel like I'm doing something that ties me directly into the music, even though what I'm doing at work is completely unmusical. I don't think any person interested in cooking per se would want to do my job, because it's not really about cooking, it's about the community of music; and there are not that many musicians who connect what I'm doing to the kind of feeling of community that I connect it to. So I am a in a particular odd little niche, which I defined for myself.

A feeling of self-confidence led to rapid promotion for someone who described herself as "a person who isn't afraid to try something new or something that I haven't had any experience in before. I also have the ability to say that I really don't know what I need to do, but I know where to find the resources from which I can learn." Another striking example of self-assurance was exhibited by a rather young graduate working in highly stressful conditions:

> *When I worked at an assisted living facility, we sometimes had people pass away, often in very dramatic ways. So I got very used to calling 911, giving CPR and Heimlich maneuvers, and dealing with strokes. I found out that I'm very good at making snap decisions about life and death under pressure.*

For the alumnus working in the environmental field, the commitment to his work stems from his deepest convictions:

> *My job is not just a job. I have a very deep personal and spiritual commitment to environmental protection and that is interwoven throughout my life. It affects everything I do. It's not a burden in the sense that some people take their work home with them and they're never away from the office. For me, it's more that I take my personal life to my job.*

A passion for his political ideals is what motivated this respondent:

> *I was always talking about political stuff with a friend, and she finally said I should run for office. At the time I was volunteering for a campaign, but I ended up making the decision to run because we really need people out there who are good solid Libertarians running for office. It was time to step up and do something. I definitely want to make a good show, and if I get elected, great, but we haven't had any Libertarian representatives in the state yet, so we'll just see what*

happens. It is something that I believe in, and most jobs just don't give you something like that; they are not usually something you love. I stay on my message, and I don't tell people what they want to hear to try to get a vote. I will outright tell somebody not to vote for me if they don't agree with me. That actually floors a lot of people.

Our graduates prided themselves on their feeling of responsibility towards their work and their ability to follow through on what they had started. One person got her job "by being the one who was able to take on a new project and follow it through from beginning to end." Another described the way in which his sense of responsibility drives his resistance to pressure exerted by parents of the students in the gymnastics school in which he teaches.

It's a very difficult dynamic there. I feel the need to honor my boss because it's his establishment and I work for him. I feel the need to honor the parents for bringing their children there. In a sense we all work for them. However, the most important thing, hands down, for both myself, my boss, and the parents, is the children. How can I best teach them to improve themselves? Any of the problems I've had have all been things that impinge on that or impede that. I've made some tough decisions that the parents didn't like, and my boss didn't like, which were based on students' safety and training. If a kid's being lazy – not if they're having a slow day, but if they're resisting me – I won't actively go after them, because I feel that that's their decision. This is part of my Sudbury Valley education: if you don't want to learn something, I can move heaven and earth and I'm still not going to get you to learn it. So I let that go.

But my one rule with children, and the children know this, is that no one may interfere with anyone else's gymnastics training. Anything that interferes with that gets adjusted, so when children who are training for competition show up late, they're put in a different group. The parents argue, "I'm paying good money. I want my kid in the competition training group." I say, "Great, you have to get your child here on time. On the days that they get here on time, they can be in that group, because I have to teach these children effectively, otherwise they will get injured. If I teach them a skill and then before a meet I say, 'Go as hard as you can,' and they get hurt, who do you look to? It's my responsibility. I take the responsibility. This is my decision and it's not for me, this is for the kids." So that's how it is, and then my sanity fits in there somewhere.

Our alumni talked a lot about their high standards in their work. The pursuit of excellence is something that is part of their everyday lives, whether they are professionals, tradespeople, or staff members at a Sudbury school.

I'm a family practice doctor, and therefore I tend to be involved in a lot of family dynamics, a lot of counseling, things like that. I enjoy it and I think I'm good at it, but it is very draining. I don't like to have the feeling, when I come home at the end of the day, that I've kind of given my all to other people and I don't have much left for my family. That's one of the hardest things about being a doctor, and I didn't anticipate when I went along this path how all-encompassing it would be. I was a person who liked to dabble in a little bit of this and a little bit of that. And between work, which involves a lot of my time, and then the time that I need to do things related to work – looking up things that I don't know, going to conferences, going to meetings – it really takes up a huge amount of my free time. But there's this part of me that knows that if I'm going to do it, I have to do a good job, so I have to do those things.

All the carpentry has been totally through word of mouth. I've never had any advertisements or even a business card, and I really have more work than I can handle. I rely on doing a good job and having people recommend me.

We never advertised. We always went by word of mouth. And we always said, "We are NOT professional painters." Because professional painters would paint in the drizzle, you know, whenever. But we are environmentalists first. So when we put toxins on surfaces, we want to make sure that they will really stay. If it rains, we always let it dry for a day or two and never paint when it's damp. We end up painting sometimes on the weekend if that is when the weather permits, and if it is raining, we take time off.

When you come and work with me in the kitchen for a couple of hours, you really do work and it's very disciplined and it is like a cooking class. That's just the way I do it. And that's kind of the way it is in the music rooms too, which has caused some unhappiness. I don't think I'm one of the most popular staff members because of that, because I've worked hard while I've been here to outfit our music rooms with great equipment, a really nice recording studio. But the way I look at equipment is a little different from the way your standard 15-year-old guy looks at his equipment lying around the floor in his room. When I was on the road, nobody screwed around with the band's equipment. If some kid was caught playing around with Joe Perry's guitar, we'd bring him out back and handcuff him to a bicycle rack and leave him there, you know? It was pretty hard core!

Quite a few people talked about their ability to extract benefits from all sorts of work situations, even those that were far from ideal. As one put it, "I think I've gotten something out of most of the jobs I have had," and added, "If nothing else, I've learned that it is not what I want to do."

Here's how one former student, a professional ballet dancer, discussed the quality of persistence as it related to his training:

A particular teacher sort of glommed onto me and sat me down and said, "Well, do you want to be a professional? Or do you want to just do this on an amateur level?" He was willing to work with me intensively, and so I said, "Well, I guess I'll do it professionally." So off we went, and off I went. I worked really, really hard; I'm not a quick study in anything in my life, but I've got a real stick-to-itiveness and a persistence and I'll get onto something and hang onto it until I get it. That's probably my greatest attribute.

The ability to solve problems was mentioned by several respondents as an important quality they possess. Typical was the following comment of a social worker:

I chose to work in a residential care center that was actually in disarray a little bit. The staff were being sort of insubordinate and kind of up in arms. You know, sort of blocking the system, lashing out against anyone in management. I thought, "Hmmm. . . there's something going on here." What I did was problem-solve for them, figure out what was happening, how I could help them, and how we could get the job done. They've been really receptive to that. They have a certain amount of respect for me as I do for them, and I think it was sort of this team effort.

A carpenter felt his creativity was a particularly noteworthy aspect of his work:

They come to me for ideas. I like it. That's what I do best. What I try to do when people ask me questions is teach them the train of thought to figure it out, and explain why I came to a certain decision – why this would be best, and here's how you think about it.

Flexibility – the ability to comfortably learn new things in new situations – is a theme mentioned by many former students, and appears as a constant background to the work history of the following person.

When I left Sudbury Valley, I didn't think I wanted to pursue an engineering degree. I was interested in electronics. I didn't know whether I had the aptitude for it. When I graduated, I based my thesis defense on becoming an electronic technician through self-study. I did that and found it difficult to get a job in the early 70's. The economy was in recession. At any rate, I ended up, because I was also involved in music and sound, working with Mach Bell's group, ThunderTrain, as a sound engineer. I did that for five years, and along the way I bought a few little electronic instruments and did some more studying on my own. I learned how to repair amplifiers and basically finished getting a technician's background. In 1980, somebody told me that a company that made professional audio equipment was looking for people. I got a job there and spent a couple of years in the production test environment as a test development technician and supervisor. I then moved into the design group as a design engineer/technician. I started taking math courses at night. I felt I didn't have enough career opportunities at this company, so I went to a head hunter, and got a position at one of the divisions of Analog Devices as a technician. Moved from that division to being a design technician. Moved into the AD Products Testing division, where they asked me to do things that normally a technician wouldn't do.

They said, "Here's a new computer automation design station. Figure out how to simulate all the specifications for this product." I said, "Oh, ok." I started opening up the books, started asking questions, and continued taking some courses at night. The company eventually realized I was doing engineering level work, and promoted me as a non-degreed engineer. A few years later, I was a senior design engineer, and a couple of years ago, I was promoted to staff design engineer.

Although quite a few respondents identified compassion as one of their key qualities, the following person exhibited this trait in an environment often portrayed as cold – that of an advisor to college students wishing to pursue a medical career:

I think it's good for them to have somebody like me advising them because they get an awful lot of pressure from their families, and they live in a high pressure environment with their peers. They tend to get tunnel vision, and they need somebody who is going to sit them down and say, "Look, this is not all that life has to offer you. It's a wonderful thing if you can go to medical school and be a doctor, but think about it before you make such a commitment. Explore a little bit. Chill out, don't give yourself a heart attack."

I think it goes over as well as it can. That message is most commonly given to students, when it's clear that they're going to have trouble getting into medical school – those whose GPA's and test scores are just not up to par. So I'm often the person who's telling them what they need to hear, but what they don't want to hear. I think it's good for them to have somebody whose perspective is a little bit different.

It's to be expected that several alumni felt that being articulate was one of their strong points in the workplace. Here is a typical response:

When I have had good job opportunities, I have generally been able to impress my employers very rapidly. That's been one of my biggest advantages. I can speak well in interviews; I do well in meetings. I'm very active in business social situations, for example. Not in terms of dinner parties or things like that, but you take me to a meeting and I will always be an active participant in what's going on. I can get into analysis and problem-solving very easily. Those are probably my biggest strengths, by far.

In the next sections we will see these qualities re-appearing in several forms, providing the framework within which former students approach the work world.

Why They Chose Their Jobs

"I was looking for what it was next that I was going to do in my life and a bit stressed out about that, and it was sort of like a brick fell out of the sky and said, 'Hello! This is what you love doing! Figure out a way to make a living!'"

They Couldn't Help It

Over half of the alumni have lifelong passions that develop organically into the ways they earn a living. For one, it is farming:

> Farming is the main passion of my life. I think about it all the time and just throw myself into it. It's something I can't imagine not doing because I enjoy it so much, and people enjoy the food so much.

For another, it was playing music, any music:

> I was performance-oriented. I'd play with three or four bands at a time, so I was playing almost every night of the week. I did studio session work, I did a lot of sit-in work, plus I had my own acts. I had an Irish act with one guy, I had a wedding band with another guy, Top 40 bands, country bands – I was a musical slut. People who knew me and liked what I played would ask, "Can I use you on this thing? I need a player."

For an ardent feminist, it was finding a venue to promote her ideals:

> Right after graduating from Sudbury Valley, I started working for Planned Parenthood. I had stated in my thesis defense that I wanted to work for an organization like Planned Parenthood, because I believed

in the pro-choice cause. It was something that I really believed in and still do, although working for them was very hard.

Several former students developed their passion for rock and roll music while at school. Here is one person who followed that passion into stardom:

> *As a student I was already working weekends as a musician. I felt that something big was coming in music. I had been going to the shows locally, when Jimmy Hendrix came to Framingham, when Led Zeppelin came to Framingham, and even though those shows didn't sell out I knew that this music was going to be something really big, and I wanted to be a part of it. And sure enough, my second year at SVS was when Woodstock happened and this whole social, youth, music, and capitalism thing all converged. So I had my own small musical group. I was only 16 at the time, but I was learning a lot from what I had seen and what I was experiencing. As soon as I left school I picked up the pace. I started to move more into Boston. By the time I was 20 years old, for local kids, I was somebody that they had seen on stages doing the local gigs and high school gigs and the battle of the bands, and I had a name for myself already and was one of the more established people in my area. A few years later, I moved into New York City, and then from New York I moved national.*

Then there was the alumnus we saw in the last chapter who fell in love with classical ballet while a young student at school, became a successful professional dancer, and then later in life discovered a new way to follow another of his lifelong passions:

> *After I finished my graduate work, I taught dance for a while at the University until I became really tired and burnt out. The whole thing was a real struggle for me. It was very fulfilling and I learned a lot from doing it, but it made me very tired. I said, "You know what? I'm just going to go play golf for a couple years and chill out and sleep." And so I went and played golf for a couple of years – I*

worked at a hotel at night to pay my bills and played a ton of golf every day. Through that process, every time somebody came along and asked the concierge about a golf course or anything related to golf, they would call me up and I'd answer the question. It got to the point where people were saying, "Where should I golf?" and I'd say, "Well, I'm golfing tomorrow. Do you want to come with me?" and we'd go. Some German people came into town one year and I brought them to a local club maker and got some clubs for them and I just thought, "Why am I not making a living doing this? It's what I love doing," and so I started a company.

I was looking for what it was next that I was going to do in my life and a bit stressed out about that, and it was sort of like a brick fell out of the sky and said, "Hello! This is what you love doing! Figure out a way to make a living!"

Occasionally, a respondent would simply follow their gut intuition into a career path. After pursuing her equestrian passions and her urge to drive commercial semis cross-country, this woman began to consider enlisting in the Air Force:

I wasn't ready to settle down. I had no clear cut goal. I didn't have anywhere to go. I had things to do but I really didn't have a plan. Looking back on it, I think the appeal to me was that this would give me some boundaries and give me a goal. It would let me push my energy down one long straight tube instead of just having all my energy dissipate north, south, east and west. I knew that I might really hate it – I was pretty much warned, "Wow, the military, you're going to hate it."

I knew I could fail without it being a disaster. I figured that it's pretty easy to get out, so what the heck, I could get the training that I want. I went to some bases to check them out, asked them to take me around and show me, and I was assured that they're pretty normal people like me. There's room for thinking minds and they're not going to pluck my brain out and replace it with Styrofoam or if they do it will be a very long process and I won't be aware of it. And it turned out to be true. I won't say it was good strategy because I don't think I really planned it as well as this may sound. It was more of an intuitive thing.

As might be expected, a great many children enroll at Sudbury Valley because they are ardently independent. Quite a few alumni retain this desire to be their own boss throughout their lives:

I didn't want to work for somebody else. I'd worked for everybody. I don't know how many different, stupid jobs I had. So I said, well, everybody that I know who has made any money has usually worked for themselves or started out that way. There's no ceiling. What you make is only dependent on how much you put into it. It really is. If you work for somebody, you're going to wind up getting to a ceiling – you're going to get to a certain point, then you ask for a raise, etc. etc., like my brother did: his ceiling was $500,000, which he bagged. The point is, in a professional position, you wind up getting ceilings. I didn't want to do that. I wanted to do something I can take and do whatever I wanted with. I figured what the hell else was I doing? I had money in my pocket so I didn't have to worry about anything. So I took what I had and I invested in me and it wound up paying off.

Over and over again, we found former students driven to pursue their occupations by a desire to fulfill long-standing dreams, passions, or gut intuitions. Other considerations played a secondary role, and they took whatever route they had to in order to continue following their primary interests, as the following young woman did:

I was acting all the time I was living in the Boston area, but not seriously. I did plays here and there. I got a lead role in a full-length independent film and that was a lot of fun. After I was done with that, I decided that I was going to move to New York and take it very seriously for at least the next couple of years, just because I loved it and it was now or never.

It's Right for Them

Sometimes a person chooses a job because it is a good fit for who they are or where they are in their lives. Sometimes they know this while they are seeking that type of work; other times they discover it happily after they have begun a particular type of work.

Several respondents found that their line of work meshes perfectly with their natural talents. A naturally shy person who cares very deeply about others chose documentary making as a way to realize an essential feature of her personality:

> I have pretty good empathetic skills so I can kind of key into people and better enable them to be who they are or express who they are. As a nonfiction film-maker, I'm very interested in this. I have no interest in doing fiction work; I have no interest in writing things and putting words in people's mouths. I'm fascinated with real people, how they live their lives and what they do. It's the greatest sort of privilege to be able to hang out with people and have them open up and reveal who they are and how they live their lives – to share that and be able to capture it and make stories out of it.

An alumnus who was seeking a particular spiritual and intellectual environment – and who also happened to like cooking and sports – found a way to satisfy all of his natural inclinations:

I was the chef at a center for holistic studies, the largest of its kind in North America. It is basically a venue for many kinds of different thought. Meditation and yoga classes are their bread and butter, but there are all kinds of other things. A Nobel Peace Prize runner-up is there every year for a program that runs from mid-March to mid-November. And really, any kind of out-there ideas would come through. It's a neat place. In return for my work, I was able to attend a workshop every year, and every year I would also take a basketball camp that was led by Phil Jackson. I got a lot out of that – I got to know Phil and I was able to hone my basketball skills.

Youthful passions didn't have to be set aside in order for this respondent to earn a living:

I've always been a gear-head through all my studio stuff, and through my contacts working in music retail, I happened to meet a friend. When I started realizing music wasn't ever going to pay the bills, a couple of opportunities came up to work at the place where he worked, a company that manufactures nonlinear digital editing video systems, and I just was persistent. I kind of snuck my way in basically at the ground level, and I worked my way up to be test manager.

An estate appraiser and auctioneer got into that field because, "I've always liked antiques. I grew up with antiques, my parents had antiques, my grandparents had antiques. They were all fairly knowledgeable about them so probably when I was six years old I knew what a Queen Anne chair was."

Another alum who grew up in an environmentally conscious home, and pursued "green" interests throughout her youth, ended up living her adult life in the same manner:

I'm a peasant. We grow a lot of our own food. We make our own firewood, and I do side work every once in a while. I work with my partner – he's a solar electricity guy – and so every once in a while

I put on the solar technician belt and help put up and install solar power. I'm also the bookkeeper for the business and I'm an artist, so I have some paintings and other artworks in area galleries.

A highly successful realtor chose that field because she felt it was a good fit for her lifestyle:

I put a lot of time into thinking about what I would like to do with the next several years of my life. I spent months thinking about it, writing about it and just kind of going over the different concepts and I finally suddenly hit on real estate because it could meet all my goals: my children were just at the age where I needed to be home in the afternoons, so I wanted all kinds of unusual hours and I wanted to have summers with them. One of my highest goals at the time was to spend more time with my children because I could see that they were growing up very quickly.

Typical of those who chose their occupation in order to further career goals that were not directly related to the job, was the following respondent:

I'm an accountant right now and that's what I've been doing for a while. It's not something that I'm particularly talented at but I think it's good exposure. It's not something that I plan on doing for the rest of my life. I wouldn't say that I don't like it, but I just view it as a stepping-stone to being an entrepreneur, having my own business. I'm basically doing it so I can learn finance, so I can run that aspect of my own company.

A devoted performing musician took work as a café manager in a large urban music school in order to combine his love of music with his passion for being immersed in a culture of people sharing a common interest:

The fact is that the culture of the rock-and-roll band is a very odd little subculture within American culture. It's basically a group of people who get together to do something creative – to make some music. They hop in a van together and play shows. It's a very odd kind of a family. Even the most egotistical bands, where one person is making all the arrangements and writing all the songs and doing everything, are much more communal affairs than you imagine, because they're still ultimately all riding in the van together, they're still all getting up there and playing their instruments, and how good it is depends on how well they mesh. The school I work in is sort of an odd place, where the general subculture of a band and the particular subculture of the school have kind of dovetailed. It is something that a lot of musicians who have been in bands can instantly identify with. I see that same dynamic and get that same sort of satisfaction with hundreds of people, at the school. It's not as intimate as the people you're actually in a band with, but when you realize that everyone is doing this for the same reason it becomes just that much more exciting. It becomes much bigger. I certainly feel a band-like kinship with a lot of the people I work with. We're all pretty much in the same boat. Most of the administrators are also musicians. They're doing that job because they love music first, and they also know they're competent in organizing something. We all have a mutual respect for each other's musical entities, but we're expressing it by getting together to make this school a reality.

To Serve Others

Twenty-one of the respondents said they chose their jobs because they are interested in teaching. Here is how two of them, who work in widely different fields, expressed it:

> I taught acting for a while and that was incredibly important to me. It was probably one of the most rewarding things I've ever done, and I actually left it because I loved it so much that I decided to get out there and do as much acting as I could before I went back to teaching. Because eventually that's definitely what I would love to go back to doing.

> Any glimmer of real interest in my subject is satisfying to see. Some students ask questions about how this impacts their life: why do we care about global warming, or why do we care about the greenhouse effect, or why do we care about floods and hurricanes? We talk about geological issues and where you build your house and where you live and why floods should be expected in certain places and not others. That's a lot of fun. I also teach a class for graduate students that's very close to the field I do research in. That's more like a peer interaction, except that I do a lot more of the talking.
> When you're teaching science, I think it's very important to keep your personal views private. It's important to try to prevent students from thinking that having a certain view will be good for them. The

whole point is to try to convince people to analyze things critically, and carefully look for evidence, without jumping to conclusions.

More than forty respondents said that they were specifically looking for a way to be of service to others. One respondent said, "I always wanted to work with people, helping people. It turns out I kind of had a knack for it." Another person joined the Coast Guard to satisfy this desire:

> *I always wanted to do something in the law enforcement field. When I left Sudbury Valley everybody was saying you need a college degree to do law enforcement and I really wasn't into going to college. So I looked into the military. I was looking for the Military Police and I talked with the Army and the Marines and the Navy, and they said they couldn't guarantee that I could be an MP. Then I talked to the Coast Guard recruiter and he said, "We don't really have a Military Police. We don't police ourselves, but we do law enforcement on a daily basis everywhere else." So I joined and I got to do four years of law enforcement in Cape May, New Jersey. That was really what drew me towards the Coast Guard, plus the whole peacetime mission – you're helping people out all the time.*

A former student who was highly trained in the martial arts found that he looked for a service feature of any job he took. One in particular led to a striking opportunity:

> *I've had a very wide selection of jobs. I think a lot of them I've done at least a little bit to touch other people. I was a new student program counselor at my university. The program included being a tour guide, and a guidance counselor, and a camp counselor all rolled up in one. I think that was a really good job – getting introduced to basically everyone that was going to be in the university community for the next year – and it allowed me to make contacts with a lot of people that are in administrative positions in the university.*

One of my greatest successes was about two years ago when there was a very large rape scare on campus. There were a number of assaults against women in broad daylight. The campus police force reacted by teaching rape aggression defense classes. I've always had a serious problem with that particular approach; in my personal opinion it's not very useful. From my experience as a resident advisor, I knew a lot of the police officers, including the one who was involved in teaching this, and I told her, "This is basically useless for rape defense." She said, "If you can do better, go ahead." So every night, I'd have thirty or forty women come in, and I'd teach them a class on what I felt was really useful – rape defense and rape awareness. A lot of people came back the next night and the next night and the next night. I had a lot of new people every night and this went on for about a month and a half. It just made me feel really good. I saw people's awareness go up and I feel like I had a small part in helping curb that terrible pattern on campus – a very small part, but a part nonetheless.

Then there was the alumnus for whom helping others seemed to be at the very core of his existence.

I went round and round on my conscientious objector status. They turned me down several times. One night, I was called for a personal appearance before the draft board. It was the night of the Stanley Cup playoffs. It was pouring rain, and it was the night after Nixon had announced the mining of the harbor at Haiphong. So here I am, sitting on the Group W bench. The draft board didn't want to be there, either, and they were not pleased with me. I said, "I work at this house," and that we were full-time volunteers. We didn't get any money, just room and board. And the guy was being antagonistic and he said, "Well if you're a full-time volunteer, who bought those clothes you're wearing? The archbishop?" I said, "Well, you know, it's funny you should ask, because it's a little embarrassing. We collect clothes for men on the street and because we don't have any money, from time to time when something fits, we'll just wear it." It was like suddenly somebody had opened the windows, birds had come in and started landing on my hand; I mean, I was suddenly genuine. They knew that I was genuinely crazy. I think the lady who was the secretary of the draft board always liked me because I was always polite when I came with my forms – I never poured any blood on her! I went outside, and I have always had the feeling that she said, "Oh, let's give it to him," and they made me a conscientious objector. I then had to spend two years doing civilian alternate service, and I did. As quickly as possible, I got a job as an operating room orderly.

For the first week, when you go to work you're a "conscientious objector" working in the operating room. But after that, you're just really somebody who's doing a lot of the jobs, and you can't quit. I sort of ended up in that hospital thing and I worked as an operating room orderly, and a regular orderly, and an occupational therapist assistant, and a central sterile supply supervisor, and a pharmacy technician, and ended up being a purchasing agent for pharmaceuticals at a well-known cancer treatment center at the end of my health career.

In these three chapters we have looked at most of the key reasons respondents gave for choosing their occupations. Figure 11 on the following page displays the full range of reasons given by the respondents, grouped into several broad categories.

Overall, as can be seen from the figure, and as was illustrated in these three chapters, by far the largest number of respondents reported that they chose their jobs because they had a passion for what they are doing, or because it fit their native talents, or because it gave them an avenue to serve others.

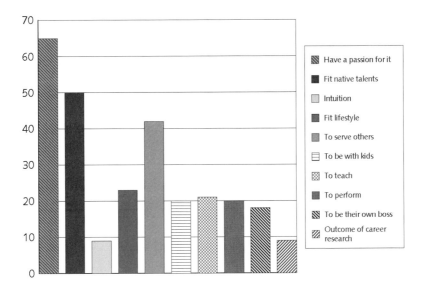

Figure 11 Respondents' explanations for why they chose their line of work. Many respondents gave more than one reason.

Why They Like Their Jobs

"Have a hard time going home at night. Too much fun working."

The Many Faces of Satisfaction

In the last section we looked at the various factors that contributed to the respondents' choices of their occupations. In this section we are going to examine their feelings about the jobs they have chosen. Inevitably, there is a lot of overlap in the language they used when replying to these two different lines of questioning: more often than not, the reason a person chose a job turned out to be validated in their work experience. The reader will recognize some of the same people they met in the last section as they read this one, but many significant new factors emerge as they talk further about their work.

When respondents were asked directly what they liked about their jobs, their answers usually encompassed a broad range of factors. Consider the following reply:

> The job that I have now is very close to being my ideal job. I'm the administrator for a town's Conservation Commission. I'm essentially in charge of a wide range of environmental work in the town, both from the standpoint of reviewing and permitting construction projects in or near environmentally sensitive areas, as well as managing about 550 acres of conservation land almost from a park ranger standpoint. And it's terrific – I love the people I work with, I love the town, I'm given a lot of freedom to structure the work environment in a way that meets my needs – it's terrific.

Being at the local level really helps. When I worked as a consultant to the federal government, it was just so far removed from what was happening on the ground. I mean, I might be writing a report that would help create a policy that might be used by a local organization to do something in a particular location, but then again it might not, and even if it did I wouldn't know about it because the end result was so far removed from the work that I did. So I really like working at the local level where I can see the results and the fruits of my labor right in front of me.

I work on so many different things in my job and they're really all interesting to me. The only part of my job that I don't like is the law enforcement side of it; if people are committing violations of the State Wetlands Protection Act or the Local Wetlands Protection Bylaw, I have to issue fines, violation notices and enforcement orders, and tell them to clean up the mess or replant trees that they've cut in prohibited areas. That can involve conflict and nobody likes conflict. I can handle it, but it's not my favorite part of the job. Aside from that, everything else I do, I love. I'm really in the right place.

In the above passage, teamwork, location, autonomy, fulfillment, variety, public service, are all seen to contribute to the respondent's high degree of pleasure in his work. Figure 12 displays the full range of reasons given in the interviews for finding work satisfying.

The reason that appeared most frequently, by a good margin, was "service to others". Other factors that appeared to stand out were "challenging work", "meaningful work", "relating to other people", "fun" and "hands on work".

In the Chapter "Who the Alumni Are", Figure 6, (p. 20) we saw that forty-three of the respondents had spent seven or more years at the school – that is, they spent at least part of what would have been their elementary school years, as well as what would have been their middle and high school years, at Sudbury Valley. When analyzing respondents' replies throughout this work, we routinely compared the distributions for all the respondents with the distributions for the forty-three very

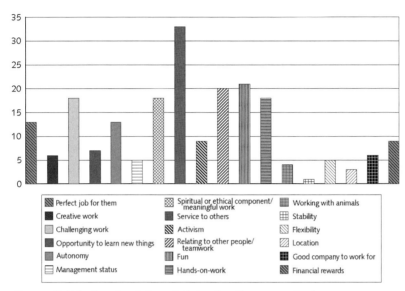

Figure 12 What makes jobs satisfying for the respondents.

long-term students. Generally, there was no significant variation between the two distributions. However, in this case we found some interesting differences, as shown in Figure 13.

Whereas 17% of the full group reported taking pleasure in their jobs from relating to other people, 33% of the long-term group described this factor as important to their work satisfaction. Having fun was mentioned by 18% and 26% of the two groups, respectively; and enjoying hands-on work was mentioned by 15% and 26% respectively. It would appear that the long-termers were a little more focused on the interpersonal aspects, the enjoyment and the experiential nature of their occupations.

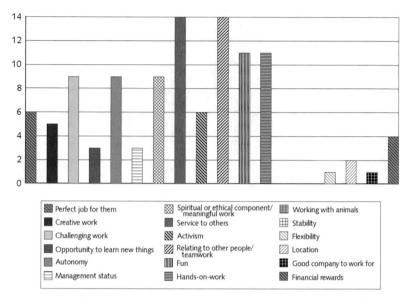

Figure 13 What makes jobs satisfying for the alumni who were long-term students.

Quite a few people were pleased that they were working in a company that was particularly enlightened. Here are two comments:

> It's a really good company. In some ways it's sort of – I'm not going to say modeled after Sudbury Valley – but a lot of its practices and policies are related to self-motivation and empowerment, so you really get to exercise personal initiative. They treat you really well, and pay you pretty well. It's a good job.

> I love the company. I like the people in the company, and the company treats me great. I've been there a long time, so I've got a lot of seniority, and I have an excellent position. I feel as though I'll probably work there until I retire.

One person waxed eloquent about the pleasure she got from being part of the creation of management guidelines for a swiftly growing company:

> *I was running a store. I was the store manager. But what we were doing was really building the infrastructure in terms of how to hire, and how to train, and how to open new stores quickly with quality staff and quality service, by following guidelines so that you could get the same product at every store, that kind of thing. So I was running a store, but I was also doing all this other stuff. We had lots of fun; we put our heart and soul into it.*

Several people mentioned the autonomy they enjoyed within the framework of their employment:

> *I like the fact that I get to make my own decisions. I'm very much on my own throughout the day. There's not a lot of supervision that I need to follow. I'm left to my own devices, for better or for worse, which I've found mostly for better. In fact, in almost all instances better.*

> *I enjoy the type of project-based work where it's three to six months in duration and then you move on to something else, and you have ownership of that project for the time that you're working on it. What I didn't like about my last company is that it took many years before you got an opportunity to really take ownership of things. You're at a fairly junior level and there's a fairly rigid hierarchy in a management consulting firm. Because my current employer's strategic planning group is smaller than the staffing levels at a large management consulting firm, you tend to get more responsibility.*

> *I really love my job and I don't consider it just a place I have to go. My approach is that what I'm being paid for is to manage a café, to make sure that there is an ample and good variety of healthful food there for people to eat and that we don't run out of things. I do that really well, but that's not necessarily a job where you start at 9:00 and*

end at 5:00. That's a job where you come in and see what's there and you have a burst of energy and you do a bunch of stuff and then either you just plow through or maybe you stop and take an hour off and do something in the middle of your day and then come back. Who's to say whether I'm going to leave at four o'clock in the afternoon or ten o'clock in the evening? It's very open, so a lot of my leisure time is actually spent at my workplace, when I'm by myself in a practice room or in a good conversation with a fellow musician. If I want to duck into a rehearsal room for an hour in the middle of the day, I just do it. If I am enjoying having a conversation with someone, I'll just do it. I'll take half an hour off to talk with someone who's interesting, and then I'll work more later.

Many people reported that their work was just plain fun for them. The following two comments were representative of the responses:

I joined a company and started making games for a living. I'm bringing joy to people now. A lot of the skills from my prior television work converted over to game design. I am doing game design, just taking all the parts – the art and the programing and all of that – and crafting the environment that people will be playing in, and the rules, and all that. Good fun – not exactly work for a living. You know, a definite artistic environment, very relaxed. You have deadlines, but after television – a deadline every six months or something is no big deal after having a deadline of 10:00 every night.

The military has treated me terrifically. For one thing, as a woman trying to make a wage and progress in any kind of a career, I think you get more fairness in the military than out. When I got eligible to retire – right about the time my first baby came – I told my boss, "It's been great, but I think it's time to hang up my Major fatigues and become a civilian." But he said, "Well, not so fast, we're starting to let people telecommute – it's working out great for the Air Force. It's very cost effective in the military to have people telecommute if you happen to be on a job that lends itself to that." So I got out and became a reservist and went right back into the military historian field and it has been great ever since. So for the past four years I've been telecommunicating for the Air Force. Currently, I do it two or three days a week.

I work at home and I'm doing a lot of transcribing and editing, mostly oral histories, lectures and interviews with people. Right now there is a real push to get stuff about Korea before the veterans are all too old to tell any stories. The World War II guys are still telling stories, but the stories are getting pretty farfetched in a lot of cases.

How can you beat it? I sit at my desk and I look out at the mountains and at the eagles and I transcribe. It's awesome. Pretty cool. I don't have to wear a uniform. I don't even know where my uniform is.

The overwhelming impression received from the interviews is of a group of people who by and large have pursued and found vocations that give them satisfaction and pleasure. The full gamut of these pleasures radiate from this person's description of farming:

It's an amazing combination of so many different skills and challenges – it's constantly creating efficient systems, it's working with natural forces, it's being outside. I'm a devoted cook and I love cooking with incredible ingredients, so it's a way to surround myself with a dream assortment of vegetables a lot of the year. And I'm a social person – I like working with employees, and I like the way we market the produce, which is that dozens of families come to the farm once a week and pick up a basket of produce. We also sell at farmers' markets – so it's very social and people just love it, which makes me feel good.

It's a wonderful way to raise a family too. I love hard work, I love using my body, I love working with machinery. I just really do love every aspect of farming, except sometimes there's just too much hard work. But I actually love it. I wake up at dawn and I'm just so excited to go work on the farm. I'm depressed when it gets dark out and I can't work anymore.

I'm doing exactly what I want to be doing, which very few people can do. I live in an unbelievably beautiful area on a beautiful farm, and I've been able to pursue my dreams at a young age.

Challenge

The enormous percentage of the interviewees who are engaged in entrepreneurial work, or are in management positions, testifies to the extent to which challenge, creativity, and constant stimulation are an integral part of their daily work life – so much so that it comes as no surprise that most of them take it for granted, and that not that many singled out these factors specifically as reasons they enjoyed their work. However, many of the remarks made on this subject caught our attention.[5]

People enjoy challenge in all sorts of occupations. A carpenter said that he likes to do "anything that's challenging, that I haven't done before and that I have to use my head a little bit about." A software engineer said, "I enjoy the feel, just being able to stretch my mind, of really being challenged over the natural course of my job." A lawyer commented, "I need a lot of stimulation, so I think change for me is good. It keeps me awake." A manager in a chain of copy and print centers remarked, "I've done a lot of different stuff. It's always kind of a little bit different, and whenever I get tired of one thing they let me

---

[5] We considered the responses that fell into the following five categories, displayed in Figures 12 and 13 on page 81-82 , as conveying the notion of "challenge": creative work, challenging work, opportunity to learn new things, autonomy, and management status.

do whatever else I want." And this comment is from a person in the retail clothing business:

> *I've been working in retail since I graduated. Well before I even went to college, I was working in retail – and to me it's interesting, it's challenging. I manage a shop, I have a lot of people under me, and I'm in charge of a lot of things. I communicate well with my clientele in a very prosperous area in London—it's very rich actually, and it's very challenging.*

Several people enjoyed the excitement of being busy in a multi-task environment.

> *I get to interact with 400 different people, which is the best part of my job. I don't go sit at a computer. I don't sit down and just do one thing. I get to deal with complex issues in what I would call a seriously intense environment. That's the best part of it. It's different every day. There's always something.*

> *I work for an Internet start-up. There's no dress code, there's no hours. It's sort of very loose. As long as you get your job done, everybody's happy. It's not really high pressure, but we have a lot of deadlines, we have a lot of things that have to happen quickly, which is sort of the nature of the business. But that's good too, because it's never ever boring. I worked at a bank for about five months and that didn't really work out.*

> *I worked for a Boston based worldwide management consulting firm. I was an off-site technology coordinator for them, so I got to work with a lot of different people in the organization, primarily vice-presidents in the company, going around and basically being their tech guy around the world, wherever they traveled. The bulk of what I had to do was this: there were about fifteen core conferences around the world that we had to schedule and they would be for anywhere between 30 and 300 people. They needed IT infrastructure to support those people*

while they were at the conference, which basically meant replicating whatever support services they had at their home offices, which they were going to expect when they showed up at your door. So it was a matter of working with a lot of different vendors, working with a lot of different IT groups within the company, really having a lot of irons in the fire at the same time.

Even temporary work unrelated to the person's primary career goals turned out to be satisfying for the respondent who got a kick out of the challenge in it:

I had a job at a real estate tax service through a temp agency. I think it was a very good experience. Now I've got two-plus years of office experience under my belt and I've juggled all kinds of tasks. I answered phones, I dealt with customers, I ran a mail room, I ran part of a department essentially when there wasn't anybody else. Time management was also important because the business is very cyclical and several times a year it is extraordinarily busy and then at other times it can be really slow. But those times when it's really busy, trying to handle that and juggle that is challenging. I remember one particular tax cycle where I was kind of my whole department, and it was so busy I was coming in early and staying late, and I still felt like I never got through the stuff.

Several alumni focused on the pleasure they got at learning new things at their jobs. A former student who worked at a large nursery while in art school found unexpected challenges:

They have at least a thousand people working for them and a lot of them are from the Dominican Republic, Puerto Rico, Mexico. So I've had to learn to speak Spanish. I've had to learn to drive and operate loaders and fork lifts and stuff. I'm working on getting my commercial driver's license. I've learned a lot of skills, and I've also learned a lot about how other people in the world, other communities in the world, act and treat each other and how they think of our society in the US. That's kind of been a big eye-opener. It's been interesting.

Another artist found himself enjoying what he was learning in a complete different domain:

> *After I started going to art school, I continued to work for a house painter from my home area. It was just the two of us, and I didn't do it so much because I needed the money, or necessarily for the love of house painting, but I did it because I learned a lot from him, and I learned a lot about being responsible for somebody else's professional life. That was a really important experience for me and I still work for him when he needs extra help.*

Another graduate looked for a succession of jobs from which he could expand his knowledge in several related areas.

> *I've never worked at anything just for the money. I like to keep it something I can learn from. I worked pressing herbal extracts immediately after I graduated SVS. I worked retail at a couple of other places, such as natural food markets. I worked at an organic farm; that was a great job. Now I work at a florist, because it involves flowers and people that I like.*

The ability to be creative in a job was a key factor mentioned by several alumni. For a fashion industry pattern maker, this was particularly important:

> *In every world there's always a little maverick fringe. I began by working in companies run by young women, starting up designers, so I worked the maverick fringe and made good friends with people who were a little different than the rest of the fashion industry. From there I moved to a larger designer which itself was actually known to be very different than the rest of the fashion industry. It was a very nice atmosphere.*

Teaching music in an inner-city high school turned out to be a unique creative outlet for an aspiring singer:

> *I taught for a year and a half at a public high school in Manhattan, one of the inner city schools. It was a really amazing experience. The diversity of my students was just astounding. I had kids from India, Dominican Republic, Africa, Puerto Rico, Jamaica, Bangladesh, Iraq, Iran.*
>
> *I built the program at that high school. My first year there they threw me into a room with a package of dry erase markers and no books, no piano, no music, no equipment, no television, no nothing. They just put me in a room and handed me 300 kids and said, "Teach music!" I built everything that program had. This was a business school, so obviously music wasn't necessarily everyone's favorite topic, but I had wonderful kids. I had no discipline problems after a while, which was sort of unusual because I was new, I was young, and I had a lot of special needs kids that were being mainstreamed and they were wild. I don't know exactly what it is. I'm good with teenagers, so I guess it worked out somehow.*

An avant garde artist, sculptor and performance artist brings creativity to the level of eccentricity:

> *As a general rule, all the things that I do tend to be sort of ongoing things so that while, yes, I try to be open to particular spontaneities that might improve a particular piece, there definitely is an overall long-term drive that is the ultimate governing factor of whatever I'm doing.*
>
> *Depending on which mode I am in, I might be spending an entire day just foraging around in a landfill looking for bits of scrap material that would be the right things for repairing the various items from one of my main collections, or I might spend an entire day just running back and forth between the different areas of the shop and working on fixing things, or I might be working entirely on my website or going out and trying to do something in terms of publicizing the project,*

schmoozing the people in galleries, etcetera, or doing performances in various venues, both to publicize my work and also just for the sake of doing it.

Even he, however, occasionally found the need to take routine jobs to earn some money – jobs from which he managed to extract useful experience each time:

For the most part I've been pretty much involved with my own projects. I mean obviously I have worked, but for the most part I've tried to get jobs where I could pick up skills that would be useful to me for my own needs – getting a paycheck and hopefully picking up a little bit of knowledge, like working in a photomat, where I got to develop my own pictures. I also worked briefly doing museum restoration work, from which I picked up a lot of good techniques.

Meaning

Many of the respondents indicated that they enjoy their work because it adds meaning to their lives. Their replies revealed a great deal about their personal value systems.[6]

Here is how a librarian put it:

> Since I've been out of college, I've been working in libraries, children's libraries, and I find that really meaningful. It's kind of my mission to change libraries to be more open. I think there's a lot of potential for libraries to use their meeting space for a whole host of things that they don't use them for now. For example, I have teenagers come into the library and they bring bands and they play music after the library is closed. This summer we put on a play where the high school students were teaching the younger kids improv acting.
>
> I think that libraries in the old-fashioned sense are unfortunately – or fortunately – kind of defunct. My vision of a library of the future is a space where information on all kinds of different platforms can be exchanged.

---

[6] We considered the responses that fell into the following four categories, displayed in Figures 12 and 13 on page 81-82, as conveying the notion of "meaning": spiritual or ethical components/meaningful work; service to others; activism; relating to other people/teamwork. As can be seen from the figures, a great many of the replies fell into those categories.

This person felt that her work transformed the entire relationship of a community to its culture:

> *I was the executive director of the Arts Council of my town for two and a half years. It certainly wasn't the pay that I really enjoyed, because as a nonprofit they didn't pay very well. But I worked on a project that had a lot of impact on the community. We took an old library building and, with a nineteen-member board of directors, we were able to raise $1,800,000 to restore it. It was remarkable because we are in a very remote area. There aren't any big industries, no high-tech corporations, so all of our funding had to come from private foundations and local individuals and small donations from businesses – a lot of really small donations and some fairly substantial ones. It was a big undertaking, something that a lot of people said couldn't be done, and now it's a cornerstone of the community and it's really being recognized.*
>
> *There are things that I initiated that have become pretty well established, like what we call the Cultural Round Table, which is a coalition of cultural organizations. It was basically a means of getting people together to talk, to have an opportunity to discuss problems and difficulties, and to enable a way to work together. There had been the feeling of competition, and this forum provided a way to schedule things so that you weren't, for instance, having performances on the same day as someone else and then ticket sales would suffer as a result, that kind of thing. That idea was then taken by the regional Arts Council, and now they're using these Cultural Round Tables and have established them in each of the six counties that make up the region. We have a Cultural Trust, which is fairly new, an endowment fund to fund the arts in the state, and they are looking for ways to distribute the money. They were going to send funds to the cities in the rural areas, but now they're finding that because of the Cultural Round Tables, they can send the money there, and then have a system set up where people can apply for the funding from a local organization. So one little tiny thing that I did has mushroomed into a really big thing.*

> *Artists are coming out of the woodwork. Now they have a place to exhibit their artwork, and a means of marketing it, and art education. That's going to impact the livability of the area, it's going to impact people wanting to come here – doctors and professionals and people like that – and it's increasing things like art fairs and sidewalk fairs. All of these activities now have a place to come together.*

A person who works in the environmental field found that his very first job after he graduated from college pointed him in the direction of a meaningful career:

> *I worked for a large environmental organization. We worked on creating a code of environmental conduct for corporations and on a system which they could use to report annually on their compliance with those principles. It was to be used by people who wanted to invest in companies that represented their own personal views, and wanted some objective way of measuring whether their corporations were, in fact, meeting those criteria. I worked with an excellent group of people, comprised of individuals from a number of nonprofit organizations in the environmental field, and from different religious organizations and institutions committed to conservation. I felt the work I was doing was very valuable because I felt we were helping to change corporate environmental practices for the better, but then in addition to that, the people I worked with were just terrific individuals and I made friendships that are continuing to this day. That work convinced me of my need for further training and education in environmental science and natural resources management. It not only led me toward graduate school, but also gave me some of the credentials I needed to get into the graduate programs I was interested in.*

Several former students commented on the pleasure they got from providing service to others. A realtor mentioned how she enjoys "the chance to work with people on what for them is one of the most important decisions they can make. I enjoy the whole process of helping them to make a good decision." A respondent who works with disturbed children in a group home setting remarked that her "goal with employment is not to be bored and to feel like I am doing something useful; this work fulfills that goal." A social worker chose her profession because "I wanted to do something that meant something to me and that contributed to the well being of the community. Since earning money was going to take up a great deal of my time, I wanted to incorporate other goals as well." Another social worker explained:

> I worked for the Public Child Welfare Agency in the city I was living in for nine years, and that was really meaningful. The bulk of the time I was a protective service case worker. I worked with children at risk of abuse and neglect and I provided the families with services. I removed the children from the home when they weren't safe and tried to reunite families that were apart. It was super meaningful work and very hard.
>
> Then I became a home finder. I trained foster and adoptive parents and made the placements. I coordinated which children went to which home, and re-evaluated the homes and lent them support. I really, really liked that job.

The former student who was a funeral director for about twenty years invested a great deal of compassion in his work:

> People make a lot of snide remarks, but it was very gratifying. People are in terrible shape when they arrive to settle their loved ones' final arrangements, and I've always been a kind, sympathetic, patient person. My work used a combination of every talent I've got. It was a good job for me as far as being rewarding in a spiritual way. I've got a whole box of letters from families thanking me for being so kind and helpful – and not trying to screw them.

A former student who took a job in a nursing home in order to pay her college tuition found satisfaction as she became highly committed to the clients and their welfare: "I run activities like arts and crafts, exercise, a whole slew of things. The nursing home residents have very high levels of dementia. I have my own floor there and I really enjoy the work." She then went on to describe an incident that illustrated the extent of her involvement:

> *My floor is for wanderers and behavioral problems. On my floor there are two women who are in their late 80's. I called them "my two little wanderers" because they wandered around but they always looked for each other. They don't know what planet we're on, they don't know what's going on, but they know each other. The administration decided to separate them. So I had a disagreement about moving one and not the other. The one they decided to move had just gotten back from the hospital and she was very frail.*
>
> *On the day of the move she was very upset, so I told one of the administrators, "I need someone else to be in the recreation activity so I can help her" – you know, I had 20 or 30 other people to look after. So she called, and someone in Social Service came up and said about my patient, "Who's Jean?" That's how well they know their clients! I explained the situation. I said, "I don't know who made this decision and I don't have any medical background, but I think it's a very bad idea because it's just going to upset both of them and I think they're going to go downhill. Jean's in a really bad state."*
>
> *Well, I got in trouble for speaking up for my residents' interests. And this has been sort of ongoing. I've seen the residents' families – they're all very upset about this – and I talked to them about it. I fully acknowledged to them that I disagreed with what the administration decided to do. So, I'm just sort of waiting for the other shoe to drop. I spend eight hours a day with these people, and I know them, and someone comes in and says, "Who's Jean?" I don't think it's right.*

The satisfaction of working with special needs children outweighs the difficulties inherent in this person's job:

> *What I'm doing right now is substitute teaching, working with special-ed kids, which I really love. The pay is so low that you might*

as well say I'm volunteering. I don't really have to be working at this point in my life; I do it just because I really enjoy it.

The kids dread it because here's a substitute and how much help can she possibly be? She doesn't know the kids, and some of the programs the kids are on are very involved, lots of subtleties.   Also, kids with special needs may not respond well to changes and different faces. That alone can set them off sometimes; it's really hard to have a stranger among them. There were a couple of times where I walked in the door and people were openly upset. By the end of the day it was like, "Thank you so much for coming!" They might as well have just said, "We really thought you'd be a dud." So it's been rewarding.

What I have found interesting is that very quickly people realize that I have some experience, I have something to bring to the table, and quite honestly I feel like now everywhere I go I'm respected. People know that when I walk in the door I'm not going to be dead weight. I'm going to be able to get the job done. Now people are calling and requesting me directly, which makes me feel good.

Service to other people is a common denominator for all alumni who got involved in teaching. The former student who became a ballet dancer and went on to become a dance instructor at the university level had this to say about his experience as a teacher:

I had a ball when I was doing it. My students would tease me; my dance classes were referred to as "philosophy classes." I would say, "Anybody can do a tendu. Who cares about the actual movement? If it doesn't mean anything. . ." So that was sort of my bent.

Teaching is not something where you get a lot of instant gratification. I'd come back two years later to do something at the university and I'd run into a former student and he'd say, "Oh, man, what you taught me two years ago has really influenced how I see life in general." They would say, "It changed my life, blah, blah, blah," and I'd be thinking, "God, why did it feel like I was pulling your damn teeth? Why couldn't you just give me something at the time?" As I age I realize that that's the way it is, and it's not about instant gratification.

But, oh, sometimes it is. You know, you have students who just take off! They hook into your style. Over the period of time that I taught there I saw people really develop. I'd teach them in one class and then the next year I would teach them again. I'd see their development and be blown away by it. It was really exciting.

Service was the prime source of satisfaction to the woman who, quite literally, went to the ends of the earth to work with an NGO:

I had never worked harder in my life than I did in East Timor. The first three months that I was there, it was still an emergency situation, and we were doing anywhere from twelve to eighteen hour days, seven days a week. But I was so charged. I enjoyed the work and it needed to get done. If you have a job in an office it can be like, "Oh, do I do the filing today or do I do it tomorrow? It can wait until tomorrow, no big deal." But when people are waiting for shelter materials and until we bring them they're going to be living under a tarp issued by the UN, it's a whole other thing. I found that very challenging, very rewarding, but it also puts a lot of pressure on you. There were days when I just didn't think we could do it. People look at you and they think you're going to be bringing them materials so they can go ahead and build a house, and you're thinking, "I know these materials are not going to come from Malaysia or Indonesia for another three weeks, and how do I explain that to these people?" So it was very rewarding, but at the same time it could be very hard. I took the work not necessarily personally, but I certainly took it to heart, so when things didn't go out when they were supposed to, that was very hard. But I actually really enjoyed the work until the very end.

Teamwork and a sense of community were sources of job satisfaction for many former students. The café manager in an urban music school saw this as a primary goal of his work:

To me the café has always been about extension of the school's community. Before I started running it, all they had was pre-made snacks, ugly food, and basically, beer and soda. I turned it into a really vibrant, fun place for everybody to eat. I started making a bunch of really tasty food. I keep the prices really low by working with simple ingredients and doing the leg work myself, rather than buying prepackaged, pre-processed stuff that you have to sell for a lot because you paid a lot for it. My basic thinking was, if people eat together, then it will be an exciting part of the community. Rather than trying to run out of the building, teachers are going to stay in and eat with their students at a table.

The community that can be built up among co-workers who share responsibility was important to this chef:

There's a real showbiz aspect to working in a kitchen. You're putting on a show and you're waiting for that time, 8:00, when the dinner's going to begin. You'd put all your effort into that and then you'd dance in the kitchen for a few hours and then there's that great feeling afterwards when you've accomplished it. There's a good brotherhood between the chefs just like there is between the players in a band. They're a rough and tumble bunch, which I am myself. They like to go out for a beer and stories afterwards. So I was actually very comfortable in that scene and it was a really good experience for me.

A bartender exclaimed, "Waitressing didn't do it for me, but bartending I absolutely adore. It's a lot of fun, because you get to talk with people." The manager of a yoga studio enjoyed her work because of the "give and take of the whole thing. Everyone's kind of evolving, somewhat together and somewhat not, and it's like a bunch of friends and a bunch of people kind of helping each other." An assistant manager in a supermarket found it "was a fairly interesting job. There were about forty employees in the department. Over half of them were from other countries, and some of them barely spoke any English. It was definitely a learning experience. Obviously you can find people to translate, so it's not like you're learning the language or anything. I found there are so many strange differences in people's attitudes from different cultures. Things you take for granted, like ways that you would phrase a question, or ways you would go about asking for something, can definitely be completely different than the way they would go about it. So it was interesting trying to manage these people. That was not something I ever predicted I would have to deal with."

A gymnastics instructor found her greatest satisfaction in fostering a sense of comradeship among her students:

> What I feel is really important in gymnastics is the camaraderie between the girls that makes it a team sport. I would have to say that if an elite gymnast walked up off the street and said to me, "Will you coach me as an elite gymnast?" I would probably recommend them to someone else. Since we don't have any other gymnasts like that right now in our gym, they would be extremely individualized, and I don't think that that's healthy for them. I think they need the companionship that they can only get from girls going through the same thing that they're going through at that time.

The relationships that he forms with clients is the key factor that makes a golf tour director like his work:

> We've got beautiful golf courses here and I love showing people. I feel like I'm sort of a golf ambassador, or an employee of the Chamber of Commerce, because I love the area so much. I bring people out and I walk them around the golf course and I tell them where their shots need to be and I get them to score ten or fifteen or twenty strokes better than they would have if they had gone out on their own. They become your best friend. I do things like make dinner reservations on the way back from the golf course, I tell them what sightseeing things they should do. So it's more than just bringing somebody out to a golf course and dropping them off.

What They Don't Like

Several former students made it clear that there were things about certain job experiences that they didn't like. Their negative comments were sometimes as illuminating as their positive ones. Here for example is what one person had to say after his foray into the world of retail giants:

> I've had a bunch of odd jobs, but an important one was working for a huge superstore chain. That opened my eyes quite a bit to corporate structure and made me realize that I never want to do it again.
>
> Although working there seemed fine at the beginning, I started to notice that it almost seemed fake, a fake smile, while behind the scenes, everyone was stressed out to the point of breaking. The face that they put forward was "Hi! How are you doing today!" Ugh. That's the way you have to act, but it went overboard because we had to act that way all the time, even to each other. If you're in a bad mood, you're in a bad mood. You couldn't show it. It was kind of weird.
>
> I ended up not being able to handle it. That kind of pressure didn't really work well for me, but I think that is true of retail business in general. It was a very high stress kind of job. It gives you more of a feeling of what's going on when you go into a store next time.

The corporate world was hardly more appealing to this artist:

I worked for an ad agency for a little while and I got to know exactly what they were about and how the whole program worked and the sequence of what you do to get into what position. That was very important information for me. I decided I didn't like it too much, and set out to pursue my own business and go into freelance work, which worked out very well.

One person said, flat out, "I don't really like being in an office from 9:00 to 5:00 every day. I don't want to deal with a computer job anymore. That's not the life I intend to live." Another couldn't stand what he perceived to be an atmosphere of falsehood:

I was a producer-director at a TV station. I ran the news department, built a new set, had a jazz show that was nominated for a Cable Ace Award. Then I left there and I went to a big-city station as an editor, but I started getting disheartened with the news. Because the big lie is that you're out to tell the truth – that it's not really about ratings, it's about telling the truth. And the real gist is, it's really just about advertisers, and you don't want to piss off the wrong people. It's just very corporate. Also I spent seven years doing local news, so most of my time was spent doing murders and fires, etc., and I wondered, "Who am I really helping with this?" I felt like all I was doing day-in and day-out was bumming out the public at home.

A dedicated women's rights activist had a job she loved turn sour when she could no longer live with the daily threat of danger:

While I was working at a Planned Parenthood clinic, we had a violent attack there. A man broke in and trashed the place. He didn't have a gun but he did have a huge brick which he threw through the reception glass window in order to break in, and a bunch of us were there. It was very scary. It's just a miracle that none of us were hurt because we were all standing right there when the glass window shattered everywhere. After this incident, which happened when I was twenty years old, I continued to work at Planned Parenthood until I was about twenty-five. I had just started working there when this happened. A year later I left – I was totally burnt out, and I took a few months off. But I wound up going back because there's a joke at Planned Parenthood: you never leave. That repeatedly happened with staff. They would leave and then come back a few months later, a year later – people always came back. When I finally left, the clinic director said to me, "How many going away parties have we thrown for you?" I said to her, "I've had three." But I have not been back since and I don't plan on going back. Ever since then I feel like I don't want to work in a place where my life's in danger every day. Reproductive freedom is something very important to me, but I don't want to work in a clinic. I don't want to live like that anymore. So I admire people who do it, and I'm proud of myself for having done it, but I don't ever want to do it again.

Danger and corruption were also the factors that drove the person who works for an international NGO away from one of her assignments:

On one difficult assignment in a third-world country, the first few months there I loved it, and then we had a problem in my office where I discovered that about 25% of the staff were committing fraud and trying to steal money from the agency through medical benefits. The idea was, if they need to see a doctor, they see a doctor, they get a receipt, and they get reimbursed. But people were writing bogus receipts. So I sort of figured out what was happening, did some investigation, talked to the country director, and I then had to fire a lot of the staff, which in any environment is a bad thing to have to do. In a country where you have 80% unemployment and you know people's children will be hungry after you fire them, it's extremely difficult. On top of that, some of the staff were very upset with me because I had discovered it and I was the front person. Even though I was not the one who made the decision for them to be dismissed, I was the one who handed them the pink slip, so there were a lot of former staff who were very unhappy with me. People were going to see witch doctors, and putting spells on me, and it got really kind of strange. So I wanted to get out of there, not so much because I wanted the comforts of home, but rather because I had staff coming up to me and saying, "Look, be careful. There's some people who are not doing good things."

On a lighter note, a person who basically loves her job as a reference librarian in a town library, discussed the things that frustrate her at times:

Well, I have days and then I have days. Sometimes I find the whole PC troubleshooting aspect of my job very wearing. My impression from talking to people and reading the literature is that pretty much all librarians find that. Before computers, it was the copier that was always broken. Librarians tend to be people who have advanced degrees who are interested in either the scholarly aspect or the working with people aspect, and then find themselves stuck with these machines as well.

Since I work in a public library, I see a broad spectrum of human beings, everybody from toddlers to their great-grandparents, and therefore I get a broader spectrum of questions than I might if I worked in an academic setting. I also don't tend to get the more scholarly sorts of inquiries. So I do have days when I feel like my brain is atrophying. In effect, I'm on a public service desk and I'm there for whatever people need from me, including "Where's the bathroom?", which is the other big joke amongst librarians. We went to school to get a Master's degree so we can tell people where the bathroom is.

One alumnus commented that "once you get something going to the point where it becomes profitable, it also becomes boring. What happens is, the boredom kicks in after a while and you do something dumb like selling the company." A direct link between a negative attitude towards a particular job and his Sudbury Valley experience is expressed by this former student:

I had a really lousy office job for a while – very, very miserable – in which I was just stunned at how people were never given the authority or trust to do their job well. There was an office manager, the owner, looking over your shoulder every moment. It was very distracting. I came to realize that was how many work places were structured, and I guess my objection to it is similar to my objections to traditional school. The idea that people can't just be told the things that have to be done and left alone to do them, but have to be micro-managed, grows out of the same culture that is created by, and created, the traditional school model. Obviously I didn't have any fun, but I think that job had a significant role in making me who I am. I think that it made me more realistic about how deep the philosophical gulf is between what I view as the way to live one's life and the way much of the world seems to view it.

Formal Study After Sudbury Valley

*"During three years of undergraduate work, attending a
Shiatsu school on the side to learn Chinese medicine, and then
four long years in chiropractic school, have led me to to the
conclusion that Sudbury Valley School is the most advanced
learning institution I have ever seen or attended. It has put
me at the top of everything I set out to do. So anyone out
there who wants to become a doctor, scientist, or Buddhist
monk, know that you have a better shot at it if you played at
SVS as a kid."*

To Pursue or Not to Pursue?

As of the time of the interviews, 98 of the 119 respondents (82 %) had pursued formal study after Sudbury Valley.[7]

Virtually all of those who did not pursue formal studies made it clear that they felt ready to go directly into the fields they wished to pursue as adults. They felt confident in their ability to learn, either through experience, from available resources, or from other people. They expressed no regrets about their decision to go straight into living their lives, and did not feel that their careers, or their lifestyles had been impeded in any way by this decision. One person explained, "I honestly learn a lot better outside a traditional classroom setting, which was probably one of the reasons why Sudbury Valley worked so well for me."

Another commented:

> I had to kind of work on my rock star lifestyle and persona from the first time I started picking up on it, and I couldn't do that in the

---

[7] In the chapter "Data", Figure 22 (p. 152) shows that our former students chose to enter formal educational situations at widely different times in their lives. Since many of the respondents are still quite young, it is possible that some of those who had not yet gone on to other schools will do so in the future.

> *constraints of public school. College really would have put me off on*
> *the sidelines for another four years.*
>
> *When I left the public school system, I really never wanted to go*
> *back into a classroom situation again. Usually that's not the way I prefer*
> *to learn. I like to follow my own instincts. I know how to reference*
> *things that I need. I feel that I'm a unique character who really doesn't*
> *need much of what's being taught in a sterile atmosphere.*

Some started their studies and changed their minds soon after, as did this person:

> *After leaving college, I thought at some point about going back. I*
> *thought it was important for a little while, because that sort of seemed*
> *to be what you did after you left high school. But then I decided that*
> *I've never really done anything the way everybody else does, so why*
> *should I start now? I haven't regretted not getting a college education*
> *yet, so, for me, college is not a pressing issue.*

Another person felt that he was just plain wasting his money:

> *After two years at college, at $17,000 a year, I decided I could*
> *probably make more money and have much less net loss if I went into*
> *computing as someone getting paid for it. And sure enough I did.*

The majority, who did go on to further formal studies, had many reasons for doing so. We grouped these into the categories shown in Figure 14.

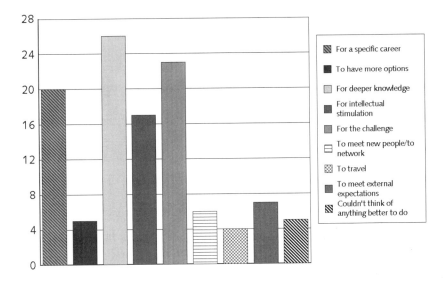

Figure 14 Respondents reasons for pursuing formal study

A significant number were studying with specific career goals in mind, as the following examples illustrate:

> *I worked for a shoe manufacturing company for twenty-four years, but since the company downsized several years ago, I have been going to college and working on starting a new career. I'm studying medicine; my ultimate goal is to become a physician's assistant, which doesn't take quite so long as becoming a doctor. I really enjoy people and I enjoy helping people. I'm also fascinated by the biology of the human body, by disease pathology, and by all the research that's going on. It's just an absolutely fascinating and overwhelming field to be in right now.*

> *I am enrolled in a double degree undergraduate program at a university for classical piano performance and music composition. It basically occupies all my time. It's something I do willingly, but it's certainly a lot of hard work.*

I went to the university to study acting, and it was definitely overwhelming on some level. I didn't realize that I was exactly like everybody else. It was kind of a shock Everybody in the acting program was the star of their high school play and considered very talented by their friends and family, and something special, so we were all exactly alike. We were all eighteen and scared and, for the most part, from someplace other than New York.

Some people went to college with a particular career in mind but found that their focus became clearer over time:

I transferred into the university I am attending as a Daycare major just to declare something. I wasn't very interested in daycare per se but I was interested in the birth-to-three population and that was the best way to get it at that time. Later I switched to Early Childhood Education as a way of getting Early Intervention. Then the university added a bunch of new majors, which was excellent for me, because they added a Child Studies major through which you could focus on the birth-to-three population and early intervention without having to take education courses. Now I can do my internship in a child-service for young mothers with their children, which is definitely what I'm interested in doing.

I took one of those quick career courses at a computer school. After I graduated from there I got a job doing drafting and designing, and then I went back to school while I was working.
I was working on getting my math skills up to a high enough level so that I could get into an engineering program, but by the time I got my math up to that level I decided I didn't want to do engineering anymore. I wanted to study linguistics, that was my main thing, and I also wanted to study some physics, so I transferred into those programs.

I went to undergrad school for psychology for a year and a half. I wasn't very happy with the decisions I had made with that school, so I took a year and a half off. I transferred to another college and became an education major with a psychology minor. Eventually I decided I wanted to keep exploring human behavior and designed an independent major, where I started taking psychology and sociology. After graduating, I did some work in child care, and residential work with troubled teenagers, mostly kids who couldn't get over the traumas of sexual abuse. That led me to undertake graduate studies in social work.

A career goal that developed from everyday experiences led this person to study in a professional culinary institute:

I started cooking for myself and then I started cooking for friends, and then I started having a big Easter brunch every year, and it just became this really fun thing for me to do. I would think, "This year I'm going to make this, and I'm going to do that . . ." People would offer to bring things, and I would let them because you're crazy if you don't let people do that, but at the same time I didn't really want people to, because I wanted to make everything myself because I enjoyed doing it so much. And also because I'm a little bit of a control freak, I will admit. It just started to hit me that I really love this and it's a great way to be creative. Also, if I really get into this professionally, there are so many different places I could take it. I can work in a test kitchen, I can work for a caterer, I can work in a restaurant, I can start my own bakery – there are millions of things I can do with a food background. There'll always be a job for me.

This is the first time that I decided I would go to school and then try to make a career out of it for myself.

As might be expected from Sudbury Valley alumni, the reasons that the most people gave for going to college were related to increasing their understanding of the world – "for deeper knowledge", "for intellectual stimulation", and "for the challenge". Some related their quest directly to their experience at school:

> *I wanted to go somewhere that kind of played off of some of Sudbury Valley's ideas about students taking on their own education and taking responsibility for their own education. And I wasn't disappointed in that regard.*

> *It's a really great school. It's a lot like Sudbury Valley School, except they have way more toys. They have every media to make art that you could ever imagine right there, all under one roof, in all these different rooms, in this huge four story brick building right next to the museum. It's very relaxed, but very serious at the same time. There are a lot of serious people there who get really wonderful art made.*

Some wanted to deepen their intellectual pursuits:

> *The main reason I was going to a university was to study Japanese language and culture. I researched where I could do that without being a part of a campus. So I moved back to Boston and studied at Harvard at the Extension School for two years which was a great experience. Because you've got access basically to the whole campus and yet you're sort of just on the periphery of things.*
> *At that time, it was a good balance in my life because I was working part-time and going to school. I didn't feel like an outsider, but I did feel like I was missing out in terms of the "college experience" that everybody talks about so much, and many people talk about as the best years of their lives. And so during the second year that I was there, I decided that go to school full-time and become a part of that college experience somewhere else.*

> *I was very interested in thinking about environmental issues and environmental protection and things like that, so I started taking the appropriate classes in that field and found myself more interested in the scientific aspects and getting into the basic science of the earth.*

> *As I started getting more into geology I realized that to go into what I think are the more interesting aspects of it, that I really like to study and enjoy, I had to go to graduate school.*

One former student was determined to get a general education in science, by hook or by crook:

> *For a long time I was a classical ballet dancer, but I've always been interested in science as well. I got into college, but I ended up running out of money. I wanted to finish my education. I had served on the university's Board with the head of the dance department while I was dancing with a ballet company there, and she had always said that if I ever wanted a free education I could just come dance for them. I was never going to dance again after I had retired, but since I had run out of money, I sort of went with my tail between my legs to her and said, "Alright, what's the deal?"*
>
> *I enrolled in the dance program there, and probably had the best dance experience of my whole career going through the dance program! But the bottom line was, I was able to take a lot of science courses.*

Others reveled in their post-SVS schooling purely for the joy of learning. "It didn't even occur to me that I should get a degree," one commented – although a degree ultimately fell in her lap. "I just realized I was interested in the sort of things they teach at a university," said another. A third "basically went to college just to get an education, as opposed to doing anything that I hoped would turn into a career. The things that I studied were what I really enjoyed. I definitely think it was worthwhile."

Several former students were well-established in their jobs, but decided to look for further intellectual stimulation in a university environment. A designer of computer games said:

> *Right now I'm pursuing my education fairly aggressively. I'm not pushing it at a fast pace, but I'm being very diligent about it. My*

grades kick ass in the stuff I'm doing now in college. I'm at Harvard Extension, so the courses are challenging and very interesting and that is definitely a nice avenue to be following at this point.

This, from a highly successful public relations person working in New York, who got her bachelor's degree several years earlier:

I'm probably not unlike a lot of people who are about to reach their thirties. I've been sort of rethinking the whole career path thing, and I decided that I want to go back to class just for the intellectual possibilities – just to have the mental challenge, and since I have a personal interest in food and food studies, I enrolled in the food studies program. I negotiated with my job that they would pay for it. I'm also thinking about applying to business school.

Quite a few people tested their opportunities in the work world and subsequently decided that going to college would open up more desirable options for them. They entered different fields, but they repeated the same litany:

Having tried doing something else, having tried the type of job that's available to those who don't have a college education, I was certainly ready for something different. [geologist]

The blue collar jobs I held in between times at university provided a lot of motivation to want to be in school and not want to have to work 70 hours a week busting my ass doing that kind of shit! [graduate student in political science]

I needed a little more challenge. I spent a lot of time in jobs that don't really go anywhere and aren't very intellectually challenging. I get enough physical activity most of the time, but I end up feeling that I would like to exercise my mind at the same time. [student, math major]

I actually thought I was not going to go to college. I had this idea somehow that I was going to have a career without going to college, but I quickly found out that the only job I could get was as a clerk in an insurance company and I decided that actually I did not want to spend the rest of my life doing that, so I went to college. [independent management consultant]

I worked for a couple years and then decided running a shoe store wasn't for me. I went to a small community college to study television broadcasting, and actually never finished because I got a job while I was an intern in the field. So it was sort of like, well, that's what I wanted college to do for me. [television producer]

I took a couple classes at community college – I took a Spanish class and I took art classes and this and that – and at some point I just kind of realized I didn't want to keep working low-paid menial jobs forever, and I needed to figure out what I wanted to do. Actually my original plan when I went back to college seriously was to be a midwife. Being a doctor followed out of that. [physician]

One alumnus went to college, and excelled, just to prove to doubters that his objections to traditional models of education were based on principle, and not on an inability to perform:

The reason I attended college was this: I was very much a critic of traditional education, including college. What I told my friends when I went off to college – and it's still true – was that I was going so that I could continue to talk about the things I disagree with in an environment like that without people saying "Oh, it's just sour grapes."

Six other alumni reported going on to college as a response to external expectations. "Since I was going to go through the motions of getting the degree," said one, "I decided that I might as well study something I liked," and he ended up majoring in mass communications and film although it did not relate to his future work. Two others went as a result of deals they made with their parents:

> After I graduated from Sudbury Valley, I worked training horses. The agreement with my folks was that I would do this until I broke an arm or leg or something, and then I'd think about going to college. Since I didn't have a clue about what I wanted to do, I thought there was no reason to spend good money going off to college till then. So I did the horse thing for a couple years.

> I got to Sudbury Valley because of an odd set of circumstances: in seventh grade I wanted to skip ahead to eighth grade, since all my friends were in eighth grade and I was intelligent enough to do so. I had some fights with the guidance counselor. I was doing very well in school – there was no reason I couldn't skip ahead a grade and be with all of the kids I considered my peers, but the guidance counselor said, "Oh! Well, skipping grades is reserved for very special cases." I thought I was a very special case! So I made a deal with my mother: if she'd let me go to this alternative school for four years – that would catch me up to all my peers instead of the five years it would take to go through the regular high school route – I would go into college early. That was our deal.
> So I went to SVS for four years, had a fantastic time, and I thought I was ready to go right into the "real world". I was managing a coffee shop at the time and I thought I could stay there and maybe purchase it someday. But when the four years were up, my mom said, "Well, now it's time to apply to college." I didn't really want to, and I sent out a half-hearted application. Little did I think they would accept me, but they did. So I went, very convinced that I would not like it, and that after two or three weeks I would just leave. But I got there and it was the greatest thing! It was so interesting, so much fun, and so easy compared to some of the processes and learning experiences I had at SVS. Basically, when college came around all I had to do was go and sit in the room and listen and I'd do well. I was way ahead of most of the other students who were sitting around me. I met a lot

of people who really did a lot for me, and adjusting was very quick and very easy.

The College Experience

Every one of the people in our survey who was interested in going to college was able to do so. In fact, it was so clearly not a problem, that only some of them even mentioned to us how they got accepted.

There were almost as many ways to get into college as there were people who mentioned it. Most do it the standard way – they take the SAT's, they write applications, and they have interviews if they can. One person, who went to a college of art, said, "I refused to submit my SAT scores, although they were high, because I wanted to get in just on the merit of my portfolio and my writing, which I did."

Still other people used their own creative work:

> I had a portfolio that I put together and I guess they were impressed enough to take me.

> They send you an application where you can fill out all the checked boxes, and also you get a space for any additional comments. I made sure to really be on top of that one, to let them know I had good stuff going on between the ears. I also sent in some sheet music that I had just recently composed, which was really the best thing I had ever done. I think that was kind of the clincher for the deal.

Another student felt her interview was her strongest recommendation:

I didn't have a transcript with grades from Sudbury Valley, of course. I decided to make an appointment with the Dean of the concentration that I was going to be studying, just to sort of touch base with him. I walked into his office, and we sat down and started talking. He asked what he could tell me about the university, since I had made this appointment. I told him that I had already decided to go there, and that I had come to tell him a little bit about myself – what I am, who I've become, and why I think I'm going to be an asset to the university. We chatted for about an hour and, without any other information, without seeing any transcripts or anything, his response to me was, "I'll see you in the fall"! That was pure Sudbury Valley.

There were many other portals to the college world. One person got in "through the back door," as she put it, and explained:

What happened was I got in as a non-matriculating student. I was taking classes with other degree-seeking students, but I wasn't one. I did that for about three years and then I actually got a job in the field I was studying. Then I decided that I wanted to go back to school and study social theory; I wanted to do more theoretical work. I thought that maybe I should apply to a school. I was about 27 years old. I got in and I studied sociology, but I ended up doing it with a focus on media. I didn't do SATs because for students who were older and had some work experience, the application process was different and they didn't require SATs.

One person commented, "I'm proud to say I'm one of the only majors in the Air Force who never took an SAT to get into college." Another managed to be accepted to college even though she "felt that my transcript that I got from Sudbury Valley did not really aid me in getting into the schools that I was most interested in getting in to. I knew I had the potential." A graduate who was determined to become a nurse took the following path:

The nursing school wasn't familiar with Sudbury Valley and they weren't sure if I could function in a structured environment. They wanted me to prove myself. So I went to college and I took some courses over the summer. They evaluated me on how I did, and I was successful.

Once accepted, the respondents faced the necessity of adjusting. Some discussed this process, Figure 15 displays how those fared during their initial exposure to college life.

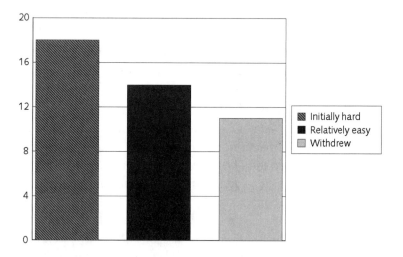

Figure 15 How respondents adjusted to formal study.

As is rather common with college freshmen, a number found the beginning hard going, because what was expected of them differed so radically from what they had been used to:

I simply was unaccustomed to the idea of grades. I was also unaccustomed to the idea that a professor would have a clear idea of what was important and what was unimportant in the subject, and that if you did not agree with that professor's assessment, you would end up being penalized in your grade. The four classes I chose for my first semester each involved very large reading lists – ten or more good-sized books each – and so, as a result, I was required to read about forty books in those first three and a half months. That was crushing. I was reading and working all the time. I didn't sleep much, didn't really do anything except go to classes and study. Of course, I learned my lesson from that and chose a set of classes with a more balanced workload in future semesters.

But the issue of not being able to focus in on what I perceived to be important within a subject, and being forced instead to simply tow the line of what the professor was telling you was important, was difficult. I learned how to play the game, as we all do, and I learned how to spit back what I knew they wanted to hear and get good grades, but that always stuck with me as a less than ideal method of learning. It was quite a contrast to my experience at Sudbury Valley, where I had been able to focus on what was important to me and stay with a subject until I was tired of it, and to really explore it to whatever depth I was interested. In college, it was really more of a cookbook – a lot of rote-memory type operations.

The same sentiments were echoed by other students:

It was hard at first, because I needed to learn what the expectations were and how to fulfill the expectations, so my first semester was actually my worst academically, as far as grades were concerned. I didn't know how to take tests – I didn't know what was expected on essay exams as opposed to multiple choice or something that was more straightforward.

It was hard at first. A lot of the time I just didn't know what to do when I had to write a paper or I had homework. I just hadn't done any of it before. But, you know, I got used to it fairly quickly – I'd say within a semester.

When I first got to college, I took a biology class. I loved biology, but had a terrible professor. I scraped by with a C- because I didn't understand academic learning. He handed me a test and I was like, "What's this for? I've already learned it! Why do you want this?" But because I can write, I got through it. The next semester I ended up doing so well in anatomy and physiology that I tutored it and I also got an A+ in psychology. It took me a whole semester of getting my ass kicked by that one course to acclimate to the academic mind-set. What I discovered is that the strength of the Sudbury Valley student in an academic setting is that Sudbury Valley students can evolve.

Some had specific difficulties that they had to cope with:

As a freshman, it was algebra that was probably the most challenging because I hadn't studied math since I was seven. It was a personal choice that I made while I was at Sudbury Valley. So after the first class, I just walked right up to the professor and said, "Listen, I've not taken an official math class since I was seven years old. Tell me what I need to do to get to the point that I can do well in this class and I will do it." She was wonderful; she gave me a couple of extra books, and said, "Study this, study that." I struggled, it was hard, but I was determined to do it and I passed.

I had some trouble adapting. I think a lot of it was expectation. I went to a college that had a reputation for being very alternative. I had pictured them being more like Sudbury Valley than in fact they were. I think if I had gone to a traditional college, the adaptation would have been easier, even though it would have been a more extreme adaptation, because I would have expected it and I would have prepared for it.

At Sudbury Valley it was really, relatively speaking, harmonious, and it was orderly. Students didn't spray-paint graffiti all over the place, and didn't trash the place, whereas on my college campus students did all those kinds of things. It was kind of shocking to me in a naive sort of way. The standard at Sudbury Valley was so much higher in terms of behavior, and in terms of discourse about issues and conflict, and that sort of thing.

For some, the solution to their discomfort with academia was withdrawal, at least for a time, before returning later to finish their college work: One person, accustomed to being allowed to pursue his interests uninterrupted at Sudbury Valley, was put off by his inability to do so in the college he chose:

> *They had a pretty good environmental program there. But I found that I had too many distractions because of my love of the environment and the outdoors! I ended up being outdoors far too much, being out on the water fishing or whatever, not getting things done. So, I had a pretty tough time.*

He withdrew, and later, when he was ready to accommodate to college reality, returned to school to obtain a degree. Another person found dorm life at odds with his growing maturity:

> *The college experience, I guess, was fun but I wasn't really ready for it at that time – it wasn't the atmosphere for me. I'm an alcoholic in recovery, and I was living in the dorms there for three months with kind of beer-swilling jocks, with whom I wasn't at odds, but I certainly didn't embrace their life style.*

A third person had this to say:

> *It wasn't difficult academically at all. I had specifically chosen a large university because Sudbury Valley was so small, and I thought, "Well, this'll be great. I can go to a big school and meet lots of people." So I did that. I went to a big school and met lots of people, but I didn't feel like I fit in with any of them. I felt like I had a level of maturity that these people were never going to achieve in their lives,*

*let alone had not achieved the first time away from home – seventeen
to eighteen-year-olds who had never experienced any freedom, so
college was quite a shock for them. So socially I think it was quite
difficult for me.*

And a musician who also worked in a high-tech recording studio found
that the music college he had chosen didn't measure up to his needs:

*They weren't as into the stuff that I wanted to do as I wanted
them to be. And the pacing was not what I was looking for. They
wanted people to start at stuff that I'd already done and was already
through with for myself, and they wouldn't let me advance as quickly
as I needed to. It was too expensive to go there for them to be holding
me back like that, so I decided to leave and pursue it on my own.*

Most of the respondents who went to college adjusted with little
or no difficulty, and they were eloquent and emphatic on the subject.
Typical were the following comments: "I thought I would have difficulty
adapting to a rigorous college schedule, but I didn't"; "Coming from
Sudbury Valley, the university setting was an easy step"; "Academically,
I didn't have much of an issue. You come with more skills, in terms
of independence and how to manage your own time, than you would
coming out of a public school where every minute of every day is set
for you"; "I performed much better than most of my fellow students. I
kept a 4.0 for a couple of years. I think the fact that I was older and
that I had worked for several years before going back to school had a
lot to do with it."
Some replies were more expansive:

*I thought that college was easy. For me the hardest thing was
working jobs while being there, and keeping up with the Joneses. I
lived in a dorm the first year, and a lot of people had money and were
not working, and were a little bit more comfortable, so that part was
hard. But academically I was fine.*

I actually think that in a lot of ways Sudbury Valley made it easier for me. I remember how my roommate and his friends would never ever work up the energy to read the book or prepare themselves for any aspect of the class until the night before the test in question, that sort of thing. And I remember feeling astounded because it seemed to me that there were more efficient ways, that you didn't have to work any harder but you could prepare yourself in a more leisurely way when you simply kept up with the reading. What used to happen was the whole campus would be in a panic just before midterms and just before finals, while my tendency was to work the opposite way. I think that's an aspect of taking charge of how you spend your own time. I made sure to get a good enough grade on the first test of the year that I was guaranteed to pass the course after the midterm exam, even if I failed the final, so that the second half of each semester I was able to walk through campus whistling and not worrying about it while everyone else was panicking.

I had none of these preconceived ideas about getting an extension on a paper or taking a makeup test. That was totally foreign to me. It was, to me, like playing school. They would say to me, "Go read one hundred pages of this book by tomorrow," and I would say, "okay." I would go home, read one hundred pages of the book, and do exactly what they told me to do, exactly when they told me to do it. It was very successful, it worked out really well for me. I was extremely invested in doing well.

It was an adjustment, but it was also clear to me that it was an adjustment for everybody. In particular, at a prestigious college like the one I attended, a lot of the students who get in there were used to being in the top 10%, the top 5%, the top 1%, whatever, of their high schools, without doing all that much work. To suddenly find that, "Oh, I'm not automatically one of the best students because everybody else around me is of a similar caliber," was a strain on a lot of people.

So, in a way, I was fortunate, because it was plain to me that it was going to be a big change.

In my first semester, I got the first letter grade I'd ever had. It was kind of a big deal in the sense that it was kind of bizarre for me. It was a good thing that I had gone to a school that didn't have grades. I think I would have been a very competitive, annoying sort of teenager, if I had been at a regular high school, trying to get all A's.

I think it was a lot easier for me than it was for a lot of my peers at college. It seemed like they had always sort of been told what to do in school, so they were used to following directions. Suddenly they had the freedom to pick their classes, and to have less time in class relative to the time it takes to do the homework, and things like that. I think that also there was not a good understanding of cause and effect: if you do your work you'll get a good grade, and if you drink yourself into a stupor and don't get your work done you'll not get a good grade, you know?

For me it wasn't that hard, because for five years I'd been in an environment where I learned that there are causes and effects, and if you want to get something done, you need to look at the steps to take to achieve that.

In spending your whole life at Sudbury Valley making your own decisions, and going after your own passions, you're constantly having to make new decisions every day and change how you are. Anything you try to do – if you decide to go apprentice with a mechanic – the Sudbury Valley student will learn faster. They'll adjust because the environment is so dynamic. So to me college, mechanic school, massage school, starting your trade or working for a living, they're the same thing – learning to acclimate. The beauty of Sudbury Valley is: you strengthen the natural abilities, and then all other things will follow.

We asked our alumni what they liked and disliked about their college experience. For respondents who made critical comments about their experience, Figure 16 shows, by category, the kinds of things they didn't like.

One person found his school just plain too easy:

> *The school was bad. The other students there just didn't know what they were doing. There were people there to get photography degrees who had never done their own printing and never developed their own film before. It got kind of old to be standing around with those people in class every day.*

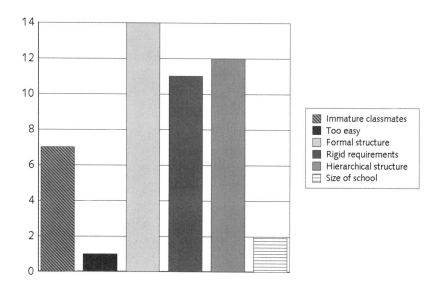

Figure 16 What respondents didn't like about their formal study situation.

For another, "it was too structured." Another felt the same distaste, but swallowed it:

> *College is more restrictive than Sudbury Valley was, but it's not too hard for a person with abilities to do what other people are telling them to do. It's a little bit harder to take control of your own self,*

*and your own time, but when you enroll in college and let that vast
quantity of money be spent on it, it's sort of the act of entering into
a contract. It seems to me it's not that big a deal to fulfill your end
of the contract.*

The rigidity of the particular school she had chosen caused one
student to be quite unhappy:

> *I realized I went to the wrong school. It was very much like the
> public school system which I had left to come to Sudbury Valley. The
> classes were arranged the same as the public high school, 50 minute
> periods for each course. My first year there I had to spend doing
> the core curriculum which was, once again, Math, English, Science
> requirements. I did it with relative ease, but I was unhappy doing
> it, because it wasn't what I was interested in. I didn't make any real
> friends there or get involved in the school at all. In the end, I realized
> what it was that I was interested in and what I wanted to pursue. I
> had three really great professors who helped me realize that politics was
> what I want to do, but I had to transfer to a school that had offerings
> more relevant to what I was interested in.*

The hierarchy of a radical college was not palatable to these
students. "Nothing could match Sudbury Valley," said one, who had
chosen a school he thought would be egalitarian, "because I found
out that my college wasn't a real democracy." Another had a similar
disillusioning experience:

> *I thought that their ideology would mesh well with what I had
> experienced at Sudbury Valley. It did to a degree. I think Sudbury
> Valley definitely prepared me well for the kind of self-motivation
> that was needed at that place, but there was definitely a lot more
> bureaucracy there than at Sudbury Valley, even though it wasn't that
> much bigger.*

The hierarchy of a traditional college was just as disturbing to these students:

> *I didn't like all the bureaucracy and I thought a lot of the rules were stupid. They tried to project themselves to be a very open liberal school, but their ideas of open and liberal were far different than mine. I felt as though the professors just wanted me to repeat back to them what they were trying to teach me, and they weren't open to my ideas and opinions.*

> *My first college was a total waste of time. The one thing I got out of it was binary thinking, which made my life in the computer world much better, but overall I found it filled with professors who weren't interested in teaching and students who weren't interested in learning. There was a certain disattachment that professors had from students. Perhaps that was driven by the institution itself in its desire to get more out of professors than just teaching students: grants and publishing papers had a higher priority than educating students while I was there.*

A number of respondents complained about the level of maturity of their classmates at college. "I wasn't in the same mind set as the people who went to high school. I was actually feeling very serious at the time, but I wasn't able to find any other serious 18 year olds," was one person's reaction. Another had an even stronger reaction:

> *The first semester that I was at college I pretty much hid in my room and didn't talk to anybody. I felt a little bit estranged from most of the people. I stayed an extra year at Sudbury Valley, so I was 19 when I went to college and the people who lived in my hall were all 17 or 18, which doesn't seem like a big difference, but to me it was. I had already lived on my own, I had been working full-time since I was 15, and most of the people who were around me had just left home and were really loud and obnoxious and drinking all the time. I was past that phase.*

Most alumni who went on to college found a lot to like about their experience. Figure 17 categorizes the things they mentioned enjoying.

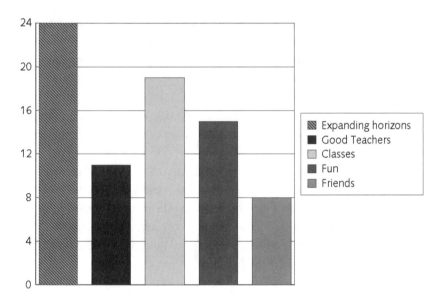

Figure 17 What respondents liked about formal study.

Quite a few people were pleased to be in an environment that broadened their life experience. "It was worthwhile academically and socially," one said. "I learned a lot. It was the first time I had lived on my own, but it was a protected environment, with a lot of support. So, it was a good way to become independent from my parents slowly. I made wonderful friends." From another: "It was filled with wonderful professors, who were there to teach and write and to give you as much as you wanted to get from them." Another found resources she had not encountered previously:

> *Computers were just starting to be available to regular people when I went to college. I did some exciting stuff with a computer*

which now you would think was a joke but, at the time, was so totally cool. You put a bunch of data into a computer and you come back the next day and it turns out the answer for you! We thought it was amazingly fast. I liked college. It was fun.

A graduate who felt that "most of my learning came after college" nevertheless had this to say:

> *I think college was a lot of fun. I certainly enjoyed the process of studying. It was kind of exciting to encounter a philosophy of education so different from Sudbury Valley. All of a sudden I went from having an education where grades were not present to an environment where they were, and where I had to figure out people and find out what their methods were and how they thought. For the first couple of years, I couldn't really understand why people weren't trying to absorb the entire subject in each class. They were trying to find these little tricks to getting a grade, when my thinking was, "God, learn about something, will you?!"*

Many people sought out professors and mentors who were particularly interesting to them. Sometimes they were in unusual places. One person, who went to four different colleges – one a year over four years – ended up in a small state school that had a poor reputation:

> *My favorite college, which is really funny, was considered the low dog of universities. It's in a really dumpy, kind of poor, town and, of all places, that was my favorite school. Because there were a few very good teachers – eccentric, really live-wired teachers – and I hadn't found them in the other schools. Sometimes in the hidden corners there are amazing things.*

A typical comment was the following: "I like the mix of students my school had. I wanted to go some place fairly small, where there was a lot of individual interaction with the faculty." A similar sentiment was expressed by this respondent:

> *I went to a community college first and then a four-year university. Thank God I did. I wanted to start off somewhere where I thought I could have access to professors, I wasn't disappointed, and the professors were very knowledgeable. They were there to help me and everyone else. I didn't get an attitude. Snobbery didn't exist. In my experience, the bigger the schools are, the less they really care about the students.*

In general, good teachers were a source of delight:

> *The school offered an immense amount of studio space. I'd literally do five different mediums every day because the buildings are all interconnected. The teachers were totally amazing and it had both a formal and informal structure. The more you put into it, the more you got out of it.*

And as for bad teachers . . .

> *It may be a weakness and it may be a strength, about Sudbury Valley students. If I have a great professor I'm all over it – I kick butt, and I kick it way beyond the expectations of the class. I'm really into learning. If the professor stinks, I have a hard time eating shit, because if there's no value, you just walk away. If what you have to teach me is useless, I'm going somewhere else.*

Plain old college classes were a kick for some students: "I'm sort of a nerd type. I like to study. I know that sounds weird, but I really liked my courses. I did really well in college. I graduated second in my class, I did a lot of honors work, I wrote a thesis, I did research, and I got to be friendly with some of the professors." For another:

> *I made a decision not to take any notes in class, just to pay attention to the instructor. It actually started from weakness – my note taking sucks. I always study from the book or from other people's notes. Finally, as I was cleaning up my notes from last quarter, I said, "Wow, I didn't use any of these." So I just look at the professor and learn. In the intensity of the academic setting, it's giving me a great chance to train, absorbing as much new information as possible. I'm very academically stimulated. When I stopped writing things down, I got a chance to focus and enjoy it more. It was rocky to start. I had to adjust a little.*

A college of art provided the ideal setting for one graduate to prepare himself for life as a professional artist:

> *I have had some amazing experiences. Recently I was in a group studio at my school. There were twelve of us and it was organized like a class, but it was a permanent studio for all twelve of us. Every week the teacher would come and we'd spent the day talking about our work and having group critiques. We would also study readings, and discuss them in class. We were all given an assignment, as a group, to develop a small body of work (in addition to whatever we were working on the time) which responded directly to a particular author. This work was developed over a semester. At the end, we all decided that it was pretty successful and cohesive and that it would make a good group show. So we put together slides and our respective statements and brought them around to different galleries, and eventually found a gallery that was interested in showing it. That was a pretty important educational experience because it not only really developed my own personal art production, but it developed the practical skills needed for getting a show together and dealing with people and marketing and stuff like that.*

All in all, one gets the impression that the respondents knew what they wanted to get out of college and went after it, enjoying what worked for them, and retaining their critical faculties about the shortcomings of academic life.

Was it Worth it?

We asked the respondents who pursued formal study after they left Sudbury Valley to reflect on their experience. The overwhelming majority felt that they had made the right decision, and that their further study had been worthwhile, as we can see from Figure 18.

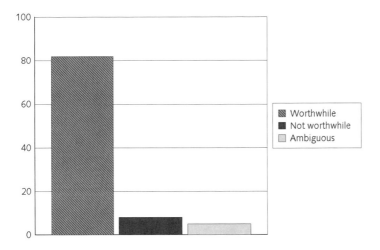

Figure18 Respondents evaluation of formal study.

The feelings of those few who were not happy that they had chosen to pursue formal education after Sudbury Valley are telling. One said:

> *I was very eager to **do**. I didn't want to have to sit and go through books. I had a full-time job when I was in college, in my field, and I learned more in my full-time job in computers than I learned the whole time at college. I felt like I had a fair amount of experience with computers and with science and math, especially from Sudbury Valley, and that most everything I did in college I had done previous to college. I have to thank Sudbury Valley for a lot of that.*

For another person, the whole college experience is still an embarrassment:

> *I still think it was a big mistake. I really do. It was an act of pure egoism, I think. I was just so afraid people would say, "Oh, the real reason you didn't go to college is because you were afraid of it." Or that they would say, "Well, look at the school you went to. You couldn't have cut it." So I think it was really pride. And I'll be honest, I'm still embarrassed by it.*

A few were ambiguous. One, in answer to the direct question of whether he thought college had been worthwhile, said:

> *In some ways yes, in some ways no. That's how it always is for music students, because usually you don't end up doing exactly what you thought you were going to do, but you're more ready to do what you do end up doing. You know, everybody wants to be a nice rich rock star, but it doesn't quite happen that way.*

But virtually all of those who went on to college felt they had made the right choice. One said, "I think college was wonderful. Liberal arts education is perfect, especially for people coming out of Sudbury Valley. There's an emphasis on writing and thinking as opposed to just learning skills which you'll apply directly in a job, and I think that type of education is definitely suited to someone who comes from

Sudbury Valley." Another commented, "I would say it was worthwhile because there are a lot of things that I just didn't know about and now I know about. I have a lot more skills, a lot more options in my life. I have a lot more things that I can do with myself and in the world in general."

Sometimes the pure joy of studying things you are interested in was enough to make college worthwhile. As one person put it, "I studied Romance Languages. I found it really fun. I love traveling and I love Italy and I love speaking the languages. It's not exactly the most lucrative thing to study, but I had a great time studying these languages."

Lots of reasons were given by different respondents for feeling that the college experience had been worthwhile. Here is a sampling:

> *I don't know how exactly my degree has served me, but I think college and the education itself is a valuable thing. I have a degree in history, but that certainly doesn't mean that I'm a history buff, or that I know really anything about history at all. What I did get is four years of reading and writing and analytical thinking, and all that sort of stuff. Whether or not the degree serves to make me better at my job I don't know – I don't really think so – but I may not even have been interviewed for the job if I didn't have a degree, so it serves that purpose.*

> *There's no guaranteed job when you graduate. There was no agent waiting to sign me when I was done. If I had gone to medical school, I would become a doctor, and would have a job in that field. It's not like that in acting school. But I met a lot of great people there, and I did learn a lot, so I think it was worthwhile. It gave me a historical overview, and also a technical overview, of what it's like to be an actor and what that means, and how to go about it.*

> *It was a very intensive program, and what I really liked about it was that the people were willing to match the effort you put into it,*

and so it was really worthwhile for me because I made it pay off a lot. It's a school where if you put in a bigger effort, you get more out of it, and I tried to take advantage of that.

I had a very positive experience in college. Part of that is because, since I was a student at Sudbury Valley, I knew what I wanted to do for a career, which was to be a therapist, and I knew that I needed to go to college in order to achieve that. So I think that part of my appreciation of college had to do with knowing that it was part of a bigger picture.

Visual media is what I do today, it's what I love. It's what I'll do in my grave. I make things. It's what I did at SVS – I drew. College exposed me to some fantastic work and some stuff that I probably wouldn't be able to discover on my own. And then the work that I did – the more academic or theoretical work – was great in terms of grounding me, giving me an understanding of what images in media mean in contemporary society. I grew up pretty much glued to the television, so I was interested in questions about how images inform our realities. Doing some more theoretical work allowed me to ask those kinds of questions and read about them.

We thought it would be interesting to look more closely at the various reasons people gave for feeling that they had benefitted from college. We compiled Figure 19 in order to display the various kinds of reasons offered, grouped by category. Not surprisingly for graduates of a school that stresses pursuit of one's interests, the two dominant reasons given were the ability to learn something interesting and to be in the company of others sharing their interests.

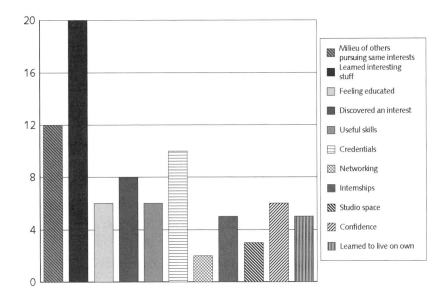

Figure 19 Benefits of formal study to respondents.

In general, when addressing the question, the respondents gave answers that showed that they had been examining the reasons for continuing their studies in a formal setting after leaving Sudbury Valley. "I took a couple of psychology courses at Harvard Extension," said one. "I learned a tremendous amount, even though they had nothing to do with what I'm doing in my career now. I enjoyed them tremendously, and still think about them quite often." Such pure joy of learning was common, as we have already seen. A person in the midst of her graduate school studies in archaeology said, "I like to learn the new things that I learn here." Others echoed this sentiment:

> I loved it. I'm one of those students who might have done well to be a fifth or sixth year senior, because there was so much that I wanted to do. I didn't get a chance to do it all.

> In terms of practical applications and the value to society, I'm not quite sure about the benefits of my graduate studies. In terms of

the fact that it was really fun stuff to do – yes! When I talk to people who are thinking about going to graduate school in math I say, "You should not do this unless you really, really like doing math. Going to graduate school is hard work, so unless you enjoy it you don't want to be doing it."

Freedom to follow through on one's interests was a significant factor in contributing to the satisfaction of these students:

Graduate school gave me more intellectual freedom, more of a sense that students should be trusted with their own drive and perceptions by that stage in their career. I had a lot of freedom and it was encouraged. With a lot of the projects, including my Master's thesis, it was completely up to me how to structure it and what to focus on. In the two graduate programs that I attended, the assumption was that you knew what you wanted to do and you knew where you were going; you just needed to have assistance to get there. You weren't looked at as a blank slate that needed to be filled with information.

I started as an illustrator. Then I got more into painting. I found that my painting style was real thick and I was actually wanting to describe things in three dimensional form, so the last couple of years, I just moved into sculpture. It has been mostly steel, but I'm starting to do a lot of mixed media using clay, plaster, plastics, whatever fits the idea that I'm working with.

Practical experience in their fields was an important benefit for some people. As one person put it, "I had the chance to do some internships that were really interesting." Another

...had good internships through my school. I had to assert myself to get what I wanted, big time. But, educationally, I would say that I learned a lot about my profession. Some of it was a waste of time, but it taught me how to be a social worker.

College often gave people a chance to work with inspiring people in their fields:

> *I was exposed to a kind of critical and theoretical world that I don't imagine I ever would have really engaged with if I hadn't been introduced to it in a kind of structured way. That has been really important to me – that, and the community in which I experienced it. As far as technical training as an artist goes, I picked up what I needed, but it's more of an individual thing.*

It was also a place to meet people, and network in the field of their interest:

> *The MBA was a great experience, but it was not because of the education I received. I don't think very many people go to business school for the education. It's more for the credentials, for the networking, and for the opportunities it gives you. Having an MBA from a prestigious school is going to open doors for you. Also, it gave me a good opportunity to interrupt my career and kind of figure out what I'm really interested in doing.*

The credentials were what was important to other people:

> *My Bachelor's degree was pretty much an exercise in square filling. I didn't learn a whole lot, but it was something I did to accomplish a goal, which was to get a commission in the military. Which I did.*

> *More than what I learned was the accomplishment, the pedigree – the fact that I could reach a milestone that a college degree represents in our society. I think that was probably the most important thing for me. I feel as though I'm an educated person. But if I didn't have at least an undergraduate degree, then by society's standards I might not be considered one.*

For others, it was the place they discovered a lasting interest. Consider, for example, the person who became a government science advisor:

> *I took a physics course because I had to when I was a freshman, and I didn't understand it. I just kept pursuing it because my intellectual curiosity was piqued. When I went to graduate school I did not do so with the intention of becoming a professional physicist. That wasn't something that I was ever interested in, but I did want to learn about the field – not necessarily to apply it. It was a great learning experience, and it's very useful training to have. It helps me enormously every day.*

And this from someone in the field of social work:

> *I started out in college thinking I was going to be a lawyer. Learning not only the academics of it, but also what it really entails to become a lawyer, showed me that it certainly did not fit my personality at that time. I was more interested in helping people just for the sake of helping people, not by potentially having to lie for them and about them. I started branching off with my co-op jobs in Human Services because it fit my niche.*

All in all, people who went on to further formal studies thought about this step, and felt they had benefitted from taking it.

Data

This chapter presents specific data concerning those alumni who sought further formal education after leaving Sudbury Valley. It is worth bearing in mind that the sample we are looking at is still relatively young, and that many of them have either not completed their schooling, or have not made up their minds with finality about whether to continue their studies (either by commencing studies at a licensing school or college, or going on to graduate or professional school).

Most of them attended traditional schools; in fact, only a smattering went on to alternative type schools. It is clear that once they decided to pursue a field, they focused on places that would give them a good education in as direct a manner as possible, and were not restricted to institutions that might provide an environment similar to the one they were accustomed to.

Figure 20 shows the number of schools of each level that the respondents attended. The characterization "other schools" refers to such institutions as art schools that are not set up as colleges, culinary arts schools, schools of massage, etc.

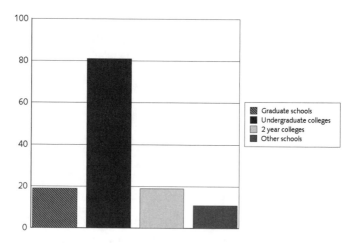

Figure 20 Categories of schools attended by respondents

Table 2 gives a complete listing of the names of the various colleges and universities attended by the respondents as of the time of their interviews.

Table 2 Colleges and Universities Attended by the Respondents
Graduate Schools

Boston College
Columbia University
Emory-Riddle University
Harvard University
Lehigh University
Life University
Massachusetts Institute of
    Technology
New School University (NY)
Rutgers University
Saint John's Seminary
Smith College

Tufts University
University of California, San
    Diego
University of Connecticut
University of Southern
    California
University of Texas
University of Wisconsin
University of Washington
William Mitchell College of Law
Yale University

Table 2   (Cont.)
Undergraduate Colleges

American University
American College in London
Antioch College
Art Institute in San Francisco
Assumption College
Babson College
Bard College
Bennington College
Berklee College of Music
Bermidji University
Boston College
Boston University
Brandies University
California School of
    Professional Psychology
Carnegie Mellon University
Catholic University
Clark University
Colorado University
Colorado Institute of Art
Columbia Business School
Columbia University
Curry College
Deaconess Nursing School
Dean College
Eastman School of Music
Emerson University
Eugene Lang College, New
    School University
Evergreen State College
Framingham Union Nursing
    School
Framingham State College
Gilford College

Goddard College
Hampshire College
Harvard Extension School
Immaculate Heart College
Johnson and Wales University
Lesley College
Linburne College (Australia)
Louisiana State University
Macalester College
Marlboro College
Massachusetts College of Art
Merrimack College
Mills College in San Francisco
Montserrat College of Art
Mount Ida College
Naropa University
New England Conservatory of
    Music
New School University (NY)
New York University
Newbury College
Northeastern University
Occidental College
Roger Williams College
Rutgers University
School of the Museum of Fine
    Arts
Smith College
Sonoma State University
Superior University
Unity College
University of Arizona, Tuscon
University of British Columbia

Table 2   (Cont.)

University of California, Berkeley	University of Massachusetts, Boston
University of California, Los Angeles	University of Rochester
University of Denver	University of Victoria
University of Grenoble, France	University of Washington
University of Houston	University of Wisconsin, Madison
University of Massachusetts, Amherst	Wesleyan University
	Wheelock College
	Worcester State College

Two Year Colleges

Berkshire Community College	Mount Wachusett Community College
Greenfield Community College	
Holliston Junior College	Santa Monica Community College
ITT Technical Institute	
Massachusetts Bay Community College	Southern Maine Technical College
Massasoit Community College	Suffolk County (NY) Community College

In Figure 21, we have grouped by category the areas of study that the respondents pursued. The figure turns out to verify what one would expect from this group. Only a few pursued studies in education, which by its nature would focus on traditional education. Most of the graduates who pursued a career in computers did so directly, without going through formal schooling. A subject such as science, where a professional career these days virtually always requires some sort of degree, rates high, as does social science, not a surprising choice for people who have developed their interpersonal skills so highly, and value them so much. The usual subjects one studies in college when one is looking for broad intellectual stimulation – liberal arts and the arts – are also well represented.

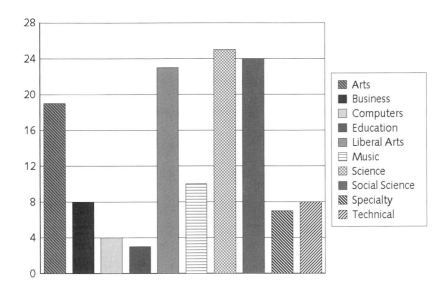

Figure 21 Areas of study pursued by respondents, grouped by category.

Table 3 names many of the specific areas of study in which our respondents specialized. They reveal a diverse range of interests.

Table 3 Specific Areas of Study Pursued by the Respondents

Accounting	Art Theory
Acting	Astronomy
Aesthetics	Ballet
Air Conditioning and	Biological Sciences
Refrigeration	Business
American Institutions	Child Studies
American Studies	Chiropractics
Anthropology	Cinematography
Architecture	Computers
Art	Criminal Justice

Table 3 (Cont.)

Culinary
Culture and Communications
Dance
Dress making and Fashion Design
Economics
Education
Electrical Engineering
EMT
Engineering
English Literature
Environmental Studies
Film
Forest Science
General Studies
Geology
Graphic Design
Hairdressing
Higher Education Administration
History
International Relations
International Development
Latin
Law
Liberal Arts
Library Information and Sciences
Linguistics
Literature
Maritime Law Enforcement
Mass Communications
Massage

Math
Media Studies
Medical Assistant
Medicine
Music / Instrumentation / Composition
Music Education
Near Eastern and Judaic Studies
Nursing
Painting
Pathology
Philosophy
Photography
Physical Therapy
Physics
Political Theory
Political Science
Psychology
Religious Studies
Research Economics
Romance Languages
Science and Automotive Technology
Sculpture
Social Work
Sociology
Spa Sciences
Television Broadcast
Theatre
Theology

As of the time of the interviews, ten people had been licensed to practice a profession (for example, CPA, Shiatsu, appraiser, cosmetologist, etc.); ten people had received an Associate's Degree; sixty people had received a Bachelor's Degree; fifteen had received a Master's Degree; two were physicians, one a lawyer, and three had received Ph.D. degrees. Quite a few were still in school, presumably pursuing degree programs, but not yet finished.

One of the phenomena we found interesting about our respondents was that quite a few of them did not rush from Sudbury Valley to another school, even though they did eventually decide to go on with their formal studies. Many of those who paused in their formal studies were pleased that when they finally went to school, they felt mature and ready, and often they looked for schools where others had made similar decisions. As one person put it:

> *The university that I attended has a program that caters to what they call "mature students," who are basically people who've gone and done something else for several years and have then decided to come back to school. That was one of the things that intrigued me about that school as opposed to the other schools that I was applying to at the time. Because I figured that would fit more with who I was, in terms of not wanting school to be the only activity in my life, and not being eighteen, and not wanting to drink beer every night of the week – those types of things.*

Another person dropped out of college, and later enrolled in the University of Massachusetts in Boston, a decision that turned out to delight him:

> *I think maturity made it a much better experience, having more life experience behind me, at that point, knowing what I wanted to learn. It was filled with wonderful professors who wanted to teach and write and were there to give you as much as you wanted to get from them.*

We were able to retrieve information from some of the interviews about the length of time that elapsed between the time people left Sudbury Valley and the time they enrolled in another school. Figure 22 displays what we know.

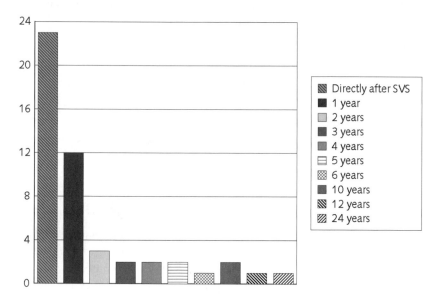

Figure 22 Length of time between leaving Sudbury Valley and beginning formal study

One interesting footnote to this data on delayed entry to college. Only one respondent – who went on to college directly after receiving his diploma from Sudbury Valley – flunked out of school; it happened during his first year at school. He went on to become a very successful computer programmer, and is currently (and very happily and success-fully) pursuing college studies while continuing to work full time and raising a family.

The Good Things in Life

"What I like about my life is that it's mine. I have a very close family, a very close knit group of friends, and a lot of wonderful people in my life. I have the opportunity to do a lot of wonderful things in my life, like riding horses. Not lots of people get to live out their dreams."

Overview

The good things in life are the things we think about when we contemplate our everyday existence. The way we feel about them determines whether our life feels fulfilled or whether it has shortcomings that cry for attention and repair. They are the answers we come up with spontaneously to the questions, "What do you like about your life?" and "What do you dislike about your life?"

As we move from one topic to another in this section, how the alumni look at their lives will gradually be revealed.

A surprising number of respondents were eloquent about the sheer pleasure they derive from the kinds of everyday things that we all want to find enjoyable. Over and over again their words convey an undertone of excitement and enthusiasm that comes through even in the printed word. Consider the responses of the following people, whose words almost rise to the level of poetry:

> You get up in the morning and you're walking around. It's like you won the lottery. We are the best, the coolest, weirdest, most interesting animals that have ever evolved. I love human beings. By God, we walked on the moon! We plumbed every depth of the entire earth! We have space ships that are almost light years away from here at this point! It doesn't get any cooler than us. I love pointing out to people how cool they are. I like how close we are at this point in life to actually functioning fully as human beings. Getting away

from all the dull, cruel, oppressive mechanical ways which have been historically how we operated. Survival is no longer an issue for us. It need not be an issue for the entire human race. Every day we get a little bit closer to understanding each other and being there for each other and losing the sense that if we don't get it, no one's going to get it for us and so we have to fight each other for it.

I love my occupation. I love where I live. I get to travel. I'm a really lucky person! I think what constitutes most people's happiness is their everyday interactions and their occupations and their friends and family. I have my family around me in New York. My parents come to visit a lot and I have a good stable base of friends and community. I love what I do. I wouldn't want to do anything else. It's so exciting. I'm really happy.

I like so much about my life. I feel like the luckiest man in the world at this point. I have a beautiful wife who's a close friend and the most wonderful woman I've ever met. I have a beautiful daughter who's turning out to be a joy every day – most of every day anyway – and I'm now living where I want to live. I'm near my close friends, I'm near my family. I live in a terrific house that we were just in the right place at the right time to buy. It's a great house and great location. After working ten years in the environmental field in a variety of jobs, I have finally found myself in my ideal job. In general, I just feel that everything has fallen into place in my life.

From a person who lives in the far north of Minnesota, the following paean:

I seem to have sidestepped the speed and the time constraints and that hurriedness that our culture seems to be so bent on. I regulate my own time. I choose what I'm going to do. My work is very varied. I can do stuff outside; I can garden when I want to use my body and have a workout, and I have a studio, my very own studio, that I go to and do artwork in. I have time to write. Another thing I like about my life is that I'm in nature a lot. I live in a field within the woods, so I kind of have the best of all worlds. The area between a woods and a field is really attractive to animals, so I see a lot of wild animals. It's got gorgeous birds flying all over the place. It feels like paradise. If I want the lake, it's just five miles away, so I can go to a beach. Life is good. Especially after traveling, I appreciate my choices even more.

The catalog of delights changes slightly from person to person but the underlying theme of satisfaction with life is the same:

I'm very happily married, very fortunate to be surrounded by a great family, and have a very good home life. I think I'm doing something in life that is very important and beneficial not only to myself, but to a lot of people around me.

I'm pretty happy with where I am in life. I'm happy with where I'm living. I'm happy with the choices I've made so far. I've got a great family, a great girlfriend, good friends. I'm looking forward to starting a good job. I think I'm quite happy. And I'm living in the greatest city on the face of the planet!

I have friends that I adore, that I can't even believe are my friends, they're so great. That's a really wonderful thing. I have a nice apartment with super roommates. I have maturity that I didn't have in the past and freedoms that I didn't have in the past. I was in a seven year relationship from the time I was 20 to 27, which was a great relationship and I still miss it, but being totally independent now is interesting and fun and an invigorating kind of experience.

And an unsolicited, lovely, compliment to the school:

I like my books, I like the internet, I like my friends, I like the fact that I went to Sudbury Valley. I think I'm able, as a result of going to Sudbury Valley, to ask questions all the time and I think that's very important.

Often we heard from alumni how thoroughly pleased they are with the various components of their lives:

> *I just feel I'm happy. I feel fulfilled. I have challenges that I like;*
> *I have my husband whom I love; I have my friends and family. I have*
> *satisfaction in what I've worked for and now reap the benefits from.*
> *These are not necessarily even huge things but just to know that we've*
> *worked for our house and now we have it – that's satisfying. I can't*
> *think of one thing I would change.*

> *What I like about my life is that it's mine. I have a very close family,*
> *a very close knit group of friends, and a lot of wonderful people in my*
> *life. I have the opportunity to do a lot of wonderful things in my life,*
> *like riding horses. Not lots of people get to live out their dreams.*

> *I like everything! I've got a great family life, I like my school, I've*
> *got a great, great group friends, I've got pretty good peace of mind. I*
> *think that those are probably – family, friends, relationships, peace of*
> *mind, and all that stuff – the best things in life.*

> *I like the fact that I'm alive. I like everything about my life. I love*
> *my work, I love the person that I'm with, I love where I live, I love the*
> *city, I love my house. I can't think of anything bad.*

As we have seen, the respondents mentioned various specific aspects of their lives that they like. We collected these into a number of categories, that are displayed in Figure 23.

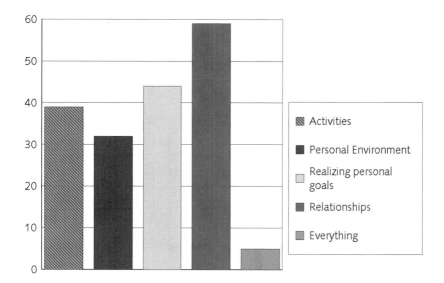

Figure 23 What respondents like about their life, grouped by category. Several respondents mentioned factors in more than one category.

By contrast, Figure 24 shows what respondents did not like about their current lives, grouped by category. The category "nothing" in this figure is actually a double negative: it represents those people who just plain have no complaints.

In the following chapters, we discuss each of these categories in turn – with the exception of the category "everything" in Figure 23, and the category "nothing" in Figure 24, neither of which needs further elaboration.

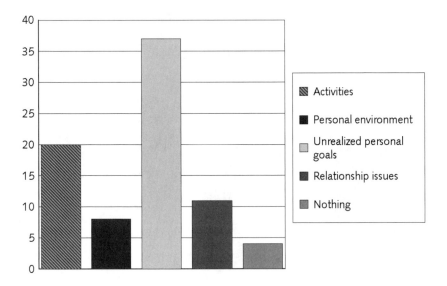

Figure 24 What respondents dislike about their life, grouped by category. Several respondents mentioned factors in more than one category and some did not reply to this question.

Personal Environment

When talking about aspects of their life that contribute to their overall well being, over a quarter of the respondents mentioned features that we grouped under the heading "personal environment" (see Figure 23). This includes such topics as the area in which they live, a community of people with which they are personal involved, their home (house, home life, etc.) and the physical comforts of their daily lives. Figure 25 breaks down their responses into these sub-categories.[8]

Several aspects of this figure are worthy of note. For seventeen people, their home stood out as a major source of pleasure. One person put it this way: "I've always been a homebody. I've always liked to stay home and I've never been a partyer. That's just who I am." Another was thrilled with fulfilling the American dream: "I'm living in a house that I own for the first time in my life. I am enjoying that and I am very comfortable in it. I'm in a different part of Massachusetts that is very beautiful and I'm enjoying learning all about it."

Half of this group emphasized the surrounding area as having special importance for them. Typical was the following comment from a photographer starting her own business:

---

[8] Since only seven people mention their personal environment as a negative factor in their lives (see Figure 24), it was not meaningful to break this down further.

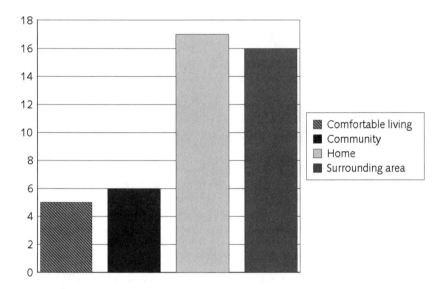

Figure 25 Characteristics of personal environment respondents mentioned as being aspects of their lives that they liked. Several people talked about more than one category.

> *It's very exciting to finally have all the things that I have wanted for a while. It's a really beautiful area here and when it's a beautiful day, I have the freedom to go out and be outside and take pictures, and that is really wonderful. Springtime here is just glorious and I used to always get spring fever and have to kind of tie myself down to my desk. So it's exciting to have those opportunities. It's sort of like Sudbury Valley, making your own structure again – figuring out what the structure of your life is; having nothing imposed.*

The same person found the isolation of working at home to be a two-edged sword, and a source of some dissatisfaction:

> *I miss certain things. I really did like certain social aspects of my job because I had a lot of friends at work. I do maintain contact*

*with everybody. But it is different working from home. It's a little
more solitary. You have to make an effort to do that and it's a little
less regular.*

She concludes that, "Overall, it's definitely well worth it."

Two respondents talked about their particular attachment to New
England:

*I really, really love New England. I'm a true New Englander
and I don't ever plan to live any place else. You never know – things
happen – but, as far as I'm concerned, this is it. This is where I'm
going to live.*

*For me, a steady, straight, kind of predictable situation is okay. I
don't mind straying once in a while and doing something different, but
I've lived in Massachusetts my whole life. And I like it here. I don't
have a desire to live anywhere else. I don't feel like I want to just take
off and live somewhere else. I've traveled of course, but coming home
always feels good. For me just being here is sort of steady.*

A surprisingly small number thought that the material comforts
of home were worthy of mention, and only a few talked about the
importance of being members of a tight-knit community. This does not
necessarily mean that most of the respondents did not care about their
personal comforts and did not value community ties, but these factors
were not foremost in their minds when they were asked to identify the
various things that they liked (or disliked) most about their lives.

The respondents were also asked a very specific question, to wit:
"Are you living in your ideal location?" Figure 26 shows how they
responded, and perhaps says something about the extent to which
these people made the effort to locate themselves in places that pleased
them. Clearly, the overwhelming majority (67%) did so, although a
significant number – thirty-one – had not, or not yet, managed to.

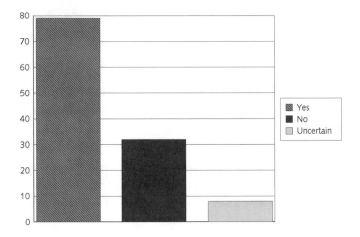

Figure 26 Respondents' replies to the question, "Are you living in your ideal location?"

A closer look at those thirty-one who do not live where they wish they did reveals where they would prefer to be living. Figure 27 shows that nineteen thought that they would rather live either in a big city, or in a different big city than the one they were living in. Sometimes that was a result of circumstances, such as still being in their university years. Eleven thought they would rather be in, basically, the middle of nowhere, as is illustrated by the respondent who said: "One thing that I feel really dissatisfied with about my life is that I live too close to a city. Every time I sit down and evaluate that, I realize that I really do much better in the country." A mere eight were hankering for suburban living.

For one person, the transplantation from New England to the Midwest was difficult to live with, and she was clear about why:

> *One of the things that drives me crazy about Minnesota is that it is a kind of churchie place. I define myself as an atheist. By that I don't mean people who believe in God are wrong and I am right. I don't know if I am right or wrong, it is just my belief. On the east*

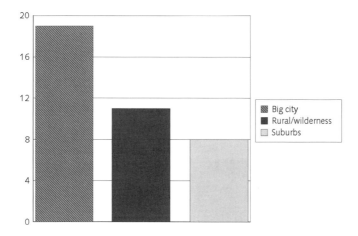

Figure 27 Where respondents currently not living in their ideal locations thought they would prefer to live. The totals for all three categories add up to more than thirty-one because several people expressed ambiguity and mentioned more than one possibility for a location they thought would be ideal.

coast I have never found people who really cared one way or the other about what I think, but out here if I say I am an atheist, it is so socially unacceptable that people will just back away and literally never speak to me again even though they have known me for months. As soon as I say it they look at me like I practice human sacrifice or something and that drives me insane. I guess people out here equate a religious person with a moral person. I do not see any connection whatsoever. I think I am an extremely moral person but it has absolutely nothing to do with being religious, because I am not.

Figure 28 shows what type of location is considered desirable by the eighty people who said they are living in their ideal locations.

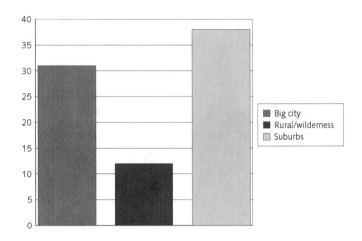

Figure 28 Where respondents live who said they are currently living in their ideal location.

Thirty-nine percent of the people living in their ideal location live in metropolitan areas, and several gave specific reasons why they like it. One said: "My rent is really reasonable. The street I live on has very nice people and I love being so close to Boston, but not in Boston. I'm very close to the T so I can get right on the T, go into Boston, be there in fifteen minutes or be in Cambridge, or wherever I want to go."

Forty-six percent live in the suburbs. Fifteen percent live in remote areas. Here is how one respondent talked about his home:

> *The place that I'm living in now is a timber frame house. I forget exactly what the inside dimensions are, but outside, it's identical to Henry David Thoreau's house in Walden. It's not very big: room for a bed, a desk, a dresser and a stove and some room to walk around, but that's pretty much it. But I don't end up spending too much time in here. I end up spending my time outside anyway.*

An interesting conclusion can be drawn from a comparison of Figures 27 and 28. The former figure relates to people who have not yet settled down in their preferred location; the latter people who say that they have. One sees a marked shift of preference for suburbs as people finally choose the location best suited to them, which is the same result that one sees in the population at large.

An additional piece of information worthy of notice can be gleaned from Figure 29, which gives an age breakdown for people who said they are not living where they ultimately want to be located. The figure shows, not surprisingly, that the older they get, the more likely they are to be happy with where they are living.

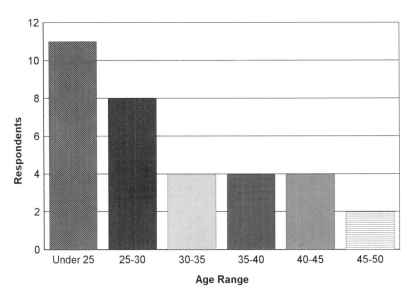

Figure 29 Age breakdown of respondents who say they are not currently living in their ideal location.

Activities

When asked what they liked about their present lives, thirty-nine alumni talked about activities that particularly pleased them. (See Figure 23, p. 159.) We grouped these responses into three categories: travel, being of service to others, and work.

Actually, only two people mentioned travel in this context. Eight talked about helping others. While it has become somewhat unfashionable to associate military service with the ideal of service to others, one person was quite articulate about the link between the two.

> I am in the Coast Guard, and I enjoy everything that I'm getting out of it. It's given me an opportunity to travel the world and be responsible. I've saved people's lives. I've stopped drugs from coming into the country. I've kept people from over-fishing. I get to do all those things that you see on TV and that really make a big difference.

Thirty-six of the thirty-nine who mentioned liking their activities referred to their current work (including, for students, university work). Often, what particularly delighted people was the freedom to pursue their passion. "I get to do what I want," said one alumnus; "I am not ever overly pressured to do anything other than what I want. It works out nicely." One person, a musician and multi-media software analyst, was keenly aware of the contrast between his happy situation and that of so many other people he knew:

> *I see people who just hate their job and it's a day-to-day grind for them. They can't stand what they do and they do it because they need the money or they just like the stability of what they're doing: it's a job and you get paid and you go home and you spend your money on your rent and whatever. And I'm really happy not to have to live that way. That to me is the most gratifying thing of all.*
>
> *On the one hand I'm doing what I want and I'm able to make a living and I don't really have to compromise what I want to do for that, and that's great! I've got a huge network of people that I work with. There's just tons of people who are my age, motivated to get things done, who are just out there kicking ass and I'm happy to be a part of that. So it's very enriching to me that I can basically do music as my job and get paid to do it and that I'm able to survive. Things have really started to come together within the past year or two.*

Twenty people cited work or college as activities in their life that they were not happy with at the time of the interview. (See Figure 24, p. 160.) Several of them were in periods of transition; their dissatisfaction focused more on their temporary situation than on the actual work that they were looking for. Thus, an aspiring young actress was less than thrilled at having to take odd jobs while she tried to break into the difficult world of entertainment:

> *There's always been an underlying dissatisfaction, because I've been pursuing acting on and off. There has certainly been more time that I've been pursuing it full steam ahead, and other times when I haven't been able to pursue it as much, for financial reasons. So there's always an underlying dissatisfaction of, "I'm not doing what I want for a living." The acting profession is unfair, and difficult to get into, and it is a lot about who you know, the right place, and the right time. A lot of it is out of my control, and that's frustrating. I wish things were different.*

A social worker who has been out of the job market while she was raising her small children, and is still not willing to be away from them for full days, was experiencing the pains of trying to find her place in the work world: "I really would like to get back into social work, and since I've been in Florida I have not been able to make that happen. I haven't been able to find a mother's hours kind of a job and I have not been willing to go back full-time. Finding really meaningful part-time work is tough to do."

Although virtually everyone who continued their education in a formal setting did so with deliberation (see the Chapter "To Pursue or Not to Pursue," p. 108), one person couldn't help expressing her annoyance at the external conditions that surrounded her studies:

> *I don't like that I'm in college. I think the lifestyle sucks. I think there's too much pressure. I like where I'm going; I like what I'm doing and where my life is leading. I just don't like the way college is forcing me to live now. I think it's awful for all college students: even if you know you want to end up doing something specific, it's still awful enough to go through.*
>
> *I wish there was another way to do it. My university forces you to live in the dorms for the first two years and eat their food. I was sick the first two years because of their food, and there's no way to get out of it. They don't value your health as much as your academics.*

Perhaps not so surprising is the reaction of one alumnus who had spent virtually all his school life at Sudbury Valley and was now a professor working in a field that he loved in a traditional academic setting. For him, his situation has a bitter-sweet ambiguity:

> *There's parts of my job that I don't like. Teaching is fun but it's only fun when you have students who are actually interested in what they're doing. For the most part, especially when I teach the more advanced courses, I do have such students. But one almost always has*

*a few students who are . . . you know, a pain in the neck and occupy
a disproportionate amount of your time. It's just one of the rules of
thumb about teaching anywhere. So there are parts of teaching that are
a real pain. That's probably as much as I want to say about that.*

Lifestyles

In order to get a more rounded picture of the kind of people our alumni are, we included some broad questions relating to lifestyle matters.

Figure 30 displays the leisure activities mentioned in the interviews.

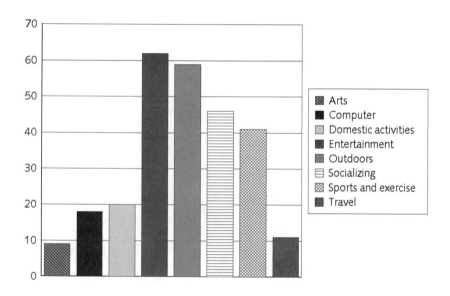

Figure 30 Respondents leisure activites

The figure reveals the group to be a fairly representative section of the general population when it comes to things they do in their spare time. Figure 31 for the most part re-enforces that impression, with a twist: there appears to be more interest in independent films than prevails in the public at large.

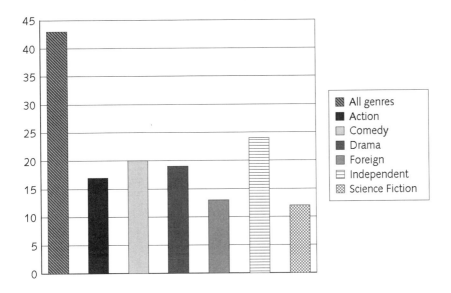

Figure 31 Respondents' cinema preferences

The respondents surprised us, however, when we asked them about their television viewing. Their answers are displayed in Figure 32. Only a handful look at sports programming, and a significant percentage of the respondents (20%) do not look at TV at all.

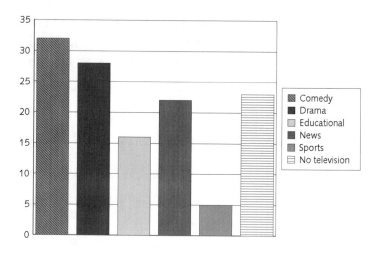

Figure 32 Respondents' television viewing preferences

The respondents do seem to read quite a bit. Figure 33 categorizes the kinds of newspapers they are interested in, and Figure 34 the types of magazines.

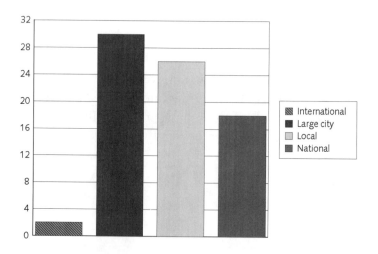

Figure 33 Respondents' newspaper preferences

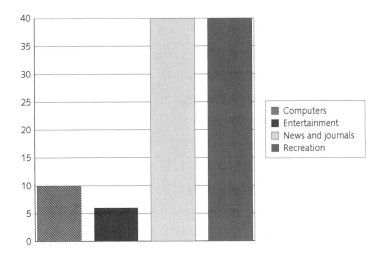

Figure 34 Respondents' magazine preferences

The kinds of books they like to read are shown in Figure 35. Although reading fiction is quite popular with this group, they seem to read an extraordinary amount of various types of non-fiction.

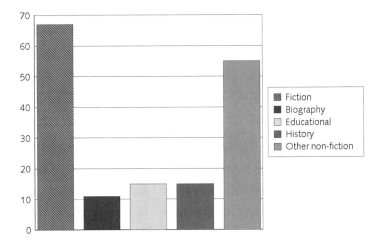

Figure35 Respondents' book preferences

Our respondents are very much rooted in the 21ˢᵗ century when it comes to their comfort using computers, as revealed in Figure 36. However, it is worth noting that we still have a few strong-minded Luddites.

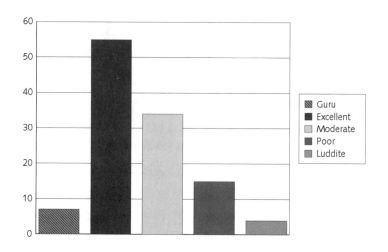

Figure 36 Respondents' familiarity with computers

Although Sudbury Valley alumni present themselves as highly individualistic people, this did not seem to stop them, in general, from joining various kinds of groups that reflected their personal interests. Figure 37 categorizes the groups they reported belonging to.

A number of the respondents turned out to be doing rather interesting and unusual things outside their work and daily routines. More than a dozen perform musically – playing in bands, singing in choruses, and performing as soloists. Quite a few have had art exhibits of one kind or another. Several write for publication. One belongs to a group that does Civil War re-enactments. One makes films; another belongs to a martial arts group that gives performances. Several are serious amateur photographers. Some participate in live-action role-playing events. A few are political activists, and one races cars just for fun.

All in all, they emerge as a very varied group of people spanning a wide range of interests, many quite unusual.

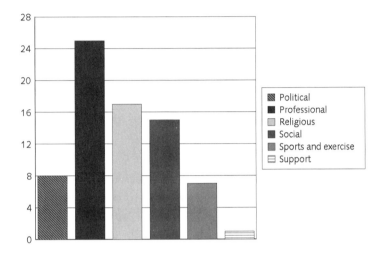

Figure 37 Respondents' group membership

Realizing Personal Goals

Many former students talked about various ways in which they had defined their own aims, and how that fit into what they liked or disliked about their lives. Thirty-seven of them mentioned these aims, sometimes wistfully, as being frustratingly elusive.[9] Figure 38 gives a breakdown of those goals.

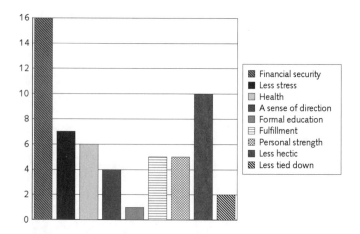

Figure 38 Unrealized personal goals, by category.

---

[9] See Figure 24, p. 160.

A closer look at the comments made by those depicted in this figure reveals people who are pursuing various types of goals, but who were unhappy at the time of the interview with the amount of progress they had made towards reaching them. For example, a graduate student felt that he didn't "like the fact that I'm still in school. I would like to be out of school and working, but I look at it as a question of delayed gratification. That would be the primary thing that kind of irritates me."

Several were still looking for a focus to their lives. As one said, "I don't have much in the way of direction at this point, so I'm kind of looking for some way to go. But I don't know how to look very actively, so I'm just kind of keeping my eyes peeled in the hope that I, and a way, will find ourselves in proximity." Another, highly successful in very demanding work, still felt that her "biggest problem is that I desperately, desperately want a career path, because I like to work and I want to be challenged, but I can't figure out exactly what it is that I should be doing and I find that very frustrating. The thing that doesn't satisfy me is my feeling of wanting to be more focused and to find something that I can set my sights on. But I think that's within my control."

Others were still waiting for a sense of fulfillment. "I'm searching a little bit to make some major decisions about where I want to live and what kind of work really fulfills me," said one. Another expressed similar concerns:

> I'm pretty stressed out by trying to find a job that actually holds my interest. I feel like my degree is kind of useless. That's what I'm feeling bad about and focusing on. Finding work that is fulfilling. Being around people that I care about. Having a good community.

None of the above people felt that the problems they expressed were intractable. Nor did people who mentioned personal weaknesses that they were struggling to overcome. "I wish I could be more aggressive," said one. "Sometimes I feel, not that people necessarily can take advantage of me, but that they feel they can, and I don't like that feeling." Another was forthright about a problem that has plagued him for his whole life: "I'm a chronic, clinically depressed person. Unless something really radical happens, that's not going to change. That's managed to a greater or lesser degree, although it's difficult." And then there's the alumnus who, despite impressive personal achievements, never gives up his quest for personal improvement:

> *I'm continually coming up against things that I'm dissatisfied with in my life, and I make huge mistakes all the time, as I think everyone does. I always try different ways to deal with that. I'm always trying different strategies for dealing with dissatisfaction or dysfunction or whatever. I guess what I do is try different approaches to the same problems. For instance, I'm chronically sort of scatter-brained and flaky and I'm constantly trying different ways to organize myself. In the last several years I've gotten really diligent about using a daybook to plan and to write things down. If someone says, "Call Al," I'll get up out of the chair and write a note and put it on the refrigerator. It sounds sort of trivial except that one of the things that causes me the most pain in my life is forgetting things and losing things and not doing things on time and that kind of stuff – for me, it's a huge issue.*

Several former students were intent on reducing the level of stress in their lives. Over and over they strike the same theme:

> *I don't like how busy I am, and how hard it is to double work and family. I'd say this is the major issue in my life.*

> *I work very hard. I wish I could work a little less hard. The hours and the type of work are both pretty demanding.*

We're just really stressed out and too busy. I think you pay a big price for living a life like that. I see people who have lots of time to spend with their kids and do this and do that and I think, wow, that's nice. That's just not my lot right now.[10]

I wish there was more time to get things done and I could get things done faster. Less people who want me to do things. So I'd have a little bit more time to go canoeing and stuff. My days just go by too fast. I'm almost always under pressure; I'm always late. If you ask me to do something, I will probably show up but I will not show up on time, and I don't even worry about it anymore. It's just not possible.

Wistful musings aside, all of these people are excited about their lives, and fundamentally satisfied with them. They just wish their lives weren't so intense.

Figure 39 is the complement of 38, and shows various categories of personal goals that people were happy to be realizing.[11] In essence, these two graphs reveal the same thing about the alumni – namely that they set goals, and they consider it important to their well-being to take steps to realize them. Satisfaction with achieving these goals is, after all, not so many steps away from dissatisfaction at not yet having achieved them.

---

[10] A major reason this respondent's family time with his children was so limited was that he was in the process of beginning a Sudbury model school for his children!

[11] The data comes from the forty-four people who identified this factor as being something they liked about their lives. See Figure 23, p. 159. Several respondents mentioned more than one personal goal.

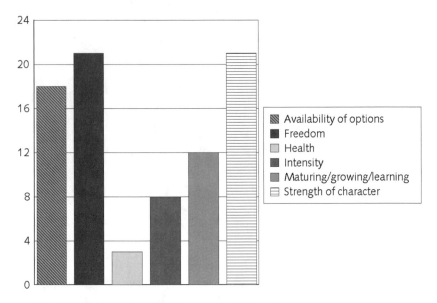

Figure 39 Personal goals being realized, by category.

Over and over again, the comments of the respondents show enthusiastic engagement with these aspects of their lives. One had this to say:

> *I like the infinite level of possibilities about my life. I like having four limbs. I really enjoy the fact that I can get up and walk anywhere in the United States. I can swing from tree to tree. I can be active and whole. It is very difficult to throw away all of the privileges that I was born with. I was born with every last privilege that you can possibly be born with. I was born white, American, and male. I'm still young. I have the use of all four limbs and all of my brain cells.*

Another talked somewhat more prosaically about his delight at the many options available to him: "I feel like I have a diverse range of opportunities and abilities, a pretty diverse range of friends, the range of things that I feel like I am fit to engage in is wide and I have had a fairly rich range of experiences."

And then there was freedom. Person after person exulted in it:

> *I feel free. I feel a lot like I did growing up at Sudbury Valley because I can just pretty much do whatever I want, aside from my school work. But since I get to choose what I want to be doing in school, I still feel free.*

> *What do I like about my life? I don't have to set an alarm clock. It's* **mine**. *Which is better than most people's.*

> *I like the fact that I'm able to pretty much do what I want. I don't feel I have to do what everybody expects me to and be one of the "normal" sort of people. I like the fact that I still get respect for being who I am, and that I don't have a lot of pressures to be who I'm not.*

Many were pleased with the strength of character that they could call upon in adversity. Here are two comments:

> *I've been down, you know? But when I'm not satisfied I'm usually pretty good about finding something, making a change, moving along, moving forward, doing something different.*

> *I like that I'm engaged and that I have two beautiful children, and that I have gone through a really tough period and done a lot of healing and managed to come out of it really well. I have some good coping techniques and a lot of strength and resilience that I didn't know I had.*

Perhaps most eloquent were those who talked about their ability to continue to grow, mature and learn:

I felt kind of bad for a little while after I left the school community. It was a big change. After, I'd say, a matter of months, certainly less than a year, things started getting different. Right now I'm happier than I've probably been in the last decade. Things seems to be getting better and better. What I think you have to do is sit back and take time with yourself, analyze different things, things that you can change, things that you might change, things that you definitely can't change, and just try to forge on ahead – try to get that picture at the end, and take the steps that you have to in order to get there all the way.

This is kind of a general broad sweeping statement – but I guess what I like about my life is my capacity to enjoy life, to be able to meet any challenges that I face without a great deal of difficulty. Probably the greatest skill that I learned attending Sudbury Valley was being able to teach myself and being able to problem-solve. By being on my own I learned how to be competent and independent and when I needed to consult someone, one of the staff members, they were always more than happy to help. I learned how to learn, and I relearned how to enjoy learning. So life is just an endless source of fascination and of pleasure for the most part.

I feel good about the changes in myself. I like myself now a lot more than I did several years ago. I am really happy to feel myself maturing into an adult. I was joking with a friend of mine who's almost fifty and she was saying how old she feels, and I was saying I'm not over the hill but the hill is in sight; and that's a good feeling. I'm getting gray hairs and I feel good as I'm entering that phase. I'm doing the most challenging, genuine thing I could do. It's definitely stretching and new and I don't know what I'll be doing or how things will be going in the future. I've just grown and changed a lot. That's a neat feeling – I think that's being alive.

A sweeping summation of the personal goals of one respondent, a graduate student, expresses his enthusiasm at feeling that he has defined them and been successful in working toward their realization:

What I like about my life is that a lot of the things that I have put forth as intentions in the last ten years – things that I have wanted in my life and things I have wanted to contribute to the world – are really coming to fruition. I'm really enjoying my schoolwork. I'm enjoying learning how to become a therapist and the work that I've begun doing as a therapist has been really rewarding. I'm very, very happy with my home life. I'm enjoying living in a residential Zen community. Spiritually and emotionally, I'm happier than I've ever been. I have strong friendships, good connections with people. I also feel that my relationship with myself is very healthy, and I'm having a good time. There's a nice balance between the serious effort being put forth in my meditation practice, and school, and work, and a nice balance of all that with having a lot of fun. I'm just really enjoying being alive right now.

Relationships

Seventy of the respondents mentioned relationship issues as being among the things that they either liked or disliked about their lives.[12] Eleven of these expressed dissatisfaction while aspiring to improve their situations. For example, a respondent still searching for the "right" significant other made these plaintive remarks:

> I think that, maybe, I would like my personal relationships with the opposite sex to be a little bit better. Being single at this point kind of stinks. But I have an equal struggle between being totally satisfied with being who I am and single and thinking "Geez, I must be missing something." The biggest thing is figuring out what I should be doing in that area. You know, I think my life is pretty good. I'd like to have a significant other to add a little bit more style to my regular guy life, but other than that it's been just fine.

Another, a recent divorcee, wasn't quite so sure how she felt:

> I like that I feel independent again. Not that I really felt not independent when I was married, but it's different and it's sort of like I'm starting over. And as far as what I don't like, I guess to an extent I don't like starting over also. It's been a little hard to adjust to being single. I was just emailing a friend earlier who was asking me how

---

[12] See Figure 23, p. 159 and Figure 24, p. 160.

I was adjusting to this non-married life, and I was saying, 'Actually, I really didn't have a problem adjusting to not being married but I've had a bit of an issue adjusting to being single again.'

A larger number by far talked about how happy they were with their relationships – primarily with family and friends:

> *I really thank my lucky stars every day that the people in my life are in my life and that I found them. I don't think that many people have such good personal connections. I think if you find one or two in your lifetime, you're lucky, and I have several of them. I just feel really, really lucky to have these deep relationships with people and I consider myself luckier than most anybody on the planet.*

> *I like being married. Liking it was really unexpected. I never saw myself getting married – I was just opposed to the whole idea of marriage as an institution – but I've changed, and it seems like my world has become more intimate.*

> *I love watching my children develop. It is just amazing. I have seen it in children before, but when they're your children, and you see day to day things, it just blows you away every day. Watching them take hold of life – especially my five year old, who has gone from being a little dependent baby into an autonomous, free thinking person, not a clone of his parents at all – that's what makes my life wonderful these days.*

Relationships with others obviously play a significant role in the lives of our respondents, as they do in everyone's life. In our study, we asked the alumni a lot of questions about the nature of their relationships. A much fuller analysis of the nuances of their attitudes towards relationships is presented in the section of this book entitled "Relationships" (see p. 241).

Income

Do former students make enough money? "Enough," of course, depends totally on your point of view. There is no objective measure for an adequate income. What we were interested in is how the alumni themselves evaluate their financial situation.

Startlingly, only fourteen of the respondents were dissatisfied with their income. Given the general level of dissatisfaction with income that one reads about among the population at large, one might have expected a larger percentage. The overwhelming majority were pleased with where they were financially – most without qualification. There were a few who, though not complaining, either expected better times in the future (for instance after their education was complete) or wouldn't object to having more now.

Figure 40 shows the responses. Note that we deliberately did not inquire about the actual incomes of the respondents. What was important to us was how satisfied they were with how much money they were making, not how much money they were making. These are two very different concepts and our respondents were very aware of this difference. Over and over again people in the study indicated that they were focused on leading satisfying lives and their attitudes towards their incomes reflected this. Here is how one of them put it:

I have a few small investments and I live extremely frugally. Part of my lifestyle choice is that I just don't spend much money and I don't run up credit card bills. I know a lot of people who feel like they have to have a nice car or they have to buy new clothes and things like that. I just don't have to have those things. Mostly my job has been developing as a person, learning, getting over some of the really heavy emotional encumbrances I had as a child, and developing relationships with people, taking care of my family and my friends, and also trying to contribute to my community. I've been very politically active throughout my life and I still am. I feel like it's important for me to dedicate a lot of my time towards improving relationships in my neighborhoods and resolving conflict in my communities and trying to do the right thing. So, I guess, in a way I see that as my job in the world and if nobody's paying me for it, I don't really mind.

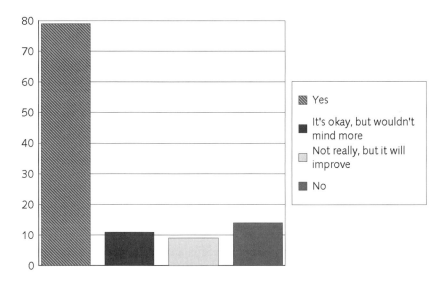

Figure 40 Respondents' satisfaction with their current level of income. Six respondents did not reply to the question.

Another person, who is immersed in the business world, had a similar indifference to his level of income: "I can live the way I want to. I've lived with a lot of money and I've lived with no money and it doesn't really matter to me."

Certainly our former students are aware of the struggles of life, and have to cope with them. But they have perspective, as the following comments illustrate:

> *New York is very expensive. It's not that I want a Mercedes or anything like that, but going out and wearing clothes appropriate to work and all that kind of stuff is very expensive and no matter how much I earn my expenses just go up. Like now I buy organic foods – that's expensive. But I'm also very happy that I can do that, and I do look back on leaner times. For example, when I was in college, if I was sick or something like that I couldn't just run to CVS and buy that big bottle of Advil. Now I can do all that stuff. Of course I have credit card debt; of course I have student loan debt; of course I don't make enough money; of course I don't have everything that I want; but I have enough money to live somewhat comfortably. I have more than I deserve. It's great.*

Some of the respondents declared unabashedly that they would be happy to have more money, but added that they had decided to be satisfied with what they had because they were conducting their lives the way they wanted to. Two typical comments:

> *What I like about my life right now is that I've made the leap over to doing what I like to do. Most days the hard work that I have to do is something I very much enjoy doing. If I could make money just a tad less tight, that would be probably one of the things I'd change just a little bit. But not to an extreme – I'm not hoping to be rich.*

Well, I just bought a house. I could always use more money, but who couldn't? I can live on what I make, but I wouldn't mind making a little more. But, you know, it's okay.

Even people who were still going to school did not allow a relative lack of money to distract them, but took it in stride. As one person put it, "I try and keep things pretty basic. As long as I can meet my bills and I have a nice place to sit down at the end of the day, I'm pretty comfortable. I'm good at doing things on a budget." Another left a succession of well-paid jobs to further her dream:

It was stressful to make the decision to go back to school and devote so much time to it, because it's financially scary, but it feels very good. I'm finally moving toward something that I want to do. Had I stayed with my previous job – which was comfortable, and I was making a big paycheck, and it was safe – I wouldn't have financial worry on my head. But other than that, I'm very happy with what I'm doing.

Over and over again, realizing the goals they set for themselves far outweighs making money, explicitly. In one person's words, "It's really hard to make a lot of money doing any of the things that I really want to focus on" – but that hasn't stopped him from going right ahead and focusing on what he wants, which in his case happens to be art and music. Or, as a brilliant inventor said, who lives in a non-electrified cottage, without running water, and runs a high-tech business on the cutting edge, "My style of living is what most people would consider poverty. And I love it."

It was not that no one had dreams of riches. This is the comment of one of the 11% who were dissatisfied: "I need to be a millionaire. Immediately! I want to work my butt off and become famous, basically. Hopefully I'll be successful through music or movies." She is working on it non-stop, and very happily at that.

Values

"I detest lies and coercion in all their forms . . . My holiest
of holies is the human body, health, intelligence, talent,
inspiration, love and the most absolute freedom, freedom from
coercion and lies, no matter how expressed."

> A.P. Chekhov, letter of October 4, 1888 to A. Plescheev,
> quoted in *Memoirs of a Non-Belonger*, Richard Pipes
> (Yale University Press; New Haven, 2003) p.89

"I'm always striving for perfection, trying to do better. I could
definitely achieve more in my life but I think that's what life
is about, to constantly pursue your dreams, to constantly
make yourself a better individual or do the best that you can
at certain things. Often times I question whether I'm a great
mother. I would love to be that tenfold."

Overview

There were many occasions for the respondents to discuss the values that they held most dear. The subject was approached explicitly when they were asked both of these questions: "What is important to you in life?" and "What things are you passionate about?" But values came up over and over again also in parenthetical remarks they made while responding to other questions.

The chapters in this section take up a broad range of ideals and values that were mentioned in interviews. We have organized them into seven large groupings, each of which is the focus of a chapter. The section ends with a self-evaluation by the respondents of whether or not they actualize their values in their daily lives.

The overwhelming impression created by the interviews is of a group of people who give a great deal of thought and attention to their value systems. One and all they reveal themselves as people who are living an examined life: these people show a palpable engagement with their ideals. From the responses, we felt that these are not abstractions that come up as answers in interviews, but are rather collections of values that infuse their lives.

The following statement, by a graduate in her late forties, could well serve as the archetypal response for the whole group. Its breadth, its obvious enthusiasm and excitement, reveal a person who has retained her youthful idealism and passions through her adult life:

I value materialistic things less and people-oriented sorts of things more. It's important to me to be able to take care of myself – to be happy on my own without being dependent on somebody else. It's important to me to get along with people and to take care of my family. And it's important to me to be able to provide a good life for my family – not just my kids, but parents and siblings and aunts and uncles – and friends.

Visual things are very important to me. It's amazing how what I see affects how I feel. I think that's because I'm an artist and I take in everything that I see. I'm passionate about my art. There's just something about creating something from nothing that gives me a sense of satisfaction like nothing else.

The environment is important to me – taking care of the environment and not wasting resources. I like being outside and I like being in nature. I spent a lot of time outside at Sudbury Valley. I used to spend a lot of time in the beech tree. That's where I received my first kiss. I spent a lot of time climbing trees. That was one of my favorite things to do. And in the winter almost every single day I would cross-country ski.

I like adventure and I'm passionate about love. I think I'm passionate about life and about living life and not letting it pass me by.

Spiritual and Ethical Values

W̄e have divided the spiritual and ethical values mentioned by the alumni as being important to them into a number of groups, as shown in figure 41.

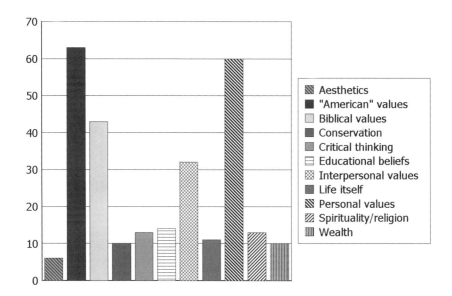

Figure 41 Spiritual and ethical values important to the respondents, grouped by category.

Under the rubric of "American" values, we include such things as egalitarianism, freedom, responsibility, respect, and rights. "Biblical" values include integrity, being a good person, justice, love, and truth. The values we group under Personal values relate to excellence, having a meaningful life, making a mark in the world, and recognition. These three groups – "American" values, "Biblical" values, and Personal values – are broad enough to merit treatment in separate chapters. They receive the most attention in the answers that the respondents gave – in fact, over half (54%) referred to one or another of the American values, half referred to personal values, and over one third (36%) talked about Biblical values. In this chapter, we look at the remaining eight categories on the graph.

The enthusiasm of some respondents when they talked about values they treasured was so wide-ranging that it could only be called a passion for life itself. The person quoted at length in the Overview to this section (p. 196) is a prime example of a reply that covers pretty much all the bases, as is the following:

> *There are millions of aspects of my life that I am passionate about: first of all, I have a wonderful 3½ year old son. And I have wonderful people – wonderful friends and family – in my life, created family as well. Also, just living life day to day and making the most of it, making things as good as they can be for that day.*

Another reply that focuses on a wide range of values is from a person deeply committed to Buddhist meditation:

> *I love practice. There's something that I really love about stepping out of my door at 5:20 A.M., crossing the street, and going to sit. I really love it. I wouldn't be doing it if I didn't love it. I'm very passionate about teaching. I love running a dojo, and seeing my students flourish in that setting. I love women – I love dating, I love getting to know people in that way, I love having relationships. I'm not in a long-term relationship right now but I'm definitely always open to it.*

I'm really passionate about the work of psychotherapy. I feel really excited about entering the field.

A young man who had fought, and overcome, an addiction to alcohol, and gone on to build a life for himself, including intensely pursuing graduate studies, had this to say:

*I'm very passionate about my standing as someone in recovery. That's very important to me. That's on kind of an emotional level, but in terms of more down-to-earth things, I'm very passionate about my wife. I love my wife very much. And I'm very passionate about – this is going to sound really nerdy – politics, and specifically about how countries interact. I take that very personally. I'm also very passionate about my origins. I'd say I **feel** very strongly.*

One person said explicitly, "Overall I value life." And she continued: "I value happiness, I value compassion, love, determination, strength and honesty." Just as explicit are the following answers, each elaborating in their own way:

*What's important to me in life? Let's see: what's **not** important to me in life? Everything's important! Having good relationships with people, true friendships, whether with family or friends or spouse – those are important. I like feeling that I have a soulmate. Feeling happy with your life and satisfied with your life and doing things that are fulfilling to you – those are important.*

I really just appreciate living every day. I love my life, and I love being human, and being who I am. There are little hardships here and there, but for the most part, I'm a pretty happy-go-lucky person, and I just enjoy life. When it comes to jobs, that's really just a secondary thing for me. Realness, happiness, and other people's happiness are important to me.

> *I'm alive, I'm in good health, I have friends, I can travel, I can think, I can earn money, I can exercise free will – I have a general appreciation of life, which a lot of people seem to lose track of.*

We included in the category Interpersonal values the seven people who were passionately against all forms of violence, and the three who were passionately involved in promoting world peace. The largest set of people who discussed interpersonal values were thirty people who stressed how important it was for them to act as caring individuals.

Several of the comments made about the other categories are worth noting. The category Aesthetics ranges from the visual arts – "I am passionate about photography and about capturing moments in time and beauty and portraying it two-dimensionally" – to theater:

> *I'm very passionate about theater. The type of theater I'm doing is creating new works and creating works that I'm very connected to and are very personal to me and personal to the actors that I'm working with. I'm very passionate about directing.*

Many respondents talked about the importance to them of spirituality or religion. Some comments were of a general nature:

> *I think it's important to have fun, but I also think it's important to live your life responsibly, both toward other people and toward the world at large, either the world as an environment or the world as a social political construct. I think it's important to have a connection to something larger than yourself. I myself am religious.*

> *I think that putting a lot of energy into spiritual development and sort of unraveling all of the knotted up places inside me – all the places that I'm stuck – is really important, so that I can be able to more fully try to accord with my life, rather than trying to make it accord with me. I'm passionate about my spiritual life.*

And, from a person living in an ashram at the time of the interview:

> *It's really intense here. I think the spiritual growth that we do here is almost like taking a wire whisk to your soul; you can think that everything's fine and the glass is clear and you come here and it sort of kicks up the soil. There are times of equilibrium, there are times of deep bliss and there are times of – I'm going to pull all my hair out. That's one of the reasons that I'm here. I always felt a lot of contentment and bliss after yoga or meditation. Or acceptance, acceptance with change, acceptance with lack of control, acceptance over everything being part of some greater divine picture that wasn't necessarily what I would have wanted or asked for.*

Some people referred to specific experiences within the framework of organized religions. "We lead a fairly spiritual lifestyle, in terms of celebrating Jewish holidays and the Sabbath and keeping God part of our life, being grateful, spiritual." And another: "I'm passionate about my Jewish life. I've worked for the last four or five years in the Jewish community and the not-for-profit community to help religious organizations become more efficient." On the other hand, organized religion could stir intense and contradictory feelings:

> *I'm sure I'll go to my grave feeling great passion about the Catholic Church. There was a Catholic church with a priest who gave a lecture in Chicago. You know, traditionally they referred in the old days to the church as "Our Mother." Well, he said, "If your mother is a prostitute, she's still your mother." And that has always stayed with me, right to this day. I am so, so angry at the Church. I was asked to leave the Paulist Fathers because they said I was too critical of the Church. I said to the rector at the time, "I thought that the Paulist Fathers were the most liberal community. As a Paulist, I thought I was supposed to be critical." He didn't like that. They could have said a lot of things. They could have said, "Well, we know you're gay." They could have said, "You're recovering from alcoholism. We can't trust that." Fine. Those are criticisms that I wouldn't have been happy about but I could*

have lived with. But to be asked to leave because I'm too critical of the Church! They might as well have said, "We're asking you to leave because you love the Church too much."

A widespread criticism of American society is its focus on wealth as a value. Only ten former students – a mere 8% – even mentioned wealth in their comments and not all of them in a positive vein. While one was passionate in his paean to wealth –

> *What I'm doing now, I'm just leading my life. Making more money. Giving myself more freedom. That's about it. The almighty dollar kinda rules it. If you make a ton of money, you have more freedom. Right? The idea is to make a whole ton of money as quickly as you can and get it the hell over with. That's what everybody tries to do. The question is how are you going to do it. You better figure it out, because if you're going to do it at $5.00 an hour, it ain't going to take you too far.*

– another excoriated it with equal passion:

> *I'm passionate about greed. I can't stand it. I think it's the poison of the world.*

Three categories of values shared an interesting characteristic – conservation, critical thinking and educational beliefs. While a relatively small number mentioned these at all (10, 13 and 14 respectively, out of 119 respondents), most of those were long term students, people who had spent seven or more years at school (7, 7, and 9 respectively, out of 43 long-timers).

Of all of the comments about conservation, we chose this one as the most outspoken. It comes from a student who arrived at school at the age of eight, a person who is an artist, a farmer, and a political activist committed to living a sustainable lifestyle.

I'm extremely passionate about water. Because I feel – not only do I feel, but I know – that water is life. Where water is, life is. So I'm real interested in seeing how we can change our relationship with water. I think that as time goes on, we're going to find that water is going to be what war is going to be over. I'm trying to imagine different ways that we can sidestep that so wars don't happen, and so that we get back in touch with what water really needs. Imagine a clean white bowl, a ceramic bowl. And then imagine that there's water in it – clear beautiful water – and then we shit in that. I think it's the Romans who started that. They started that way back when and everybody has taken it on and it's just a really poor use of water. That's one of the things I'm very passionate about. I just want to see change on that front. Living on Lake Superior here, there's lots of talk about diverting Lake Superior. To where? To Arizona, of course! Because they need it, you know? That's one thing that can really get my dander up.

Not surprisingly, several of the people who experienced Sudbury Valley expressed deep feelings about educational values. Some were emotional reactions to traditional schooling, such as the following:

I'm passionate about disliking the public school system in the United States. I think in general it's a very brutal system. The most damning aspect about the public schools is the fact that the teachers know who's going to succeed and who is not. They know very well who's going to succeed, they help these people along, and then the rest of them they throw to the far wind.

I'm passionate about education not being punitive. I'm really militant about it. Nobody will listen to me but I'm passionate about it nonetheless. I haven't really been able to find anybody near where I live to share that militancy with, because everybody is like, "Well, I walked a mile to school, so my kid should walk a mile to school."

For one, the contrast between the traditional system and Sudbury Valley was almost painful:

> *When I was a therapist, I would meet kids who were very unhappy – I mean, they were brilliant, creative, just incredible kids and somehow the system just wasn't accessing them. It was taking them away from their true essence. It was asking them to regurgitate, it was asking them to sit still. It was asking them to suffocate from the lack of being able to express themselves.*
>
> *Sudbury Valley was a taste of euphoria in so many ways that I think we all keep striving for it. You don't get a sample of that and then not feel that it's your job to pursue it, or manifest it, or create that environment for others.*

Another took an additional step and founded a Sudbury model school:

> *I think that – together with my wife, very much because of her – starting this school is a tremendous statement of respect and concern for the well-being of other people's children. That's a very, very, very concrete thing that we're doing. It's not just some moral value that we hold, but it's actions that we're taking as well.*

Perhaps the message they all convey can be summed up in one person's simple statement:

> *I feel passionately about children. I feel passionately about children and people treating them right.*

"American" Values

Sudbury Valley has always been closely linked with the distinctly American complex of values. In the words of one of the school's earliest publications, "For education in America today, the grand strategy must be to make the schools the embodiment of the American Dream for young and old alike – to make the schools bastions of Individual Rights, Political Democracy, and Equal Opportunity for all people and for all time."[13] So it is not surprising that a broad spectrum of American values were mentioned as especially important to many of the alumni.[14] Figure 42 shows a breakdown of the numbers of people who talked about specific values we identified as particularly "American."

The alumni were extremely articulate when they described how they felt. Quite a few alumni ascribed their passion for American values to their experience at the school.

> I believe that you should give people the freedom to do what they want to do. Sudbury Valley School is one of the organizations that actually helped me out because I already believed in that and they, of course, allowed that. The school gave everybody, whether it's a young kid or I don't care who it is, the freedom to do what they want to do.

[13] *The Crisis in American Education: an Analysis and a Proposal* (The Sudbury Valley School Press: Framingham, MA, 1970, reprinted 1999) p.45.
[14] Over half – see Figure 41, p. 197.

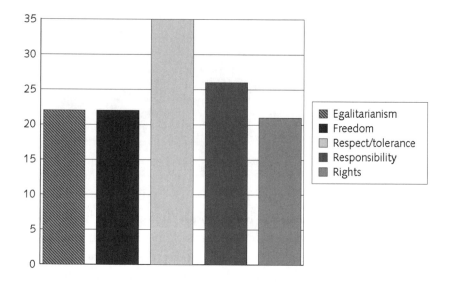

Figure 42 "American" values mentioned by the respondents, grouped by category. Many respondents talked about more than one category.

I'm committed to democracy. One of the things I am passionate about is politics. I've always been interested in politics. I guess the way I'd explain it is that I developed a view of society while I was at Sudbury Valley and of how a society could work. Sudbury Valley was a small society – around 100 people most of the time I was there. But there was fairness and there was democracy and there was self-rule and that gave me kind of a blueprint. Where I see that blueprint failing or not being mirrored in the society at large has troubled me, troubled me greatly. Those types of issues are very important to me.

The theme of freedom is a familiar one for these former students, most of whom have worked hard to embody it in their lives. As one put it, "I think having freedom is probably most important to me, freedom not to be restricted by other people's ideals, and freedom to pursue what I'm interested in." Or, in more down to earth language, "One of the things that's kind of neat about being an adult is that you can, within economic constraints, choose where you're going to live, choose where you're going to go in your own car, choose who you're going to associate with. I like it." Another respondent takes the idea of freedom as far as it will go:

> *I guess freedom is the absolute most important thing. And this freedom has to do with more than just being able to go walk around outside or something like that. It has to do with being free from the emotions, free from human habits – the typical human habits. I like to try to just be as free as possible – you know, body, emotions, mind. I guess if I were to take it to another level, I'd say that I'd also want to be able to fly, in order to complete my freedom. I guess I would like there to be no limitations, no limitations at all.*

Not unexpectedly, individual liberties and individual rights are front and center in this group of people. One alumnus recalls awakening to this issue at a very early age, and the results of this awakening:

> *I've always been very easily angered by anything that seems to be unfair. When I was in public school, when I was 7, 8, 9, I used to rebel and tell people that they were being unfair, that they were denying us freedom of assembly, freedom of speech, and so forth. I guess I'm still passionate about that but at the time it was a very gut thing. It was: here's what I'm going through, here's what other people around me are going through, and I'm surprised they're not reacting to it the same way I am. And it's unfair. It's always been a matter of deep importance to me that people be given the freedoms that are their rights by birth as human beings, and I hated not seeing it in school.*
>
> *It's one of the reasons I'm so deeply interested in history. We've watched the development of the ideas of fundamental human rights among various groups during the 15th, 16th, and 17th centuries, and of course in the United States. Seeing how people have worked or fought for those things and, to some extent, a morbid interest in what*

various people had to put up with over time, has always interested me. I'd say that is a passion.

I was probably born tending to be a person who was always trying to make sure that things were done fairly. I think I was born with that tendency, I think that my parents reinforced that tendency, I think that my rebellion against school reinforced that tendency, and I think the fact that my rebellion against school succeeded and I was taken out and sent some place else reinforced that tendency.

That "someplace else" was Sudbury Valley School. A former student, who has become a public advocate lawyer, talks about being "very angry about any kind of discrimination – sexism, bigotry, anything like that. These things make me furious, they really get to me." Another person who works in social welfare says: "I am very passionate about child rights. The short prison sentences for convicted sex offenders irritate me completely; the person who gets caught with marijuana often spends more time in jail than the person who molests a child." Then there is the graduate who extends his range even farther:

I'm pretty passionate about one's civil rights. I'm passionately against bigotry and things violent – harm to basically any person or animal. I'm very strong on animal rights as well!

Freedom of speech was a major theme too, "being able to speak my mind." Someone else discoursed on the subject at length:

I'm passionate about my role as a citizen in a democracy. A lot of people have the attitude, "Well, if you don't have the solution, you should just shut up and do what you're told." They're missing all of the things we've been taught about democracy. Your job as a citizen is to tell the people whose professional job it is to run the country that they're screwing up. Your job is to dissent. Robert Kennedy said this. Mahatma Gandhi said this. All of the founding fathers wanted the ability to dissent from what was going on and they didn't have it in their power, so they said, "this is what we're going to do. We're going to make a system where we get to dissent." I'm passionate about being able to do that.

As for responsibility, perhaps nothing could say it more pithily than this:

I'm passionate about personal responsibility – to yourself, your family, your community.

"Biblical" Values

We hen asked about what was most important to them in their lives, or what they were passionate about, forty-three of the respondents mentioned one or more of the values we have referred to as "Biblical values".[15] Figure 43 displays the particular values mentioned, and the number who mentioned each. All of these values have a prominent place in the day to day life of Sudbury Valley – indeed, are sometimes referred to as its "curriculum".

The values stressed by more respondents than any other are those that we grouped together under the heading of Integrity. "I'm passionate about doing what I say I'm going to do, and maintaining some sense of, for lack of a better term, honor," was how one person put it. A second felt that he should "always do stuff in such a way that you could never actually be blackmailed, say, because you're not afraid of what you're doing. Whatever you're going to do, you should not be afraid of doing that thing. I believe in honesty." From another:

> *Something that I've just put together lately in my mind is that my example is very important. What I am to the world influences people around me more than I ever realized. It's almost like there's always somebody who looks up to you. It doesn't even seem to matter how old you are. How I am is what is important; that I present myself as*

---

[15] See Figure 41, p. 197.

a person of – I want to say dignity but it's not really a good word – of honesty and truth.

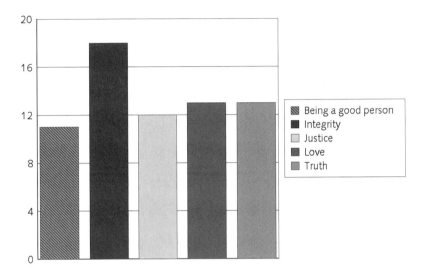

Figure 43 "Biblical" values mentioned by respondents, grouped by category. Many mentioned more than one category.

For an artist, integrity had practical consequences:

> *I do not have a stupid job. I was offered a lot of money – not a lot, but a lot to me – to sell my music for car commercials and things like that. I'll never do anything like that. I'll never sell my soul or sell my art in that way. I'll never make it into a commercial. I'm always very honest with people and with myself. Every second of my day, I'm always doing something that I feel passionately about. I never compromise and do something that I just kind of like because I think I have to.*

"Doing the right thing", as one person phrased it, loomed large for several people. One person felt that doing good brings its own rewards: "I try to treat people right, and hopefully it'll come back to me." Another felt that doing good was a way to repay life for its bounty: "I place a high value on working to do good. I think it's good to hold a position that gives back."

Other people were clear about the value of the search for truth in their lives. Here is one example:

> *I'm passionate about truth and science: finding things out – finding out how the world around us works, how we work at the sort of mechanical, chemical, biophysical level. Like how do I work? How do I think? How does my dog work? What's different about the way that I work and the way my dog works? Discovery, self-evaluation, and evaluation of the world around us, and that's sort of science – trying to figure out what is true. I guess truth is something that maybe you never really know. But I like to work on trying to understand.*

Another felt that the way to truth was through clarity of vision that allowed him to see the path that is often obscured.

> *Clarity of vision is the most valuable things in life. I'd rather have that than anything else. Being able to see things clearly. Following the path of least resistance in making any kind of decision. The water course way. Just being observant enough to tell what you're meant to do next. Which direction you're supposed to go. Not swimming against the stream. Not being a brick in the river.*

In many ways, the ultimate Biblical value is justice, as in the exhortation,[16] "Justice, justice shalt thou pursue," a theme repeated with great frequency. The latter day version of this imprecation is provided by one of the respondents:

> *I'm passionate about justice. I really can't stand any kind of injustice, no matter how small or big. I react to it. I stand up for*

---

[16] Deuteronomy, Ch.16, v.20

people a lot. I probably stand up for other people more than I stand up for myself.

"Personal" Values

H alf of the respondents in this survey were very specific about the particular set of personal values that were most important to them,[17] all of which are among those most highly esteemed in our culture. Figure 44 displays the values mentioned.

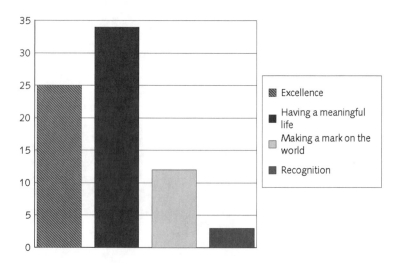

Figure 44 Personal goals valued by the respondents. Several mentioned more than one.

---

[17] See Figure 41, p. 197.

For some respondents, the pursuit of excellence informed every activity in their lives. "The most important thing to me," said one, "is to do a good job of raising my children. Then I guess the other things that are important are doing a good job at my job and at my relationship with my husband." Here are two more examples:

> *If you decide to do something, do it in a real way with your best energy and your best will, as well as you can do it. That feels like kind of a core thing to me, not that I always succeed in doing that, but it's a yardstick.*
>
> *I realize what I said is kind of abstract, but somehow that feels like the most important thing and everything else that I can say feels unduly concrete. Music is important to me and I value music, and careful thinking is important to me and I value that, and good writing is important to me and I value that. The parts of my research that seem really sort of critical and interesting I feel passionate about. And teaching; when I get very involved with a graduate student, it's something that I often feel passionate about. And my family I feel passionate about in various ways. These are all specific examples of my general desire I talked about above.*

> *I'm always striving for perfection, trying to do better. I could definitely achieve more in my life but I think that's what life is about, to constantly pursue your dreams, to constantly make yourself a better individual or do the best that you can at certain things. Often times I question whether I'm a great mother. I would love to be that tenfold.*

Leading a meaningful life was of primary importance to many of the alumni, and they were particularly articulate in describing their feelings about this. For some, this meant giving the maximum significance to their own personal development, as the following example illustrates:

> *I think the number one thing is just to have a pretty firm grip on who you are, your personal identity, what you're looking for out of life,*

and getting that. My motto is, "Get shit done." Always. There's always stuff to be done. I'm in a career path that's certainly not fulfilling for 98% of the people who are in it. Music is a total gamble, it's always a risk for everyone. I've seen people I've known with careers that have been ten years, twenty years long, and they've come to the rise and then the fall. Trying to maintain a musical career is a serious risk for everyone. I've taken the risk and I've done pretty well so far, but that could all change in the next three months, you know? But that's the choice that I've made and I'm going to live with it and try to keep that from happening for as long as I can. I think that having your identity pretty solid in your mind and what you're looking to get out of life is really the key to enjoying it. I really have invested every amount of passion and drive that I can into doing what I do. It takes up like every minute of my day. From the minute I wake up till the minute I sleep, it's all I think about or do.

For others, life had to have a combination of self-fulfillment and service to others. One respondent, a staff member at Sudbury Valley as well as a graduate, expressed it this way:

I like to be around the energy of Sudbury Valley School and I think I bring a lot of energy to the school as well. I feel so fortunate to be anxious to get to work every day and to feel that I'm really making a difference and that there's great meaning to every day.

Another:

I want to live a substantive and deep life. I don't want to skirt over the meaty and tough emotions and experiences that being in a committed and long-term relationship brings. I'm consciously looking for that, looking for that sort of deep, true experience, and I definitely credit my Sudbury Valley years with learning how to do that. I want to live a life of vision and compassion, of service to humanity and to yourself – to individual and societal development.

The theme of service to humanity came up frequently. This from somebody working happily in the business world:

> *When I graduated from Sudbury Valley my plan was to become a diplomat or do something big to help the world. I'm a little less idealistic now but I still would love to be in a position at some point where I'm really contributing to the betterment of the world. My values are very humanistic. I'm a pretty sensitive guy and kind of driven by emotions.*

And this from an academician:

> *I like to feel that at some level, in some way, I'm making the world a better place. I also like to interact with people a lot in a relatively positive way. This relates to why I'm a geologist and why I teach geology: people need to take the natural world into consideration when making decisions. I think the best way for people to do that is to have a better understanding of the natural world, although there are situations where I think some government coercion could be appropriate. That's one thing I'm passionate about.*

For one graduate, a meaningful life entailed being a role model for others and winning their respect.

> *It's on my mind a lot that I want to try and combine social change with personal enjoyment, combine a job with something that makes a difference. I don't feel like I've converged in that way yet. But, I have in other ways, just not related to my job. My involvement with various charities, whether it's just on a financial basis or a little bit more, like the Big Brother/Little Brother thing, keeps me feeling like I'm giving back a little bit, because as you get older, you start to realize how privileged we are in general.*
>
> *I feel good because people around me have told me that the way I live my life on a day to day basis makes them . . . how can I explain it? They respect the amount of integrity that I have in my day to day*

life. For example, at work, guys will say, "Oh, did you get this latest piece of software?" and I'll say, "No, I don't have it." "Oh, I'll give it to you." And I say, "No, I'm not going to do that because I don't believe in stealing software," and they're like "Oh wow, really? I never thought about that." And then people say, "Oh, I get it."

Or the fact that I don't eat beef or pork and I'm always explaining to people why I feel that way. I don't feel judgmental about it, but people have told me that it's nice to see someone who thinks consciously about the decisions they make to the extent that I do. I don't want to sound conceited. I know it does sound that way, but the truth is I have had feedback that way a lot of my life and I'm kind of proud of that.

Valuing Relationships

During the interviews, many aspects of interpersonal relationships were identified as having particular value in the respondents' lives.[18] We divided these into several major categories as shown in Figure 45.

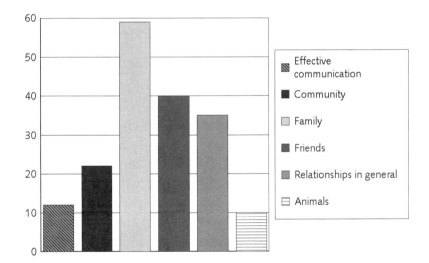

Figure 45 Aspects of interpersonal relationships respondents value highly.

---

[18] Relationships are treated in more depth in the section beginning on p. 239.

Under Communication we grouped the twelve responses that focused on effective verbal interaction with other people. Almost twice as many respondents talked about the importance of establishing and supporting a sense of community in their lives. One person was mindful of this in every aspect of his daily life:

> *I feel it's important to be part of your community. When I buy most of my stuff, if anybody in the area is in the business of selling something, I go to them first. I've basically never bought anything at a Walmart. I don't really buy cheap stuff. I buy stuff from people that are local and I try to support the community as best I can that way.*

Thirty-five respondents talked about the importance in their lives of relationships in general, and the amount of attention and emotional energy that they devote to them. Comments like the following abound in the responses: "I am very passionate about personal relationships with other people. I think that's the most important thing." "I really pride myself on the quality of my relationships with other people and I spend a lot of time nurturing those and enjoying them." "I guess priority number one would be relationships with other people, whether it is with the opposite sex or just with friends." "A lot of my emotional energy and a lot of my interest goes into the relationships that I have."

A third of the respondents particularly mentioned the importance of friendship as a value. "Friendship is a pretty high one. I hate to sound cliched, but I am talking about companionship, friendship of all sorts, keeping stimulating contact." "What's important to me? My friends. We were given the opportunity at Sudbury Valley to meet people that we want to be friends with for the rest of our lives because we had so much time just to socialize and to work that out."

Quite a few – ten – talked about the importance of their relationships to animals.

I love my animals – they're really central in my life. I volunteer sometimes, if I'm living in one place long enough, usually at an animal shelter or veterinary clinic. Most recently I have been working at the University of Massachusetts, which has the Hadley Farm, as a stable hand.

I am passionate about animals being treated right. Very few things upset me more than people who neglect or abuse animals. I'm personally a vegetarian and I don't wear leather for moral reasons. As far as I'm concerned, when it comes to food and that sort of thing, that's everybody's individual choice. But when it comes to pets or even wild animals, people who mistreat them in any way upset me.

Half of the respondents declared that they considered their relationships with their family to be primary in their lives.

What's important to me in life is my wife, my kids, my job – pretty much in that order. Pretty much everything I do is for my wife and my kids. The amount of work that I do to make sure that they get everything that they need, and the amount of off-time and on-time that I spend at work versus the off-time and on-time that I spend with my kids – I just try to find a nice happy balance. I usually do put in many long hours at work – I sometimes work both days on the weekends – but then I'll take an extended weekend off and just spend all my time with my family.

A parent with children with a chronic illness said: "What am I passionate about? My kids; that's really the only thing that comes to mind. Nothing can set me off quicker than issues that affect my kids, in both positive and negative ways. Both when they're being praised or when I feel like they're being criticized." A person who had difficulty conceiving commented, "I'm passionate about my children and how much I wanted them in my life. I was super motivated to get kids in my life." Another person who had children late in life said, "I'm passionate about family. I was forty-one when I had my first child. It's all been new to me, what most people learn in their twenties. I'm also passionate about upholding the kind of values I think are important for our family."

One respondent focused on his responsibility as a parent:

> I'm focused on my children right now, on passing down what I think are important – I don't want to say the words "family values" – things for them to know and to understand, yet things that they have to learn on their own. I'm figuring out that I don't have control, but I probably have a little bit of influence, and that's important to me, figuring out how to do this in a way that will make me very happy and proud when I'm an old man and my kids are out there in the world doing what they're doing.

Many of the respondents did not distinguish between family and friends when talking about what was most important to them, as in the comment:

> My family and friends will always be the most important thing to me, because whatever I do in life, my human connection with people and my emotional connection with people is always going to be most important. I won't be able to sustain myself just on having a good career or having material things. I need human contact and communication with people that really understand me to help deal with the pressures of life.

This sentiment was echoed by many others: "Most important to me is taking care of the people I care about – friends and family, making sure that they're OK, taking care of them." Another placed a high value on "spending time with my mother, who I have a very close relationship with, and four or five really close friends that I sort of split my time between. It's time consuming to really be there for people when they need you and that's my favorite thing to concentrate on – my relations with my kids and my relationships with my friends and my family."

A rising star in local government expressed his feelings on the subject this way:

> *Politics is one thing that is important to me. Especially now that I've had a daughter, I am very passionate about relationships with family members and with friends. A lot of my emotional energy and a lot of my interest goes into the relationships I have. I have great joy in watching my daughter develop into a toddler. It's such an important part of my life, even beyond what I could have imagined and what I could have foreseen. The relationships that I have with family and friends is even more of a passion than politics. Politics is more on the thinking side of things, whereas relationships I have with family and friends is more on the emotional side, which is a force more powerful. So I'm really enjoying being a father and a husband and it's becoming an even more important part of my life every day.*

Many alumni talked about the importance of activities that gave concrete expression to interpersonal values. Figure 46 groups their responses into three categories: activities that promote public health ("I'm passionate about people being safe on all levels – that we eat safe food, that we keep ourselves safe and society does what it can to keep us safe."); political activity; and engaging in activities that help people.

A powerful comment on political activism was the following:

> *I'm a part of a Green political party. I've also started groups and I'm part of them, like the group called North Guard that forms and then disappears back into the woods, depending on its need. We stopped low-flight military flight corridors and we stopped a sulfuric acid dump right next to Lake Superior.*
>
> *We were the first group ever to stop a tank base. We just had so many people and so much information. We used conventional*

methods, and we were really lucky. They were going up to the Iron Range which is a very poor area of iron mining. It was a bust and boom situation; the iron mining had stopped and the people up there really needed work. They said, "Well, this tank base is going to bring a lot of jobs." So we went up there and had position papers on what its effects would be on hunting, tourism, logging, just all sorts of different things, and showed that they really were not going to bring any jobs up there. When that all transpired at a meeting, the people of the area decided they didn't want it and the military backed off.

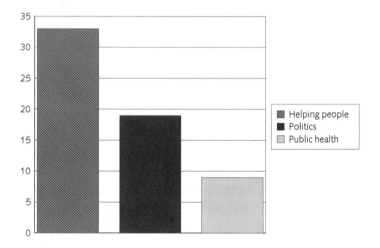

Figure 46 Types of activities that give concrete expression to interpersonal values important to the respondents.

What is important is learning how to live well in this life and enjoy oneself and not trash this planet at the same time. What's important is to know what that balance is, that quality of life that I see as being lost – chunks of it are being lost – and people are trashing the planet more. So it's real important to me to see how we can bridge that gap.

The extent to which helping other people added value to their own lives – as it did for thirty-three of the respondents – was remarked upon by people with a wide range of interests and vocations. It was particularly interesting to see how this value played a role in such a variety of different lifestyles. From a social worker:

> *I like to empower people, to get them to see themselves for who they really are. That's really an important aspect of my personality and I certainly try to provoke that in every person with whom I come in contact in my professional environment. I like to think of myself as a good professional, somebody who works really hard, and is outspoken, and is able to motivate people.*

From a librarian:

> *When you see something like an earthquake in India, it seems like if you were a Red Cross volunteer or a doctor there's a lot of immediate need that could be met. So, sometimes I feel that being a public librarian in a fairly well-to-do suburban town isn't necessarily being on the front lines of where help is most needed, but in general, I do feel I'm needed.*

From a person training to be a therapist:

> *Trying to be of some use to other people is really important. Keeping some perspective also – like that I'm not a Messiah and I can't take away other people's pain and I can't solve anything for them – but trying to be somehow useful, whether it's through teaching, or through therapy, or just lending some kind of help to a situation that needs it.*

From a lawyer who works within an organization that provides legal help to low income people:

> *In my present job I feel like I really do help people. Most of my clients are very grateful for my help. They are going through very tough situations and I feel good about what I do and how I treat other people, so that gives me satisfaction.*

An EMT said that his work was all about helping people, "one of the things that I'm passionate about." Another person said, "Part of the reason that I worked at Planned Parenthood is because I wanted to make a change and wanted to make a difference in people's lives." In the end, she had to quite her job because, "My life was in danger working at Planned Parenthood. There are no if's, and's, or but's about it."

Finally, in a more general vein:

> I like to help people with problem solving, like last minute problem solving. It is very gratifying to help somebody and watch the light dawn, watch when somebody who has been having trouble with something suddenly realizes how to deal with it. To think that you might help accomplish that is really quite a nice thing and is also part of what makes me occasionally interested in teaching, because it is really quite nice to be able to be a resource for somebody and to help them come into their own knowledge of something.

Values of Self-Realization

O ften, the things that alumni found important in their lives reflected the goals they set for themselves. We collected these under the overall rubric of self-realization, and divided the responses among several groups of categories, as shown in Figure 47.

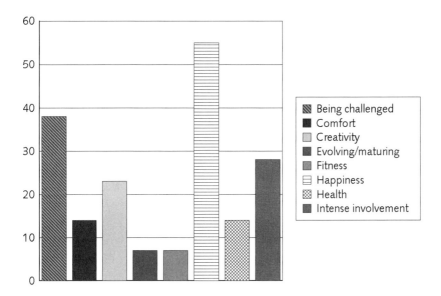

Figure 47 Aspects of self-realization that are important to respondents.

We were intrigued by the results shown in this graph. Four of these categories – comfort, evolving/maturing, fitness, and health – received the least attention in the responses, although it is clear from the overall zest for living reflected in the interviews that these categories play a significant role in the lives of the alumni. Perhaps their lack of prominence in the responses is due to the fact that most of them take these aspects of their lives for granted as an expected foundation for a satisfactory life.

Thus, for example, virtually none of the correspondents were ascetics, but only fourteen thought that "comfort" was worth mentioning. One of these is a person who grew up, as she says, in a somewhat unusual home, which served as a virtual museum, and with parents who devoted a tremendous amount of their attention to being curators. Here is what she had to say:

> [Laughing] I like to have a nice living environment. I think maybe I feel this way because of the years of growing up in my parents' house, which was really cold and damp, and they didn't seem to believe in food or cleaning – you know, they're eccentric; they had their pianos! I like to have a well-stocked refrigerator, and comfortable, clean places to sit down if I want to. I want to be able to roll around on the floor without coming up with pieces of – I don't know – clumps of dog hair and bits of piano wire and razor blades stuck in me.

The same number mentioned "health". One, a recovering alcoholic, is constantly aware of the work he has to put into maintaining his stability: "My own personal well-being, bodily and spiritually, comes first." Only after that did he talk about "comforts – a nice place to live, enjoying a job." Another person, fighting a life-long battle with eating disorders, talked at length about the value of health in her life:

> One of the major things in my life is body image and dealing with being overweight, as well as having bulimia. I'm finding it more and

more interesting that, from my own personal experience and that of people I know, the longest lasting improvements having to do with body issues come about by not thinking about them at all – by just doing yoga or some kind of meditation, where you're working with wherever you are that day and thinking of it more as a meditation and then letting go of the more superficial aspects of things. I find it fascinating how your life literally becomes a part of you physically, and in the same way you can actually heal it. You have all the control in the world to heal yourself, but you have to be able to just sit and let whatever it is go through you and accept what it is and deal with it and let go of it, which is really hard to do.

Only seven people talked about fitness, and seven talked about evolving and maturing as standing out as a factor that they are consciously aware of in their lives. For one, it is the center of life:

The meaning of life for me is to learn and to evolve. Part of that I was born with and part of it came from the Kung Fu philosophy. Nothing in Kung Fu is ever perfect; it can always be more perfect. So anything I do I can always improve. I feel best and I feel the most joy in life when I have the chance to improve something.

And for another alumnus, the focus on the maturing process derives from a fundamental impatience with the pace of it in her life:

I'm not happy with how I am right now. I want to be better. For example, I think I'm impatient and I don't want to be impatient. I think I'm sometimes intolerant and I don't like that about me – it bothers me that I'm not as tolerant as I want to be. I'm sometimes very short-tempered with things that I shouldn't be short-tempered with. Like at the end of the day I say, "Oh my God, why did I freak out about that?" I literally go to bed every night and say to myself, "I wish I had handled this better today."

I try to work on things like that every day of my life. It's wicked hard! If I make any progress, it's small. I think in some ways, I've definitely improved and in other ways if I have, it's in such small increments as to not even count. But that's not what I want. I want to change it today. I don't want to look back in ten years and say, "Wow! I was really intolerant and impatient! Now that I'm old I'm glad I'm not!" I want it to happen now. I'm impatient, I want it now!

By contrast, close to half of the respondents held "happiness" to be of central importance to them. They defined this concept in a variety of ways. One person equates it with learning to live in a positive way:

I've gone through various stages. I think I've kind of come full-circle. When I was in my late teens and twenties, I tended to be quite cynical, oftentimes negative and frustrated – not with life in general but with politics, with the state of education, with the state of our society. I was really quite cynical until I was probably in my mid-thirties, and then I did a turnaround, and I learned to dwell on all the positive and uplifting sides of life. What brought about this change was the futility of being cynical and negative all the time, and realizing that was a pointless dead end and certainly a joyless way to be. There can be a lot of fun and humor in cynicism but that only goes so far in terms of satisfaction and amusement. So I think I just matured and it's wonderful being on the bright side and focusing on the good things rather than the bad.

This alumnus has learned to define happiness as a balance between taking as much as possible from every moment and meeting his obligations:

My family's days are remarkably alike, in a funny way, even though they're really completely unalike in terms of what we do and when we do it. We just don't plan a lot. We leave a lot of room open for what people are in the mood for and how people are feeling in that particular moment and how that particular day is coming together. We kind of make a little plan in the morning and kind of revisit it in the afternoon. The goal is for everyone to be happy, rather than to stick to some foreordained plan.

I know it's a lifestyle that would drive a lot of people crazy, but I actually think that it's a lot more enjoyable and relaxed than most people allow themselves to be. We do a lot of very tribal lying around in bed, watching television, or reading books, or just sort of talking to each other, where we're not really doing anything, but just being together as a family, which I think of as really old-fashioned in a way. It's kind of what families have probably done for millennia, but it's not something I think a lot of people make space to do. Certainly not to the degree that we tend to do it, because for us, that's the most fun in our day, just relaxing with the kids.

The next person was working toward, but maybe not quite achieving, the same balance:

I think the most important thing is trying to be happy. Here is what I mean: I think that you work hard, you provide for yourself and perhaps others, but at the end of the day, life is definitely short. As you get older you realize that life is really short and it's about enjoying the day. Now, I'm saying that, but do I live that? No. You know, you work, get to work early, work late, not enjoy it as much as you could. But I do think I value happiness. I mean, if it's a beautiful nice day, breeze blowing, air smells nice and clean, and your health is good, you can't take that for granted.

For several people happiness meant not allowing themselves to remain in situations where they felt unhappy:

I try to take everything with a grain of salt and have fun and I feel like I have a pretty good sense of humor about things, which I think is important to keeping happy. So, I've been pretty satisfied with all the different stages of my life. If I was so unsatisfied that I was really unhappy, then I would have made a change to make myself happy.

I really want to do something that I'm happy doing. It took me a while to figure that out. I worked for a while feeling, "Well, this is alright," and then I realized, "No, I don't want to do this for the rest of my life." So working in a field that I'm really interested in has become very important to me. I'm very excited to be going into Egyptology, and to be able to focus on that.

I had a great childhood and I owe a lot of that to Sudbury Valley. I'm not somebody that grew up with a lot of anger when thinking about things that went wrong when I was younger, because really I've had a great life and I'm happy now too. I don't see that changing. If anything comes up – everybody has to deal with certain things – I deal with it just fine, and I can deal with anything that comes to me.

I'm quite happy. My philosophy is that if you're not happy, you're not doing it right. So if I'm ever not happy with something, I change it. It's kind of bending your path to make sure that what you're doing gives you options that you're going to enjoy. So as you're going down that path, you always head toward the directions that will end up giving you those options rather than the ones you don't like. The ones that get you in trouble from past experience, you don't do again. So it's really not a conscious thing so much as something you learn as you go, and you avoid situations and things that you have found, in the past, you really didn't enjoy that much.

Perhaps the most succinct statement on this topic was the simple declaration: "Happiness! I just want to have a joyful life. That's the most important thing to me. It doesn't really matter what I'm doing. I just appreciate being alive."

A third of the respondents placed a very high premium on being challenged in life – "not stagnating," as one person put it. One alumnus defined this as "experiencing lots of different things and being able to really experience bad things as well as good things, just as a part of life and not as something to avoid at all costs." Another talked about "tremendous variety in my life. That's what I like. And what I don't like is that it's too busy. Two sides of the same coin I guess. I have a very stimulating and challenging job. I have a good, solid family life. I try to keep myself intellectually stimulated through my graduate work. And I occasionally get the chance to explore my artistic side a bit with music."

Closely related to valuing challenge was the feeling that creativity was central to a good life. One person defined herself as "kind of a creative, free spirit." Another sought "a job where I can be creative." A jewelry designer exulted:

> I'm passionate about my work. A big part of my work is doing hands-on painting. I'm passionate about having the ability to express my creativity in whatever way it comes at the moment – having that avenue fully open is something that is very important to me.

Two of the alumni were successful inventors:

> The biggest thing I love is building stuff. I love making things from the design phase to the actual testing and running phase and that's what I spend most of my time doing.

> I'm passionate about my input to things. I want to make a difference. I got a United States patent on a snowboard invention. I really didn't know what I'd do with it. But I said, "I gotta get a patent." It gave me a sense of accomplishment.

Not surprising for former members of the Sudbury Valley community was the number who placed special importance on living a life of intense involvement. The following excerpts speak for themselves:

> I have a real passion towards things like healing and working with energy, auras, and I'm kind of into the psychic power thing. It just never ends – there's always something I'm interested in. I don't know

what I want to do in the future, because I just want to do everything – but I can't. I have to choose, because there's not enough time.

I just throw myself into one intense environment after another. There's always immersion. There have been times in my life when I sat around in frustration over what I am or I'm not doing, but I can always find at those times the things that I passionately want to strive for or do. Right now, I'm involved in a lifestyle where I'm fully immersed in every activity that I do, even if it's washing dishes, and I want to strive to do my best at whatever comes my way. There's always something pushing me past the boundaries that I thought I had which defined who I was.

The amount of interest that I'm able to take in things is probably my favorite thing in life. I seem to be interested in just about anything and have the ability to become passionate about something and become very involved with it. That's the thing I feel most fortunate about.

What I love is pursuing my passion. In this lifetime, it's my journey to know the body and to explore the aspect of becoming a healer in many, many forms. I'm getting a chance to do that and it gives me a great sense of joy to make my dream happen. I'm not going to chiropractic school to fill a prerequisite. I'm in school doing what it is that I want to do with the rest of my life. Everything I do, I do with a focus.

I know that when you're in a difficult situation, it will change, it will pass, and you just have to keep at it and not give up. I have inner resources. I think that choosing to do something that you actually want to do gives you tremendous energy. A lot of people lose their energy by not doing what they want to do because it seems too hard or scary. I think that one reason my wife and I have so much energy together as a family is that we're doing exactly what we want to do, with a no-holds-barred kind of attitude. That gives us a lot of energy – I wouldn't be able to work like this doing a job I hated.

I am passionate about just about everything. How shall I put it into words? One of the things I love about the West Coast of North America is the jagged coastline, the contrast between the mountains and the ocean, and being by the ocean. I love to go to the ocean. I love to be at the beach in the summer when it's hot, especially Cape Cod beaches, the really sandy ones. I'm passionate in sort of a fiery way – good and bad, I think – about everything I do, and my life in general. I love something, I hate something else. I might hate the same thing that I love ten minutes later.

Living One's Values

When we asked the respondents directly, "What is important to you in life?" and "What are you passionate about?" we were asking them to talk about their values. It was clear from the breadth and depth of the responses that these questions are constantly being considered by our alumni. Furthermore, from the intensity with which they answered, we received the very strong impression that these were values that the respondents tried to concretize in the pursuit of their daily lives.

We did not want to rely solely on this impression, so we put the question directly: "Do you feel your life reflects your values?" Figure 48 displays the replies.

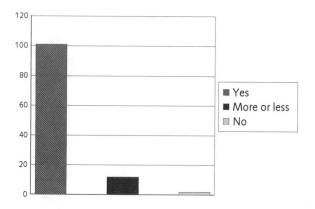

Figure 48 "Does your life reflect your values?"

Perhaps the ultimate achievement for each of us is to live true to our own value system. The overwhelming majority (86%) felt their practices were in agreement with their ideals. As one person put it, "It's not easy to do, and it's a struggle, but, yes, I've worked very hard to make that so." Another 11% felt that they were pretty much in tune: "It's not perfect, but I'm getting there," was how one person put it.

The examined life is one which combines reflection with action. The responses given by the alumni in the various chapters of this section show them to be, as a group, exemplars of people conscious of their values and how to realize them.

Relationships

"I'm sure my level of comfort [dealing with people] starts
completely at the school — starts out with this notion of being
comfortable in non-hierarchical situations where everyone
puts in their own contribution and makes the whole thing a
community."

How Alumni Deal With People

Figure 49 gives an overview of how the respondents rated their own social skills.

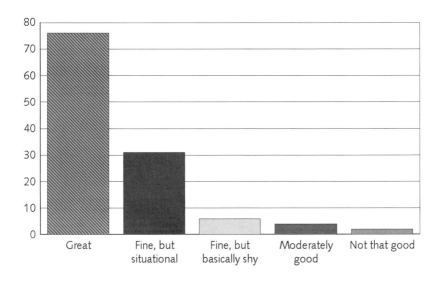

Figure 49 How respondents rated their ability to relate to others.

Most respondents feel that they have adequate social skills to deal with their daily lives. An impressive 64% are quite confident in their abilities to relate to others. Another 26% feel that in most situations they did very well. People made comments such as, "My strong suit is that I get along with people"; "In terms of communicating with people, I am comfortable, sometimes too comfortable"; "I don't always get my point across successfully, but I'm always comfortable trying." or:

> I'm quite comfortable. I have a hard time **not** communicating.
> I think communication is probably one of the most important things
> to me, whether it's verbal or otherwise; whether it be in friendship,
> business, love, family, or a stranger on the street. I feel communication
> is number one in a lot of ways in life, and I feel very good about being
> able to.

Some people voiced qualifications about their social skills. Shyness was most often mentioned.   Twenty respondents said they had dealt with it at some point in their lives. Most of them found the effort to conquer or sidestep their intrinsic reserve to be worthwhile. Here's how some of them put it:

> I've certainly always been shy, but I think that I do what I can to,
> if not overcome that, at least cover it up as much as possible.

> Maybe at first I'm not so comfortable. I'm not good at making the
> initial contact with people and getting to know people right up front, but
> once I do that initial breaking of the ice then I'm very comfortable.

> I'm one of these people that's shy at first, even painfully shy. But
> it depends on the context. If I have a role – if I'm working in a public
> place, like the library – then I'm very outgoing, but I'm not as outgoing
> at a party full of people that I don't know.

> I feel overwhelmed sometimes in an onslaught of people that I'm not
> familiar with; however, I do not feel as though I can't handle myself.

One person put her shyness in a broader cultural context:

> *In general, I'm a fairly reserved person, not the life-of-the-party, hail-fellow-well-met kind of person. I have that New England thing. In New England, if you're in a public place and there's someone else there whom you don't know, it's polite to ignore them. Whereas, in other parts of the country, like in the South, if you're in a public place and there's someone there you don't know, it's polite to maybe introduce yourself to them, say something nice to them. So, I have more of the New England model.*

Several people mentioned shyness as something they had suffered from when they were young but was now a memory from the distant past. Typical was this comment:

> *Until I was about 14, I was very shy. Now, I feel intensely comfortable – wickedly comfortable – so overall I'm very happy with my level of social comfort.*

Other factors – such as the size of the group or its constitution – affected the respondents in specific social contexts. Here are some typical comments:

> *I definitely don't feel comfortable communicating with other people in a large group, but in small groups or one-on-one I feel fairly comfortable.*[19]

> *With strangers I'm relatively reserved but once I get to know people I'm incredibly comfortable communicating with them.*

> *I think that I communicate effectively in political circles and in the sciences and I communicate effectively to people that are close to me.*

---

[19] An unusual twist on this theme was provided by one respondent who said, "I'm not a great talker one-on-one. It's not a forum I feel comfortable in."

> *I'm not a good salesman so there are certain areas of communication where I don't do as well. I imagine that I don't come across to people as being fun. I'm not the life of the party.*

One former student, aiming for an elective office, said:

> *I'm fairly comfortable a lot of the time. It depends on the person, the context, whatever. I'm a lot more comfortable if I know someone, but I'm getting better at communicating with people I don't know as well; that's an essential skill for me right now.*

Another felt she was a little too straightforward for her own good:

> *I have a problem with being more authentic than other people. It makes people uncomfortable sometimes. I'd have to say my biggest challenge is to develop a social elegance, but one that is authentic.*

Yet another felt hampered by his slowness of response: "I've always been a kind of quiet, not very social person. When I have to make decisions involving what somebody's saying to me right then and there, it doesn't work out so well."

Then there was the person who started out feeling high on his communication skills, and after he came into contact with some excellent communicators started to have some doubts:

> *I don't think it's one of my strengths anymore. When I left SVS I felt I was the great communicator and I think it's one of the reasons I jumped on that microphone and really felt that I was going to be the next John Lennon. As I got older I started to shut my mouth a little bit more and open up my ears and listen to a lot of the intelligent and not-so-intelligent things that were being said. Now I am around some very good communicators, some very persuasive speakers, and some people that have very clear opinions on a wide range of subjects. And*

I'm kind of feeling back in the dust on a lot of that. Whether I really am or not, I'm not sure.

Finally, there is the respondent who has trouble figuring out what to say when . . .

> *I am very good at the part of communicating that involves actually telling people stuff. I am not necessarily good at the part of communicating that involves telling people **about** stuff, and I have a hard time figuring out the distinction. When I do figure it out and the time comes to actually tell people about something – tell people that something has happened, describe something to people, documenting something for some purpose – I am pretty good at it.*

Several respondents mentioned various ways in which they are more comfortable with non-verbal means of communication. One felt he was more of a doer than a talker: "I often don't feel like I can really communicate verbally. I'm much more of a doer. I've always felt like I proved myself by my actions and results." Another said: "I hate communicating with people! I think that's why I do art." Then there was the person who said:

> *I feel passionate about communication and art. Those are the key things in my life. I'm more comfortable communicating through writing and through art, through film and video especially, than I am just speaking one-on-one to people.*

Several people mentioned situations that helped them deal with others. One person found that she had taken a job that turned out to be particularly helpful:

> *I love talking to people. That was something that was hard for me to attain because I was really shy as a kid. Actually, being behind a bar was the best thing I ever did for that. I'd pretty much overcome*

it before that, but that's definitely helped. I was getting better and better all along, kind of pushing myself, putting myself in uncomfortable situations and seeing how I handled it, and trying to move forward all the time.

Another person felt that he had broken down some barriers to relationships with others simply by growing up and getting married:

I've made a lot of progress in just a few years. Of course, with age comes security, and with security comes self-confidence. So today I'd say I'm very comfortable interacting with people. I think that guys are always worried about furthering their status in their relationships, and if you're in a long-term relationship you don't really worry as much about that anymore. That takes a whole threat off your life and it allows you to interact with people in a much more genuine manner.

Handling Different Types of Relationships

Figure 50 shows the various categories of personal relationships mentioned by the respondents.

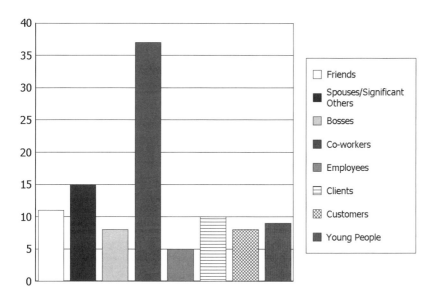

Figure 50 Categories of personal relationships mentioned by the respondents. Many people didn't single out any particular category, while others described interactions with more than one category.

When talking about intimate relationships, several respondents noted that the closer the other person was to them, the less at ease they were – somewhat the opposite of what one might expect. As one person put it, "It's easier to have problems with people who I know really well. I think that's probably because there's more of an emotional attachment and a different level of what you expect, so the way you interact is different." On the other hand, many respondents showed lots of ingenuity in dealing with spouses and significant others. One noted that he was great at negotiating compromises "because I'm married, and I have to be – I better be, otherwise my ass is not going to be married very long!" Or, as another put it, "I'm married so I do a lot of compromising with my wife." His definition of the word "compromise"? – "Usually it's whatever she wants is fine." Then there is the couple that runs a business together, and had to learn to get along through trial and error:

> *He aggravated me and I aggravated him – that's normal I guess. At first, in the back of the store all my merchandise would get pushed out of the way and then it wouldn't get put back in the right place even though I'd show him five times; he wouldn't do it and I'd get mad. And he was supposed to be handling more of the business side of it, and he just was not good with that. We got into a lot of stress. Now it's good because we understand each other's strengths and limitations, and we're working on being accepting of that. I'm doing what I'm good at and he's doing what he's good at and we're getting along better because of it.*

One respondent was able to bridge a cultural gap that was causing him difficulty:

> *When my girl friend feels upset she doesn't like to talk about it, or at least doesn't like to say anything right away. She's from Japan, and in Japan it's a lot different when it comes to people expressing their feelings. Initially it was hard adjusting to that because I felt our*

problems could be resolved quickly by just talking. Once she did talk about a problem, it would be resolved, and I would say, "See? We could have resolved this so long ago." But I had to learn how to adapt to that new situation.

Dealing with your boss can be a sensitive matter. Fairly typical was one person's comment that "I don't have a problem speaking to my superiors in a way that is professional and appropriate, but lets them know exactly what's going on. I have definitely learned to challenge authority and do it in the proper way."

Here is a respondent's analysis of her relationship with a rather mercurial boss:

I have a rather difficult boss and we get along very well. I'm not interested in getting swept up in people's dramas. That's not my thing. I don't want to be yelling and screaming all the time for no reason other than to be neurotic. My boss has got kind of a diva mentality. I think I understand that part of her hysteria is that she feels very insecure and so my being very calm and competent and reliable takes the edge off somewhat. With a lot of people she'll start yelling, and they either start yelling back, or they become defensive, or they start crying and wonder what's wrong with them. She even said one time, "I think you're one of the few people I've ever worked with that I haven't made cry." And I said, "Yeah, and you're never going to." We've established the fact that she can't take her anger out on me.

On the other hand, another former student was not quite as self-confident in the face of an angry superior:

I'm having an issue with my boss at the moment. I feel that he's doing something wrong but I don't want to confront him on it because of the repercussions that there will be.

Her desire to avoid conflict is a reaction she shares with other people, most of whom come to this stance less out of fear than out of a desire to get along:

> *I've worked for so many different kinds of people that I've learned how to make things easier, how to not rub everyone the wrong way all the time. Not that you have to keep the peace at all costs; if you feel strongly about something, you should speak your mind. But in matters that are just day-to-day life, you learn to cope with people being different individuals.*

Most respondents feel competent and understanding when it comes to dealing on a day-to-day basis with co-workers. Typical was one person who said of herself, "I'm the person that gets along with everybody. In my workplace, I find it very easy to find some common ground with everybody." Another felt that his boss promoted him to manager because he got along so well with his co-workers. A third, while finding it frustrating "when we're working as a team and they're not holding up their end of the team," added, "I certainly don't yell or anything. I have learned fairly well to just take each other's differences and walk away and let them be different." More pointed was one person's clear understanding that "you're surrounded by people in the workplace that you wouldn't choose to be around necessarily and you have to get used to it."

Several respondents consciously avoided getting involved in disputes that went on between various people they worked with: "I try not to involve myself in office politics; it's pretty brutal." Or, as an actress put it, "I just try to be as professional as possible, and not get involved in the drama of things backstage." One respondent, a realtor, commented:

> *If a co-worker stepped out of line and tried to take a customer of mine or do something that was just not right, that would put that co-worker into conflict with me and I would try to find some way to address it that would result in a different course of action and also*

in that co-worker not doing it again. That has happened only rarely and whatever I did apparently had enough effect so that it didn't happen again.

Cooperative work environments demand a high degree of interpersonal skill. Here is what one person said about his work life:

> *Most of the things I've been involved with have been non-hierarchical structures. My own businesses I've run not as a boss, but as part co-op, even when they're kind of my idea. I've always only really been comfortable working with people when they're as excited about, and invested in, what we're doing as I am. I've been in bands, and when it's not a successful money-making band, you're all doing it because you like the music that you create together, and they tend to be very cooperative too. There are certain people who write the songs and kind of decide the direction the band is going, and I'm usually one of those people, but other than that, everyone's there because they want to be there. Everyone's doing something together that they make together in that spot.*

If dealing with a boss is a tricky matter, being a boss is no less challenging. The respondents who found themselves in this situation strove to treat their subordinates with respect. Here is what a construction foreman had to say:

> *I try to listen to what they have to say and then I tell them what I feel we should do. We usually try to take a little of what they know and a little of what I know and try to figure out the best and safest way to do what we have to do, whether it be forming some colossally huge, dangerous, one-sided concrete pour that could break and spill out eleven yards of concrete on us, or simply just the way we should build something. That's the only way that you can do something – to listen to both sides and then pick a little bit from each one and try to come up with the best situation out of whatever you're doing.*

One person felt a responsibility to mediate disputes between subordinates, doing so with the help of her insights into human behavior:

> *I'm good at verbalizing what's actually going on and getting people to see that they're actually kind of saying the same thing but just in two different ways – that there's a conflict because communication has broken down. They normally accept this. I think that's one of the things that has given me a lot of respect. It usually starts out when one person comes to you to tell you the horrible thing that the other person did to them, or how mean they are, or how they can't work with this person, and then when you get the two of them together and you sort it out with them, there's a great reward for everybody.*

Another respondent was particularly sensitive to the value of positive feedback for the people under his management:

> *I'm going to come down on you if you make a mistake, but I will praise you if you do well. That's one of the things that doesn't happen at our job that often. Sometimes people say, "Well, it's just my job. I'm just doing my job." And I say, "Yeah, you're doing your job and you're doing a great job at what you do. You're making my life easier and I appreciate it." Just saying something like that to an employee makes them that much more dedicated and interested.*

Former students who are professionals dealing with clients, or who are working with people in the arts, often expressed the same sort of egalitarian philosophy that we saw above with the person who was the key figure in a band. As a director of stage plays put it:

> *I can't stand directors who stonewall. The kind of theater I do is very inclusive and positive. I love the actors' point of view. I don't think I could direct if I didn't listen to the actors because they're doing the work when it comes down to it. They're the ones on stage and they have to feel comfortable with what they're doing.*

Here is what a producer of documentary films had to say about the way that she dealt with her film projects:

> *As a documentary film-maker I feel like I can approach people and talk to them and genuinely meet them. In the work that I do I have to meet people without judgement and just go about understanding who they are and what they believe, not letting myself get in the way, because that's what's interesting to me and what will be, I think, interesting for an audience. So I'm good at communicating in that kind of way and establishing those kinds of relationships.*

A lawyer, who works for an organization that provides services to indigent clients, had this to say:

> *I get along with clients extremely well because I am very open, not judgmental at all. I do not make judgments if they are using drugs or doing whatever. I tell them, "I am not going to make judgments. I am just going to tell you how the legal system sees it and what you can do to maximize your chances." They also like me because I have a sense of humor.*

A doctor, who copes with a wide variety of patients, developed a detached view to avoid aggravation and conflict:

> *There's definitely a certain number of people out there who are looking for trouble. A lot of people are sort of dissatisfied with the whole medical world and they come to you with an attitude like, "Okay, all doctors are screw-ups, but I'm going to give you a chance." So there are a lot of fairly difficult people who I see, and I guess I do fairly well with all that. My philosophy is that there's a million patients out there and I want to have a day that's filled with people I look forward to seeing when they are on my schedule. So if some patients don't like me and they move on to another doctor, that's fine.*

A government official who has local code-enforcement responsibilities showed flexibility when dealing with reasonable requests:

> *There are compromises all the time. The law is not always clear, so you have to interpret. There might be three or four ways of doing something that will achieve the same end. So I might want it done one way and then I'll have a builder come in and say, "Well, listen, you know, it's going to be ten times as expensive for me to do it that way. If I do it this other way, you'll end up with the same results but it will cost me ten times less." I'll allow them to do that.*

From a foreman's point of view:

> *I have to deal with a lot of people every day from other contractors that might be on the job site too, and the general contractors that are overseeing projects, to people that are just at their houses where I'm doing work. I don't have any problems ever talking to anybody like that.*

Respondents who deal with customers have other challenges. One, who arranges expensive golf excursions, expressed a sentiment similar to the physician quoted above:

> *I had some clients last week who were just – ugh!! I came home and talked to my girlfriend and said, "The only way I can describe this woman is that she was the least spiritual person I've ever met." All she was worried about was her nails and her hair. You know, you deal with that and you're friendly – I don't need to voice my opinion to them because they're clients and you move on and concentrate on other clients who are worth working with.*

A more humorous perspective is provided by an estate appraiser and auctioneer who describes how he handles touchy clientele:

Everybody seems to think their stuff is worth much more than it really is. "My Oriental rug in the living room is definitely worth more than you say!" Or they say, "Oh, that belonged to my grandmother!" – except that well, maybe she bought it two days before she died in 1982. Did that ever occur to you? She wasn't out buying things when she was three years old! Or where something's just blatantly a piece of crap they tell me, "Somebody told me this was worth a lot of money!" And then they look at me like I'm trying to screw them out of something that's worth a thousand dollars. But I'm very diplomatic. You never can be annoyed, you never can get angry. Sometimes I'll just look at my watch and say, "Oh, I have to phone a minister. I have to right now." And I'll just go into my office and sit down and have a cup of coffee and a cigarette for about ten minutes – if they were really being a pain in the ass.

A few of our respondents talked about dealing with young people, either in a school setting or in other settings. Most were comfortable in their relationships with kids, and had a lot of insight on why that was true. One said:

It's been difficult for me coming back into a school setting with young kids because I'd been away from young kids for a really long time. My memory wasn't that good as to how delicate my psyche was in early adolescence and how you really do listen to what adults are saying and form opinions. When I was 13, I was quick to look for things that I might see in a negative light. So I've tried to moderate a little bit and if I don't have something nice to say to anybody, maybe not say anything, at least a little more than I used to.

When I was a kid, I was drawn into music because I saw it as being the one place where there wouldn't be rules and you could kind of do your own thing, man, and it's going to be all free and easy. But once I got a little bit more into it I realized, hey, we've got to preserve this equipment and there's a tremendous discipline to doing it if you want to have it there all year, and maybe next year and the year after. My attitude is, if you want to use the gear, you have to take ownership of that gear. I'm going to hold you to the rules. I'm going to enforce the rules. It's hard for a kid who's used to just leaving his guitar or amp on, and his guitar cord lying on the ground.

Someone who works with children in inner-city schools commented:

You have to be firm. You have to really try not to accuse them of doing anything wrong in particular, you just have to state your own truth from your point of view and be firm. For as much as, on the surface, they would like you to cave, they don't really want you to cave. Their lives are full of shifting things which are not stable. I think that they're happier when they know that there are lines [they can't cross] as long as you don't do it in a negative way.

Long-term Relationships

In the interviews, respondents were asked to evaluate their ability to form and maintain long-term relationships. Virtually all of them (110 of the 119 interviewees) talked about it, and of those only five described themselves as "poor" in that area – such as the one who said bluntly, "I have never been very successful in that regard." Another lamented, "I felt pretty good when I was much younger and I had one; I'm questioning a little bit now."

For the vast majority, the pithy response, "I feel very good about it," was the norm. Many people added some comments by way of explanation:

> I've always been someone who tends to have long-term relationships rather than short-term relationships, even with friends. And it seems to be the same with my husband so far. We've been together for eight and a half years now . . . just got married recently . . . so I would say, yes, I do well in this area.

> I feel very good about it. I've always been very serious about my relationships, ever since the first one.

> I'm pretty confident in myself and my ability to connect with other people. Of course, there are always hesitations, but overall, it's the confidence in myself that comes through in my relationships.

> *It's never been a problem. I have a very strong and healthy marriage, and I feel pretty confident in my ability to get into healthy relationships and stick with them.*

And then there was this: "Apparently, people seem to think that I'm good at it, because they keep asking me to marry them. But, uh, I didn't actually agree to any of them until recently."

Several people talked about the effort that they are willing to put into making such relationships work. "I know how to be myself and I know how to give my partner permission to be himself," said one. "Nobody is good at it. You have to work at it, make a commitment to it and not throw in the towel," said another. A third person elaborated:

> *I want to live a substantive and deep life. I don't want to skirt over the meaty and tough emotions and experiences that being in a committed and long-term relationship brings. I feel that I'm consciously looking for that sort of deep, true experience, and I definitely do credit my Sudbury Valley years with learning how to do that.*

We obtained information about the length of people's long-term relationships from fifty-six of the respondents. The results are shown in Figure 51. The number of relationships lasting more than ten years is relatively low due to the age range of people involved in the study.

Some of the alumni ascribed their success at forming extended relationships to the modeling that they observed at home, either as a reaction:

> *I definitely have some issues about that. They're probably very much related to the fact that my parents got divorced, therefore I didn't necessarily have the very best example growing up. But I did have a successful long-term relationship for seven years.*

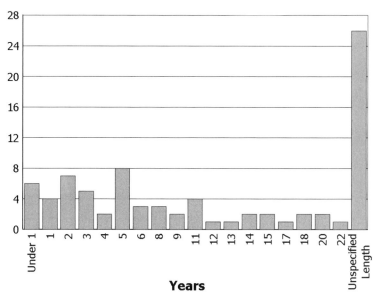

Figure 51 Length of prior and current long-term relationships.

or, more commonly, as a result of a stable home life during childhood:

> I think a big part of it is growing up in a stable, intact marriage. I watched my parents negotiate a marriage that stayed together for my entire life, and I just kind of learned what works, or at least how you negotiate staying together and that kind of stuff. The other side of it is that I'm just very confident about what I think and what I feel, and I think a big part of that can be attributed to the kind of freedom I had to decide my own education and figure things out for myself and succeed and fail with things on my own.

Aspects of Personal Relationships

Respondents described many aspects of the way they interact with other people, and of the qualities they look for in satisfactory interactions. Figure 52 displays the number of respondents who commented on each aspect or quality.

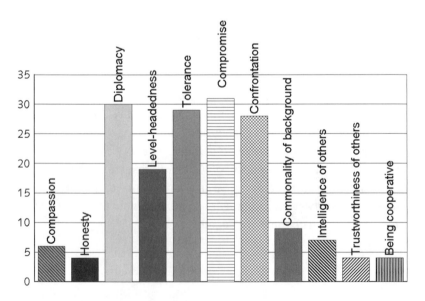

Figure 52 Aspects of personal relationships commented on by the respondents.

The theme of compassion and sensitivity to others came up often. One person found travel to be especially worthwhile because, "It teaches you compassion. Being in another country and not being able to speak the language, you have to rely on other people's compassion for you and their kindness, and I feel like I try to bring that to my lifestyle here in New York, or just living anywhere." Compassion led another to want to extend a helping hand, and succeed:

> *I tend to draw people out. They tell me things that they wouldn't tell anybody else. I've found that quite a few times I connected with a lot of people who were having troubles through depression support chat rooms. I think there were about six or seven suicides that I really had a hand in preventing. That was something that made me feel good during a period when I was in pretty bad shape, and made me realize that maybe I have a gift in communicating with people.*

One respondent found himself still working to improve his sense of identification with others:

> *A challenge that I've had throughout my life, which I'm still learning how to deal with, is communicating with people who aren't comfortable communicating. I've really had to learn to let it go when they don't want to talk, or if the timing is not right to have a conversation. It is still a challenge. It's something I'm getting a lot better at but it's definitely habitual for me to want other people to communicate with me on my timetable; so I'm kind of retraining myself to reflexively want to give them space, basing the solution on what they want rather than what I want.*

For another, compassion wasn't always a blessing: "I guess I'm very sensitive to people's hangups and issues; if they bring it into the workplace, and they kind of project it out onto other people, that can kind of bother me."

Many talked about honesty. One was not so sure it was always a good thing: "My mouth gets me in trouble sometimes, maybe because I am passionate about things. No fear about telling it like it is. Sometimes it may or may not be appropriate." But another had no doubts: "If I think someone is being insincere, I will tell them. I don't have a problem with that." For others, honesty was an essential component of making things work:

> I'm one of those people who is apt to lay things on the table, confront situations through communication for the purpose of moving forward, or helping somebody else to understand something.

> If I have a conflict with one of my kids' teachers or if I'm not happy with something that's going on in their school or the way their friends are treating them, I'll usually just communicate with whoever I need to solve it.

Then there was the maverick who was bold enough to apply this value to the corporate world:

> I've learned to be up-front and honest. I don't brown-nose or bullshit. That's not my style. I wasn't taught that. And you know what? The corporate world is a lot about faking it. I'm not. Other people might say, "Well, the most professional way to do things would be to candy-coat it a little bit. Don't show your emotion on a subject, don't show your passion so much." If I'm pissed off about something I don't go crazy, but I'll say, "I'm not happy with this; this isn't working."

As we see in Figure 52 (p. 260), many former students placed a high value on possessing the art of diplomacy. A few referred to this explicitly, such as the one who proudly declared, "Many people have described me as being a chameleon and have told me I missed my calling, that I should have been a diplomat. I have, it seems to me, a relatively unusual ability to really, really experience what others are experiencing."

The same notion was expressed by someone else in the following words: "I am sort of a social chameleon. What makes me feel comfortable is making other people feel comfortable, so I just fall into whatever pattern I need to hang out with somebody and to get along with them. I almost never get into arguments." Another thought of her way of interacting with people "as sort of an art form - being able to feel people out quickly and figure out what they need and when I should shut up and when I should talk based on the individual I'm dealing with at that time."

Quite a few respondents prided themselves on being able to stay cool and level-headed in situations where others were agitated. As one put it, "My first reaction is usually to step back and really think about it for a while before I react or act." Another said his tendency was to react "just by being quiet and not adding more fuel to the fire." One respondent talked about being

> *very relaxed and calm when dealing with people in social situations. I almost always take the stance that it doesn't cost me anything to be nice, so I'll just go along unless something starts getting totally unreasonable on the other side of it.*

A person operating in the hi-tech sector was particularly proud of his abilities in this regard:

> *Most of the time, I'm the cool headed person at work who calms everyone down from getting too excited. I don't worry about little things. I wouldn't say detached, I'm just saying that relative to everyone else, I think that I tend to be more levelheaded; I don't get spun up. We have to deal with the customers and customer service representatives from the manufacturers, and I'm the only one who can deal with customers without getting in a tizzy.*

For another respondent, staying detached was still a work in progress:

> *I have been trying for several years to work on being able to recognize an argument without passion or prejudice and see whether it is a sound argument, whether it is something that can actually prove me wrong. I sometimes say to people, "Well, I guess I have to let you win that one because you have out-argued me. I will give that to you, but it is difficult." In order to do that you have to step away from the emotional effects of an issue and that can be hard – hard to change what you think about something if it means that you have to override how you feel about it.*

Staying cool is not always a sign of equanimity in conflict situations. Sometimes it is just a result of suppressed emotions, as for the person who felt she kept things "bottled up for whatever reason," so that nothing makes her angry.

Several students mentioned being quite tolerant in their interactions. As one put it, "You say something that pisses me off. Keep going. Doesn't bother me." Or, in somewhat more elegant language, "If you understand that everyone's coming from a different perspective, then I think it's much easier to get along with people."

For one respondent, actualizing this value has taken some steady effort:

> *Tolerance is something that I've learned over time. It was definitely a learned thing. Being intolerant was something that got me into a lot of trouble and I've certainly learned to temper that. I don't always like the temperament, but in the grand scheme of things it makes everybody's life easier. And as long as you're able to accomplish your common goals, that's the most important outcome.*

More pithily: "Life's too short to hold a grudge against anybody."

For others for whom tolerance was a central value, the challenge is not quite met:

> *I think sometimes I can be a little bit bull-headed and whatever – insistent – and just get on people's nerves. That is a problem that I have, of being intolerant, of being judgmental and holding people to a standard that's unrealistic.*

> *I have a hard time getting along with the people at work who are old men stuck in their ways, and a real hard time getting along with people who are racist or just really, really stupid people.*

Intelligence was seen as an important factor by some. For example, one said: "If it's somebody reasonably intelligent, then I usually don't have any trouble communicating with them." To others, trust was important: "As long as I feel that people are trustworthy, I have no problem relating to them." How cooperative the other party in a social interaction appeared was sometimes mentioned as significant:

> *If the other person is pretty open and like-minded, then within minutes of meeting them I'm pretty comfortable with them. But if they're edgy and not comfortable with themselves, then I tend to be thrown off.*

Commonality of background was also, not unexpectedly, mentioned:

> *I've found, particularly over the past few years, that it's much easier to get along with people from Sudbury Valley. For the most part non-SVS people have surprised me with their hangups. Partly it's about people that I've been friends with a long time. I suppose the very fact that we went to the same school and that our parents sent us there implies that we must have something in common, we might share some similar values. I also think Sudbury Valley students have*

a tendency to be less uptight, more easygoing, more trustworthy at times than non-SVS students.

And then, perhaps feeling wary of making such judgments, he added, "That's a horrible generalization."

Weaving throughout the interviews was the clear recognition that relating to other people is a complex and subtle matter that is influenced by many factors, some internal, some external, which have to be taken into account in developing social competence.

Conflict, Confrontation and Compromise

Former students adopt a wide range of strategies to deal with conflict situations. Some seek to avoid conflict at almost any cost. One, when asked how she handles such situations, had a one-word reply: "Withdraw." Another answered, "When things cannot be resolved, I walk away from the situation if I can." A third person said emphatically:

> If it's a conflict of interest and ideas, I'm pretty ready to get into an argument over something that's just an ideal, but in a real confrontation, I like to try and just defuse and back down. I just don't like fights. I definitely don't like fights.

And still others avoid conflict by caving: "I am so non-confrontational in my personal relationships that I wonder if I'm good at negotiating, because I doubt that I'm even good at getting to the negotiation, at bringing things up"; or, more succinctly, "I give away the store."

The overwhelming majority of respondents, however, looked for ways to promote compromise. For some, it was a practical matter; an entrepreneur stated simply, "I deal with customers every day. You try dealing with the public every day, you'll learn compromise quick."

A recurrent theme was the extent to which respondents took pains to examine both sides of any issue in which they were embroiled:

I handle it by stating what my needs are in the situation and finding out what their needs are and then I'll say what I would be willing to do to meet them halfway and see if they agree. That usually works pretty well. It's fairly simple. In every situation.

For most things, if the person who I'm talking to has some reasoning behind what they're saying then I can usually find some kind of middle ground.

I am pretty good at negotiating compromises. I like to make a really strong argument for something, and I think that a lot of people don't make strong arguments. People bicker a lot, they yell back and forth, because they haven't formed a logical argument. I take an idea or an issue and try arguing it myself from both sides to see what I can come up with in the middle.

Another spoke of "trying to find a compromise, but at the same time not backing down; stating my position, and then trying to see what the other person really wanted and come to something that's, hopefully, mutually satisfactory." Someone else felt ready, albeit reluctantly, to yield to superior arguments: "I will tend to become fairly stridently attached to a position until someone can actually dissuade me." One ruefully commented, "A lot of people get very set in their ways and are not willing to listen to an argument. They will refuse to accept evidence that they might be wrong. When you are dealing with someone like that there really is not much you can do. You kind of have to give up and work damage control."

The ability to be even-handed in a dispute made many of them good mediators. As one put it, "I'm pretty good at playing devil's advocate actually, so I can mediate very easily. If two people have a conflict with each other and come to me for advice, I'm very good at helping them resolve that." Another "would go about defusing the situation by trying to make each person see the other person's point of view and trying to make them recognize that they're both coming to the same table, but just at different sides of it."

Often, the challenge in conflict situations is to set aside one's ego in looking for a resolution that works. "I don't have a strong pride of authorship in situations," commented one person. " If I feel that I am the best person to be making a decision on something, I will forcefully try to make that decision. But if I feel that someone else involved in the situation has more knowledge on the subject and can make a better decision, I will gladly defer to them because my interest is in having the best outcome." A person who manages a group was clear on this subject: "I'm a compromiser because I know I may not have the best idea. I tend to evaluate ideas based on merit, because it's to my own advantage."

For all the value they place on compromise, many former students felt that there was a line they would not cross in trying to find common ground with others in a dispute:

> *What I've learned is that everyone's got conflicting views and ideas about things, and a lot of times there's just no one answer. I think I'm pretty good at seeing both sides of things. But you can't be indecisive about things because sometimes you have to push your way through. There's this delicate balance of seeing everyone's view and being strong-willed yourself.*

> *Usually I'll present my point, listen to their point, and then argue for my point. But lately I've been trying to just see the other person's point and alter my point of view to fit theirs, unless it's something that I feel strongly about. Because it seems like people are way too critical over small stuff and pretty much everything's really small. But if it was something big to me then I'd present my point of view and make a strong case for it, even to the point of dropping it and coming back to it later and presenting my point again.*

Usually I tend to be non-confrontational. So if there's something that isn't a very important thing but could be confrontational, I probably won't bring it up. But if it was something I really felt was important, even though it might create some kind of conflict, I'd want to bring it up.

One former student wished he was better at meeting people halfway: "I like to be able to do what I want to do without having to negotiate with anybody. I'm not very good at compromising. I'm getting better. I realize what my shortcomings are and I work on them." On the other hand another, a long term student, had little use for the concept of compromise:

I don't necessarily believe in compromise. Compromise, at least in our culture, often is used as a way of saying that whenever two people disagree there must be a way to at least not anger both of them by finding something in the middle. I don't necessarily think that everyone has to be satisfied in order to be treated fairly. If all people are free to do something that is just plain wrong to do – hurting someone else, that sort of thing – it doesn't strike me that there's room for compromise.

Quite a few respondents did not find any need to turn away from conflict. As one put it, "If I have a conflict, I'll usually just communicate with whoever I need to solve it. I don't avoid it." Another said, "I definitely like to confront anything that's on my mind. If I have a disagreement with somebody, it bugs me until I get it out. I'm somebody that can get it pretty much out there right away, because I don't see a reason to let it go." For others, there was a distinction between personal and non-personal matters:

I wish that I could handle situations that come up with myself the way I can handle situations that come up with other people. I tend to get really wrapped up in something pretty quickly and can get pretty fiery about it.

I can be really good at [dealing with conflict] or I can be really bad. I was a family therapist. I definitely did that kind of mediating, but when it becomes a personal thing and it's your particular issue being thrown in your face, it's not always so easy. Sometimes, when a conflict arises, it sort of feels like "This is it. We don't get along." and it has a finality to it and what I keep finding over and over is that it's never like that.

When I'm at work I'm very professional and I don't generally have personality conflicts with co-workers. I am very comfortable communicating with patients, staff, people I don't really know; but I have a hard time with family and friends. It's when you get to know me a lot better that it can get more complicated. I think it's probably because there's more of an emotional kind of attachment and just a different level of what you expect from a person and the way you interact is different. So on that level I think I could actually be difficult to get along with.

What sort of role does anger fill in the lives of these people? Not much for the person who said, "Nothing makes me angry; I don't get stressed or angry easily." Nor, until he explodes, for the man who related that he "came from a family where you didn't deal with conflict until it reached the boiling point. So that has definitely been something that my wife has been very patient about in dealing with me. She is a person who wears her life on her sleeve and I'm a person who has that shirt locked away in the closet in the attic." On the other hand, this former student has put a great deal of effort into anger management:

I have a tendency to go for long walks, hour or two-hour long walks. I kind of just seem to let things run through and then I have to really take a deep breath when I'm talking to the person. I used to just cry whenever I would talk to them, no matter how much I thought about it or tried to think it was going to be fine and I was going to be calm. But now, for some reason I can just at least be present for the most part and deal with whatever is going to happen. Trying to say what I need to say is so hard that sometimes I just agree to whatever the other person's saying. And then trying to say what I need to say without being a bitch is even harder.

All in all, the picture that emerges from the responses is that of a group of people who by and large are not afraid of expressing their opinions, are not belligerent, and are practiced at accepting differences and compromising where necessary.

Parenting

Thirty eight of the respondents had children. Fourteen had one child, twenty had two, and four had three. There were also four who were expecting their first child. Figure 53 shows the age of respondents at the birth of their first child. Most of the alumni are starting their families in their late twenties and thirties, which is consistent with the trends in the general population.

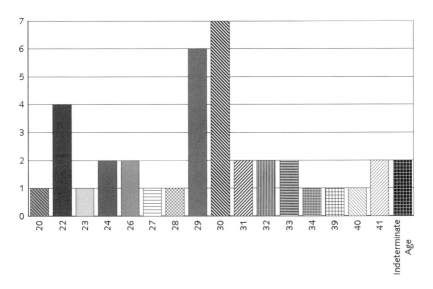

Figure 53 Age of respondents at birth of first child.

Figure 54, which depicts their age at marriage, is much flatter across the full age range; if anything, it is slightly weighted towards the early twenties. Clearly the age at which the respondents decide to begin families is independent of the age at which they decide to marry.

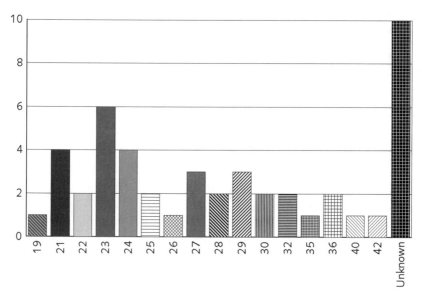

Figure 54 Age at marriage.

The comments of the respondents who had children revealed that they had given a great deal of thought to parenting. One person expounded at length on various aspects of child-rearing, covering a lot of topics that others mentioned as well:

> *I feel that I'm a good parent. I think parenting is difficult, and that at some level you disappoint your children no matter what you do. They always need you in ways which you can't necessarily fulfill because of time constraints, especially when you have two children, because a lot of times they both need different things and there's only one of you there, and so you can't really be there for both of them*

equally. When two parents are both there, well, one can get read to while the other gets played basketball with. But if only one of you is there, someone's going to have to compromise. That's just reality. I think if children know that you're basically there for them and that you love them, then they can deal with those compromises.

The older you get the easier it is to deal with not getting your way right away, but I think that when you're very little it's even hard to understand that you might have to wait twenty minutes to get something, because that's just not a block of time you deal with as a two year old. You deal with NOW, and so, to be told "well, wait 20 minutes" is not really reasonable for a two year old. They feel, "I seek something that I require and I am turned away." To me, it's about being sensitive to the fact that someone's powerless and has to trust completely in another person.

So you make a lot of hard choices, but fundamentally, my wife and I have gone to pretty extreme lengths to make sure our children are well parented. We made a decision for my wife not to work during the early childhood of each of our children. So for the first three years of our first daughter's life, she wasn't working. She was just with her full time and now our younger child is three and my wife hasn't worked since she was born. So they've had a full time mother for that chunk, even though that was an economically tricky decision. We prioritized it as important that one parent should be home to really be there for the child.

We feel like if you put a lot of time in it early, then the child is more independent later, that they're a healthier person. Our nine year old is quite independent, much more so than a lot of nine year olds. I think she pretty much bears out the theory that if you're secure early on, you actually end up needing much less attention later on because you're more of an independent person; you're not seeking approval as much. I think that is the goal of good parenting.

A respondent raising her children on her own showed the same concern about being present for them:

The reason I chose this job is I was just getting a divorce. It is very close to my home and I can keep regular hours and it gave me the flexibility that I needed in terms of what was happening with my kids at the time. I can leave basically at 4:30 every day. That is why I gave up the income that I could have earned; as a single parent I could not work the 60-70 hours a week that would have required.

Another respondent's comments reflect his profound respect for his children:

I think the best thing about kids is actually learning their point of view on the world and actually using that to your advantage. It makes a big difference to be able to get down to a two-year-old's point of view on the world and see it in their eyes, see the innocence and everything.

That same parent was keenly aware of his role as a model:

I feel like I'm a good person and if I instill the same values in my son hopefully he'll turn out like me.

Then there was the former student who expected respect from her children in return for the respect she accorded them, a point of view about child-rearing that she attributed to her experience at Sudbury Valley.

My kids do chores. They're not called chores, they're just their responsibilities. They're fine with it. They don't get paid for picking up their room, or for helping out around the house, or anything like that. They're just part of a community, which is our home, and they have to help out. That definitely comes from Sudbury Valley, from realizing that small children can be respectful, can be responsible, can control themselves enough not to hurt other people, can be sensitive to what's going on around them. They can be treated with respect and you can expect them to treat you with respect. All of that comes from Sudbury Valley.

We asked people where they found out how to go about raising their children. Some people couldn't quite pinpoint any particular sources of information: "Like most people, I learned from a mix of sources. I got some help from books, some experience through Sudbury Valley, some through parents and grandparents, some through people I met while traveling and observed parenting their children, just lots and lots of different sources." Most remembered particular ways in which they developed their style of parenting. Figure 55 groups the answers we received into categories.

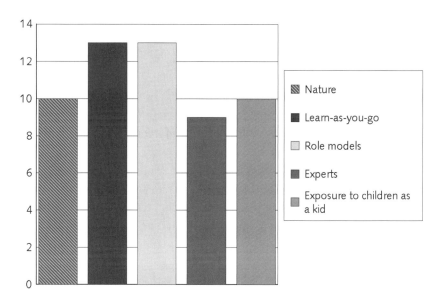

Figure 55 Sources from which respondents learned parenting skills. Several respondents cited more than one source.

Nature turned out to be a powerful factor for ten respondents. "I just knew my whole life that I was going to be a parent. I didn't know when or how or with who, I just knew it was the natural thing to do," was the way one expressed it. In the same vein, another commented: "Once I had kids, most of the time I just sort of do what seems like the best thing to do, you know? I didn't think about it much. It just came naturally." Another put it this way: "I did it by the seat of my pants. I really, really wanted to be a parent very badly and thought that I would be good at it. I love kids, babysat really young, loved to take care of friends' babies and so forth and just sort of came by it naturally, although I think it's a very difficult endeavor."

One mother recalled the transformation she underwent through pregnancy and childbirth:

> *Amazingly there's a little thing called hormones that helps a lot, when you're a woman. You start out being pregnant thinking, "I can't do this! I can't handle this! Oh my gosh, I'm not ready for this!" and then your body starts telling you, "Yes you are," and all these hormones start going. I really believe, from my experience of being pregnant, that nature gives the woman nine months – not just the child, but she gives the woman nine months – to prepare her to be a mother and to give her that time to nest and to read about it and study and talk to other moms.*
>
> *And then instinct just came out. I read Mothering Magazine. I breast-fed my daughter for a long time; we co-slept for a long time; she eats almost completely vegetarian, mostly organic foods. I guess most of it really is just instinctive on my part.*

Then there were those who said they picked up their style through experience, "trial and error," as one put it. " I wasn't trained, so it was pretty much on the job experience. I kind of would critique myself and watch other people too, and try to do things better when I thought I could improve."

Learning from experience, of course, involves learning from your children as well:

It just kind of happens. It's something that you make up as you go along, I guess. That's the way I feel about it. Just about every day when you have kids this young, it feels like you learn something new about how to deal with your kids and what's the best thing to do with them, with whatever instance you're trying to deal with, whether it be potty-training or trying to get them to eat their vegetables or explaining something that's happening in their world around them. It's on-the-job training.

His older brother, also a parent, put it this way: "I have everything to offer them and I have everything to learn from them. So it's pretty much a learning experience with my children and every day I learn something new."

And for one mother, enjoying young children was a new experience:

I had never been one to babysit. I never wanted to babysit. I didn't like little children. I never had that aching desire to hang out with kids and do that stuff. I knew that I wanted to sort of give to a kid what I received as a kid. I didn't ever change a diaper until my son was born. But, you do it. You do what you have to do, because you choose it. I chose to be a mom and, by hook or by crook, I was going to do what it took. Believe me, there's plenty of mistakes being made throughout this process. He's brilliant and he's wonderful. He's a great little kid. He's taught me a lot, that's for sure.

The respondents who cited role models as their source of inspiration often referred to their family, generally in a positive way. "I pretty much just had in my mindset the way my family raised me, and they didn't really do anything wrong," said one. He added, "I learned a lot of the compassion stuff from my wife because she's a very compassionate person."

Another is extremely grateful for the influence of his own upbringing:

> *Most of what I learned was from observing my own parents as they parented myself and my brother, who also went to Sudbury Valley. I've talked with people and really just observed people who I felt were good parents and saw how they handled situations and how they handled child-rearing. But I really think a lot of it comes down to whether a person had good parents themselves, because really, from what I've seen, most people raise their children the way that they themselves were raised. So I guess I just feel lucky that I had good parents.*

For one, his parents were the perfect negative model: "I learned from everything that I didn't like about my parents and everything I loved about my grandparents."

A sibling, as well as parents, played a big part for one person:

> *Probably I learned most from the role models in my house – to begin with, from the parenting I received. Also I have a younger brother who's seven and a half years younger than I, and my big brother and I played a role in parenting him as well. My parents parented him, but we learned how to take care of a baby and how to take care of a toddler and things like that in the family.*

Another felt that, "most significant is that I have a much younger brother. My brother is ten years younger than I am, so when he was born and growing up I was old enough to remember and notice what it was like to have a really little kid around. And I feel like that was the most significant thing in terms of evaluating how I felt about wanting to have kids."

In the early years of the school, several staff members brought their infant children and toddlers to school. Their presence made a deep impression on many of the students. The next quote is from a physician.

> *I've always paid a lot of attention to how other people parented. I would say that was probably one of my big interests when I was at Sudbury Valley, seeing how other people were raising their children and stuff like that. And it was something that I studied in college, cross-cultural child-rearing, so it's always been a big interest of mine. It definitely influences the way I raise my kids and how I counsel new parents who often want to do certain things but feel like they're not sure if it's okay.*

A graduate who, as a student, often babysat in several of the staff families, cited the different parenting techniques she observed as a source of inspiration. Another said this about the influence of staff parents at the school:

> *I think I'm a very good parent, and I think I'm a good parent due to the people at Sudbury Valley. Being around people there and seeing the way that they cared for their children, and the way that they cared for all of us, and about all of us, has made me a better parent. The one thing that I've done, that I get the most recognition for, is my parenting. It is the one thing that I'm the proudest of.*

People who cited experts as an important source of information covered a wide range, from one who studied child development at the Center for Early Education in Los Angeles, to another whose wife got a degree in Parenting from Goddard College, to others who fondly remembered a seminar they attended on the subject while a student at Sudbury Valley. One graduate whose child has a handicapping disease, acknowledged a debt to the child's therapists: "Actually you learn a lot about parenting from the therapists because you learn how to teach kids stuff, and how to get them to focus, and all the things that the therapists have to do. I learned a lot by watching them."

Most of the people who cited exposure to children when they were young as a major influence on their parenting styles made specific reference to their experience at Sudbury Valley:

I think a lot of what I knew was what I learned at Sudbury Valley School, just being involved in that multi-generational thing where you have the whole age range in one pool. There were never really any boundaries between age, so I think that in some ways you had kind of a mentoring thing, and that I think is what my wife and I try to do with our son – mentor him rather than teach him.

I really had very little exposure to young children until I had my first child. And most of the exposure until then was the age-mixing at Sudbury Valley. I had good close relationships with a lot of very young children at school when I was a teenager and that definitely helped me.

At Sudbury Valley I was exposed to, I lived with, and had as part of my community, a wide range of ages. That meant that when I was 15, 16 or 17, I might be in a situation where I was effectively caring for a much smaller person. Even though the relationship between the big kids and the little kids is not official, if there is a little kid there, somebody is supervising them, and it may not be a staff member. If there is a 10 year old kid and 5 year old kid, the 10 year old will look out for the 5 year old; and if there is a 15 year old and a 10 year old, the 15 year old will look out for the 10 year old, and so on. So there is that sense of watching and making sure that people are okay. A lot of the parenting I do really involves relating that way to a child.

The Sudbury Valley Angle

S udbury Valley's literature describes the school as an environment that is particularly well-suited for the development of social skills. Mentions of this aspect of their school experience popped up in many of the interviews, as we have seen. This is not so surprising given the age mixing, the open environment, the expectation of difference among people, and even the peer-oriented judicial system that are part and parcel of the school experience. Overall, many respondents felt that the school environment encouraged them to develop their interpersonal skills in a way that proved beneficial not only during their school years, but also throughout their adult lives. As one person put it, "I am really tolerant and I've pretty much seen everything. At Sudbury Valley, people were so completely different and what some people would say is really 'out there' just became standard everyday for me. Nothing surprises me anymore." Or, stated a bit differently, "At Sudbury Valley, you communicate with so many different people of so many different ages that I've always felt comfortable communicating with people. It's just come very easily to me."

Some credit their time at Sudbury Valley with helping them get over specific problems: "Before I was at Sudbury Valley I was a very, very shy person. I've gotten comfortable with talking to people, those I know and those I don't know. I'm a very talky person." Others were more general in giving Sudbury Valley credit: "Sudbury Valley was the best socially formative experience – that and live-action role-playing."

For one respondent, Sudbury Valley was critical in contributing to his ability to deal with teenagers at work as an adult:

> *I have a lot of teenagers that I work with. They can have teenager attitudes and that can be hard to deal with. I have to stop and think, "I've been there. I know what being a teenager is about. I know this is not really them." I think that Sudbury Valley helped me with that. Being with all different age people, interacting together all day, you get to understand you have to treat everybody equally, but you have to take age into account. A little kid might say something that you shouldn't really get offended by, or a teenager that you might get offended by, but then you think back and you say "Well, you know, they're just a kid, they didn't really mean that, they haven't learned self-control."*

In general, the atmosphere in school, when it was mentioned by the respondents, was seen as conducive to the development of tolerance, communication skills, and the overall ability to be fairly at ease with a wide variety of people in all kinds of settings:

> *I'm sure my level of comfort [dealing with people] starts completely at the school – starts out with this notion of being comfortable in non-hierarchical situations where everyone puts in their own contribution and makes the whole thing a community. I think the idea of a community, being as important to me as it is, definitely has to do with the fact that I grew up in a community. I grew up with this huge group of people that I felt were my friends; some personal friends, others just friends in that we were all at this same place that was important to all of us. That's a community: it means that you all agree that this thing is important and worth working towards.*

Perhaps the influence of the school's environment is best summed up in the following quote:

You learn mutual respect and caring for other people at Sudbury Valley because you're part of a social system which encourages you to think about the effect your actions are going to have on somebody else. It definitely fosters helping out other people and thinking about the community at large and not just about yourself. I think those values are fostered at the school.

Resilience and Flexibility

"I'm like water. If something doesn't work, I figure out another way to do it. I go around the rock."

Changes and Setbacks

We were interested in finding out what character traits our alumni brought into play when dealing with major upheavals in their lives. With that in mind, we asked them whether they had experienced any major changes or setbacks in their lives, and for those that answered "yes", we asked how they handled these changes. The following two chapters explore their replies.

We purposely did not probe into the exact nature of the changes or setbacks that respondents experienced. We felt that we were on the verge of invading their privacy if we were to delve into these areas. We focused our attention on the way they deal with these situations, in order to gain additional insight into their character.

Nevertheless, many respondents volunteered information about specific incidents in their lives that they felt were significant. We have grouped this information into three general categories, as shown in Figure 56.

A few words of explanation about these categories. By "internal" we mean events that were driven from within, such as major decisions that were made through personal choice rather than through some external force (for example, deciding to pursue further study, to move to a new location, or to seek a new job); problems with substance abuse; and advances in growth or maturity that, upon reflection, appear to be major turning points. As one person put it, "I don't feel like I've had any real major setbacks, just the ones I present to myself."

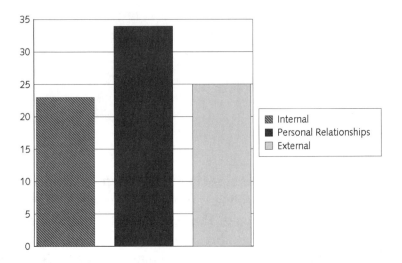

Figure 56 Types of changes and setbacks experienced by the respondents. Several people mentioned more than one category.

Under "personal relationships" we include life transforming events such as the beginning or termination of a long-term relationship; the birth of a child; or the death of someone important in their lives.

By "external" we mean changes or setbacks that were driven by outside forces and not the result of personal choice. Examples of this include being required to move to a new location for a job; problems encountered in the workplace or in the course of pursuing an advanced education (such as being placed in a difficult dormitory situations); or injuries received in automobile accidents (reported by three people).

It is very likely that similar experiences were encountered by other respondents who reported having major changes or setbacks in their lives, but did not tell us what they were. It is also important to remember that we are only dealing with people who reported having changes and setbacks that they considered to be major events in their lives. In all likelihood, there were respondents who experienced the same kinds of changes and setbacks, but simply dealt with them as part of the natural course of their lives, such as the person who said. "I would consider a setback something you never move past, and I would not consider that I ever had anything I didn't move past. Not that there weren't hard things to move past, but . . ."

Resources to Deal with Change

What inner resources did the alumni call into play when confronted with what they considered to be major turning points in their lives? We grouped the replies that they gave to that question into the categories shown in Figure 57. These same categories would surely be among those mentioned by any population sample when asked the same question. Notably absent, however, was any mention of repression, denial, sublimation, or even therapy – tools that many people use to deal with changes of fortune (and that some of the respondents may have used, but not mentioned).

Of particular interest in this figure is the distribution of the responses. Far more people identify themselves as using perseverance, trust and self-confidence than the number who make reference to the other categories. It is tempting to speculate that this is somehow related to the high value placed on these three resources in the educational environment of Sudbury Valley. One alumnus, talking about his ability to persevere, explicitly ties this to the school:

> *There are all sorts of resources that you can fall back on and when you're dissatisfied with something. There's always a possible way of changing. And so I just get back to work, knowing that if you work hard enough and go for something different or a change of direction you can always do it. Probably that dates back to the school.*

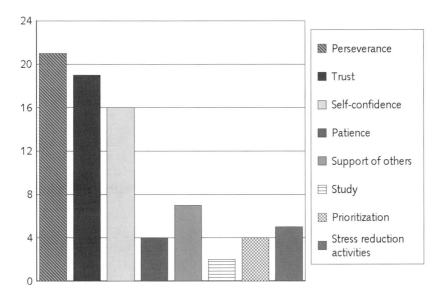

Figure 57 Resources used by respondents to handle major changes and setbacks. Some respondents mentioned more than one.

Another credits her perseverance to her parents:

> *I feel like I'm pretty adaptable. I handle changes pretty well. My parents taught me, "no complaining and you get through it." You do what you can to make your situation better.*

One person invokes it in his struggle with alcoholism: "I had a struggle for a long time, primarily as a result of alcoholism. It took me a long time to get a handle on it. I just kept coming back until I did it."

For many people, perseverance seemed to be a simple fact of their lives. Here are some sample comments:

> *I have a strong will. I just don't give up very easily.*

> *I guess I build up a lot of determination instead of just being sorry for myself.*

> *I'm definitely really dedicated and I work really hard. When there's an obstacle in my path I work harder to get through it, and I've succeeded so far even though it hasn't been easy.*

and:

> *I handle the challenges of life by getting up every morning. People that stay in bed, stay in bed. If you don't get up, your feet don't hit the floor.*

The people who invoked trust expressed a faith that the world ultimately permits a positive outcome. "There is not any certainty," said one. "I have this belief that there is always possibility."

Not everyone would share this alumnus' confidence: "A couple of times we were out in the ocean and it was just so scary, you had to close your eyes and say, 'Everything's going to be fine. I have to trust in the boat, I have to trust in the people who are driving the boat, and everything's going to be fine.'"

Another person had this to say:

> *I guess I've kind of just developed faith that the world is not going to fall out from under my feet every five minutes, and even if it does it's okay, you know? Things always seem to end up okay, or at least how they're best supposed to be, even if you're supposed to learn something.*

Or, in slightly different words:

> *I trust things will unfold in the way that's for the best, whether that means it presents a situation that's going to be uncomfortable for a while but you need to go through it for your own process of evolution, or*

whether you need to help somebody else through it. My inner resources are trusting, and being willing to take the actions needed – to take the risks – as long as it's for what feels like the right thing.

For one person, going through a painful separation, trust in God was his ultimate salvation:

There was a decent amount of depression going on and I knew that I had my friends there for me, and above that I just had to let time take it's course, because there was a union and then that union was broken. Time, of course, is a healer. Positive thinking does wonders. I prayed to God.

The people who said that they called upon their self-confidence when life buffeted them about expressed themselves with particular clarity. "I knew that I'd be all right. I knew I could handle it, because I know I am strong." "It's always there. I always know. I always feel confident, whether or not I'm scared or happy. I feel confident in my own abilities to make the best possible decision." "I handle a lot of things by building up an identity, a way of seeing myself as being a sort of tough do-what-needs-to-be-done kind of person."

Some former students illustrated their self-confidence with an incident from their lives. This young woman is an aspiring operatic singer who taught in an inner-city school:

The same thing that made me get up and teach a room full of inner city kids with handicaps, diversity, and special needs, when I was a new teacher with no experience and not quit, is the thing that helped me deal with the ridiculous things that have happened over the past year. When the shit goes down, something in me says, "NO! I'm going to do this." It's the same thing that makes me want to get out there and compete for roles in an audition. Obviously, you know you're going to get shot down. There are people out there who are older,

*and they've had more experience, but you have to get out there, and
you have to try. If I don't try, that's going to bother me.*

An alumnus who left school thinking he would pursue a career in
music, had to face an unsettling realization:

> *As far as the transition from music to a different career is concerned,
> what I relied on most was my integrity. My sense of integrity didn't
> match up with what I was heading into. The importance to me of being
> self-reliant didn't match what I was finding in the entertainment field,
> where you rely upon other people and other people's opinions to a really
> outrageous degree. I refused to let someone else control my fate.*

Here's a particularly striking tale:

> *One of the darkest periods I had was when I was pregnant, and
> then right after I had my baby, because my husband was out of work,
> I was out of work, things were really looking bleak for us financially.
> My husband then got a job, but he was working in a chain factory
> doing 12-hour shifts, and I never saw him. We were living near the
> beach, but I never liked that town. I never liked living there because
> it was just too chaotic and too frenzied and I never saw the color
> green – there were no trees there at all. The ocean was beautiful,
> but I was living right next to a biker bar and I was in this mindset of,
> "Oh, is this going to be it? Is this going to be my adult life? I'm not
> going to see my husband, we're going to be stressed, poor, and broke."
> Then I thought about it and I said, "No. I learned at Sudbury Valley
> that I can make my own future. I don't have to accept this; we can
> move forward." I just drew upon a lot of the knowledge that I kind
> of inadvertently picked up at the school, and then it was my decision
> to go camping for the summer. It was scary, but I said, "Let's do it!
> Let's just save some money by camping and be out in nature and leave
> this beach." Because we were there camping we got the opportunity
> for the store. And then again it was scary to go into that, but I just
> knew that I could handle it if I wanted to.*

As we have seen in Figure 57 (p. 293), the last five categories were mentioned by relatively few respondents. Several interesting comments were made by people who said that when faced with the necessity for major life changes they stepped back to examine their priorities. Here is an example:

> *What I've always done is try to pinpoint why I'm not satisfied or what it is I'm unhappy about and then try to figure out what I can do, if anything, to change that. How I can look at something differently or change what I'm doing in my life. Change the job if it was a job. There have been moments when I've been unfulfilled personally because I've dropped something that is very important to me, like photography, or like horseback riding. At these times, I realize I have to bring my focus back again and do the things that I love to do, to get that center back.*

A striking commitment to prioritization is depicted in the following account by a former student going away to school for the first time and faced with overwhelming financial pressures:

> *My first semester at college, I slept in the car for probably the second half of the semester because I had no place to stay. I'd wake up in the morning and I'd try to go to the gym where I could take a shower, and then I would just go straight to class. That was really hard, but I was happier that way than actually having to get up and do the same job every single day – get on the computer at work, do some drawings, do some animation or whatever they'd want me to do that day. Also I didn't like being bossed around. Since I was entry-level at my first job, they pretty much asked me to do things that I thought were completely ridiculous, and that I refused to do every time, which ended up resulting in the loss of a job. But that's alright. I wouldn't go that far just to make a few bucks, no way.*

This person faced a critical turning point in the course of her graduate work, which made her re-examine her priorities:

> *I had entered expecting to go for a Ph.D., which in the Humanities can be a ten year experience, even though you're hoping it will be more like six years. It can be a very long haul. People tend to take a very long time to write their dissertations. I just realized that the particular style of inquiry that was taking place at my university – but to be fair I think it was everywhere – wasn't really the way I wanted to work. So, I took a year off to say "Okay, well what about that? What do we do now?" and I concluded that the first thing to do would be to return and finish the Master's degree – which was, in effect, dropping out of the Ph.D. program. But it was, after all, a graduate degree and was something to show for what I had done. It was important to me because at the end of my first year, I was so unhappy that I almost ran away. I finished everything and I left.*
>
> *So it was important to me to come back to it, to find a way to cope with it on my own terms and to enjoy completing the degree. I definitely felt that I was there for a specific purpose. So I felt much more in control.*

The most moving depiction we heard of the struggles involved in confronting a major problem, and the resources called upon, is the following account given by an alumnus who is a graduate student studying foreign affairs:

> *I had some really rough years. The first four to five years when I got out of Sudbury Valley were very difficult. I am a recovering alcoholic. I've been clean for about seven years now and the first two years when I was trying to get my life back together, sober up and everything, those were very, very difficult times. I had been essentially cut off from my family, and I was living in really desperate conditions, making next to no money, and really, really struggling. So a few years were really miserable.*

Getting clean was probably the most major change in my adult life.

It's always easy to look at something like that in retrospect. When it's happening to you, you're not always very happy about it. You're ambiguous and you're a little bit weirded out by it. I think that I felt that I didn't have the choice because – well I had a choice – but I felt like my options were pretty crappy. I didn't want to end up a zombie, or with a needle hanging out of my arm, or living on the streets. And I didn't want to wind up in prison. I felt like shit. So I didn't think my options were so hot, you know? I felt like I was doing something that I had to do because I couldn't continue on the way I had been.

I am very satisfied with the way that I handled it. I tapped into resources I didn't know I had. I guess that's the best way to put it. A lot of it had to do with having an open mind. Having the will to have an open mind was very important – not placing restrictions on an open mind. Part of that had to do with my experience at Sudbury Valley. You were going to a pretty different school and so you developed an open mind, and that helped; but I also tapped into resources I didn't know I had. It's difficult to put into words, but I guess it's the ability to experience pain and then use that as a catalyst for change.

Attitudes Towards Change

Quite a few of the people interviewed talked about their mindset about changes and upheavals in their lives. We grouped their comments into the categories shown in Figure 58. These categories are, of necessity, somewhat amorphous and overlapping; attitudes by nature do not yield to sharp delineations. We have used colloquial expressions to characterize them. Taken as a group, they reveal various facets of the respondents' adaptability to change and determination to overcome obstacles. What struck us in particular was that no one expressed fear of change or a temptation to give up when faced with serious setbacks.

That there is no certainty in life was best expressed in this former student's words:

> I always realized that nothing has to be permanent, but nobody is going to change it for me. I have to do it myself. I mean, things aren't just going to fix themselves. So if there's a pattern to be broken or a change to be made, you've got to do it yourself. I'm satisfied with the way I've handled things.

Of course, uncertainty implies risk, but that doesn't have to be daunting: "Every major decision – like every time things get bleak – it seems that I'm presented with some sort of an opportunity to make things better but I have to be willing to take that chance and to believe that I can manifest it and accomplish it. So far, these feelings haven't steered me wrong."

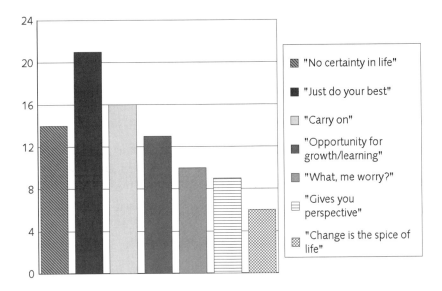

Figure 58 Respondents' attitudes towards changes and setbacks. Some people gave answers that fit into more than one category.

An integral part of doing your best is to not be plagued, afterwards, with second thoughts and regrets. This woman seems to have mastered that art: "I guess things all worked themselves out fairly enough. There are always things that you could have handled differently. 20-20 hindsight, right? It doesn't matter after the fact, does it?"

Sheer grit is what it sometimes takes to get through situations life presents you with – the ability to just plain carry on: "I just kept doing what I was doing until I finally started feeling better." Here are some other ways this attitude was expressed:

> *In most cases, what I would do is just try to get back to something I was familiar with, such as working and the personal contact that gives you, and as you're doing that, you keep your day to day life going*

smoothly, and after awhile the solutions come and you end up slowly working around and getting a new house, new partner, whatever it takes, and the pain goes away slowly.

I got a divorce. That was a change and I don't know if it was a setback ultimately. When you're going through it, it feels like a setback, but when there's some time and space between it, you realize that things work out and you move on. You just move on to something where you're happy.

It was definitely my choice to become a single mother. I could have stayed in a mediocre situation. I looked at that and I said, "No, I'm not going to do that. I'll venture forward and take the lumps as they come; this is the right thing to do." I know my son will gain from it.

This person has a more casual attitude:

I tend to just kind of roll along with whatever's going on at any given time. I'm not an incredibly driven person, to be honest. So most of the time I'll just go along with whatever's happening. I'll make modest efforts to try and dig myself out of whatever hole I'm in, but I don't generally take huge advantage of my lucky breaks either.

A particularly positive attitude towards the hard transitions in life was that expressed by the alumni who viewed them as ultimately beneficial to their growth. As one person put it: "I have gone through a really tough period and done a lot of healing and managed to come out of it really well. I have some good coping techniques and a lot of strength and resilience that I didn't know I had." Several elaborated at greater length:

My natural tendency is to question why I got married to this woman in the first place. So I could say I made a terrible choice, but I also think that I learned quite a bit from the whole experience. I could have learned all that without having married her, but that's the choice that I made and I try not to beat myself up over it.

I'm trying to look at it in the most positive way possible, because a lot of other very positive things in my life have happened that I think wouldn't have necessarily happened if I had not chosen to marry my ex-wife. I realized that there are just certain moments that help you realize what's important in life and this was one of them.

A lot of things that didn't go the way I wanted them to, but in retrospect, they helped me with that improving thing. You know what I mean? I learned a lot from the things that I went through that weren't necessarily a lot of fun to go through, but I don't think I'd have the character that I have now if I hadn't gone through them.

You're constantly changing, even though the foundation of who you are may stay the same. I definitely feel constant change, and I think it's important to go through. Sometimes it's just little gradual things and other times an experience might shine a different perspective on something. I think constantly growing is the most important thing there is.

The saying is, "Life is what happens when you're making other plans." To me – this is the warrior's perspective – there are no good and bad experiences, just opportunities to learn. So I've gotten my heart stepped on a few times in relationships, and there have been academic issues here and there, not big, but things to struggle through. Life is a struggle. I get into the struggle. I'm at my best when I'm into the challenge. Bring it on.

Ever since I was a kid I wanted to be a professional musician. I wanted to be a rock star as a little kid. Actually, in my thesis defense, one of the things I said was, "Rich or poor, famous or unknown, I will be a professional musician." I have thought about that a lot since then. "Oh my goodness, I didn't become a professional musician really and what does that mean? I said I would in my thesis defense." I think what I chalk it up to is that I learned along the way – as I started to know more and more about the industry and the life style – I started to grow as a person, I realized that was not necessarily what I really wanted. I loved playing music. I gave it my best, but by the end, I didn't really feel that's what I wanted. I feel that changed along the way. But, even so, even though intellectually I knew that, I definitely had a lot of problems making the switch from pursuing music as a career to doing something else and sort of putting it on the back burner. It was tough for a little while, but now that I'm through that, I feel like it's definitely the right thing to do and if I ever wanted to go back and do music again, in a more professional way, I would look at it in a totally different way. That I'm really happy about.

In addition, some felt that change gave them a new perspective: "Pardon the phrase, but when the shit hits the fan is when I'm the most calm and cool and able to take one step at a time in handling things, and see it from a different perspective. As my husband says, I may sweat the small stuff but when it comes to the big stuff I'm a pillar of sanity."

Then there are those who thrive on change, such as the alumnus who said, "I make a point of effecting major changes," or the ones who made the following comments:

I like change. I thrive on change, and as sort of a superficial example, moving into the house I'm in now is, I believe, the 21st time I've set up housekeeping in about 25 years; so you know, you do the math. People are like "Aren't you tired of it?" I like it, I like getting a fresh start. And I've lived in some nice places before. Even leaving the house I thought was the house of my dreams when I got divorced and tearing down my belongings from a 4-bedroom house to about 500 pounds so I could afford to take them with me, I really liked.

The influence that the school had on me is a lot more than you even realize when you're there. I think that the way that the school is set up, and the philosophy behind the school, sets you up for life.

It's a realistic version of what happens when you come out; I handle change really well. I'm pretty adaptable.

When people found out that my wife was pregnant, they'd say, "Wow, your lives are gonna change," and they said it in the most derogatory way, like you don't know what you're getting yourself into, or, just you wait. It was almost insulting, and my response always was, "You know what? I like change! I like things to change! I don't like to stagnate, I like things to move, and I like to discover and learn." Without change, life would be pretty damn boring. Watching that kid come out into the world, and experiencing that whole miracle – yeah, everything does change, and it's for the better.

Major Influences

"One thing that was very influential was a phrase my dad used to say. It was just something he'd say sometimes about an employee. He would say he liked someone because this person looks around, sees what needs to be done and does it, and I've always wanted to be the person who looks around, sees what needs to be done and then does it."

People

Even though we realize that there is no generally accepted way of objectively determining what the key influences have been in any person's life, we were interested in finding out what the respondents thought those influences were. When people tell you what they think influenced their lives in a major way, they are revealing aspects of their own personalities that they think are important.

The alumni talked about influences from several angles. They talked about particular people who had major impact on them; they talked about experiences that they thought were turning points in their character formation; and they talked about specific aspects of their character that they felt had been affected by some outside influence. This chapter will deal with the first of these subjects; the others will be taken up in the following two chapters.

In Figure 59 we have shown the various categories of people that were mentioned as influential. The Figure contains results only for those respondents who reported particular people as being major influences in their lives

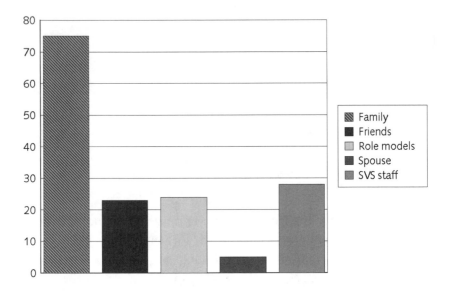

Figure 59 People respondents felt were major influences. Some mentioned more than one category.

A perfect example of a response that ranged over several of the categories in this figure is the following:

> *My mother and father absolutely always have been role models, and some of the staff that are still at the school who were founders had great impact on me, because they were doing something impossible and making it happen against the grain. And that's exactly what I wanted to do when I left school, with a vengeance. I have always, in all kinds of situations, thought, "What would Hanna say in this situation?" Trying to get into her head a little bit served me really well. I've got a lot of role models. I won't run through them all. But I do tend to, depending on what the situation is, try to put my head into, "What would Julia Child do in this situation?" "What would Jimmy Stewart say?" I do that and it just works well for me.*

Not surprisingly, the majority of the respondents talked about the important role various members of their family played. Several singled out their mother for special mention.

My mother has played a really big role. She's helped guide me, not so much with, "You should do this," but I can come to her and discuss things with her. She's not strict, so if I want to do something that she doesn't agree with, she has usually said, "Well, OK, but you'll probably regret it." And then usually I'll regret it. Now it's a little different because I've been working for a while and I don't spend as much time at home as I did during my teenage years. It's kind of become more of a friendship relationship.

My mother is really sort of my personal hero. She is a great parent and I try to emulate her in the way I treat other people, as well as the way I parent my own children. I don't think I'm as good at it as she was, but I try. My mother never raised her voice in our entire childhood, never raised her voice, ever. And I just don't know how many people you can say that about. She's a very nurturing person and an oriented-towards-other-people kind of person – kind and spiritual and ethical. A lot of things she told me, and philosophies of life that she has, I hold to be true now.

My mom dealt with cancer. She was given five years to live, and the bravery that went into that and the amazing courage – amazing. I don't have an ounce of courage compared to her. And she lived through it and she did it and she taught me some things about life, about courage.

Some singled out their fathers, such as the following alum:

I always used to think that I was right and that I knew everything. It wasn't until the last five years or so when I actually got married and started having issues, dealing with my wife's illness and then kids later on, that I realized that everything that my father said was actually right. I just kind of looked back on everything that my father ever taught me or did for me and realized that he was doing the right thing. I just didn't realize it at the time. That helps me when other people, who have more experience than me, and are older and have more knowledge, say something's right and I think they're wrong, to actually look and see why possibly they may be right.

Others talked about both of their parents:

I think my parents are big influences. Many of my values and my politics come from them but also, more importantly, how I feel about myself and how I have relationships come from them – even my mannerisms and the music I listen to. All of that I think comes from them. The foods I eat comes from them, everything.

My parents were always outrageously daring in doing exactly what they wanted to do, are just constant life-long learners, and live life to a very high standard of excellence and integrity. I didn't realize how profoundly it affected me until I was an adult and I saw how fearful and out of touch so many other young adults were with their inner passions – all these people who were going into things that they weren't really interested in just because it was safe and easy, and how different my value system and moral compass was from that.

The interplay of family and friends in this person's life as a teen enabled her to recognize her true nature:

I had a really good upbringing. I'm lucky. I have very loving parents, that's definitely part of it. No matter how I pushed their buttons, they were always really supportive of me. Even if they hadn't sent me to Sudbury Valley, there would have been some other way that they would have tried to bring me back into a place of personal power.
Sudbury Valley was huge. Sudbury Valley was really huge. Not just as a space or place or a system of beliefs, but the relationships that I had there have been so solid – the foundation of love, and the

friendships. I don't always see my own divinity, but I know when I look in the eyes of my friends from Sudbury Valley, that they do see it in me.

Another person's family purposely helped her create a group of friends that have played an important role in her life:

I have what my family lovingly refers to as a strong support network. My parents raised me with a whole group of parents and their children and I call them my surrogate mothers and fathers. I have a lot of very strong adult males and females that were in my life from the time that I was an infant up through now – people I rely on, people who are still in my life that have helped me in various different ways at various different times.

A musician recalled the effect a much older student had on him while he was attending school: "Mark Bell gave me my first guitar lessons, and taught me a lot about rock and roll and who was what. He was a major influence on me early on." An artist, who was eight when he enrolled at SVS, turned to older students for every facet of his education: "My major influences tend to come from mentor figures. That started at Sudbury Valley as a kind of mode of operation for me, taking advice from older people and really inquiring about stuff, and it continues now. Whatever situation I'm in I tend to find mentors, whether it's at school or in a job or whatever."

Another person appreciated the lasting impressions of someone who stood up to the system:

I have a friend who's a social worker, and she is a personal hero of mine because she is really super ethical. When you work for a big bureaucracy like DSS – often they ask you to compromise your values. Sometimes you kind of have to do it, because you're ordered to go against what your gut tells you to do with a person. This friend of mine got herself into a lot of trouble by saying, "No, that is inappropriate. I am not going to do that. I'm going to do it my own way." I try to emulate her.

It is not unusual for adults to talk about how their lives were impacted by encounters with certain teachers. Usually this impact relates to academic or career interests. When the Sudbury Valley alumni talked about the effect staff members had on them, it was in an altogether different context:

> *There are quite a few people who have had influences on me, and I can name them all right now – they would be all the staff members at Sudbury Valley. They gave me so many chances growing up. They were always so forgiving. I got into more trouble than just about anybody, but they always let me come back and they always treated me well. I have definitely come to appreciate that, and I did before I left. I had come to appreciate it some years before I left in fact, probably around the time when I was about twelve years old. They gave me the feeling that they still believe in me as a person, no matter what I've done. They still look at me the same way, and that makes me really happy.*

> *Danny was certainly a major influence for the years that I knew him. He was a pretty dynamic guy. I never was exposed to that type of person when I was growing up – not just him, but that whole group was pretty fascinating to me. You know, in retrospect, there are lots of people like that out there in the world. They're not a dime a dozen, but there are a lot of intelligent, creative people in the world. I just hadn't met any of them at the time. He was the first one I had really ever known who was at that level.*

> *Mimsy has been a major influence in my life because she's showered me with love my entire life and has given me a great deal of strength. She's very caring. She tries very hard to try to make you happy. She's a very good role model in terms of work and intelligence and striving, and working hard and achieving.*

For one respondent, the influence of staff and family were complementary:

> You can't really pin it down to a certain person because there was so much. The way the school was, when your parents aren't bringing you up, the staff is bringing you up. I was there from the time I was five and graduated at seventeen. So when your parents aren't there the staff are really guiding you and raising you, to an extent. There is a certain level of influence that they all had and certain things you took from each one of them. On the whole, there really was a major effect from each one of them.

Several people named role models who were particularly influential, and elaborated on the specific inspiration they provided:

> Cherry Jones. She's a big theater actress. She's been around; she's in her mid forties. She's been acting since her twenties. I saw her perform once, on stage, and I've seen her speak a couple times. She's a great actress, but she also seems like a genuinely nice person. And accessible. She is so not a theater diva. She describes herself as a workhorse. She just kind of goes where the work is. This is what she's interested in, and what she wants to do, and, she's very humble. I find that really admirable.

> In college I had some amazing influences: my choral director, Dr. Abercrombie, and Dr. Karpinski, my ear training and oral theory teacher. They were so musical and they were so steeped in it that without even trying, music just came pouring out of them. I really respected their intelligence and their expertise and also I really respected the way that they were able to effortlessly evoke the best in me.
> In the same way, my opera director right now, Tony Amatto, who owns the Amatto opera company where I sing, is also a huge inspiration. He's a master at his craft. He gets on stage and he can instantly transform into any character. When you see it demonstrated,

*suddenly you're like, "Oh, my God! That's the way it should be!"
He knows every word to just about every opera in every language.
He can sing it, he can conduct it and he can multi-task. He can be
directing the orchestra, the singers. He can be on stage, in the pit, it
doesn't matter. He knows all the cues, he knows every entrance and
at the same time, he has the presence of mind to pay attention to the
slightest detail. When I first started singing with him and I was in the
chorus and I was covering tiny little supporting roles, he really paid
attention to me. When I was on stage and the leads were on stage,
he would sometimes stop the action and come over and correct my
body posture, even though I was the smallest character. He told me
he saw something in me and he wanted to bring out the best in me
even though I wasn't the main character. I was so grateful to him for
that. He's an amazing man. My friends and I joke about it, how it
would be really funny if somebody made an opera production where
Tony was every character.*

Experiences

Alumni often singled out particular experiences as key influences on the course of their lives. For example, one person who undertook international travel at a tender age felt that this had a profound impact on his life:

> I was fifteen when I went to Europe for a summer. I was very young. Most people do a European backpacking trip from the U.S. when they're in college. I was fifteen and I was going around by myself with a backpack, which was just an awesome experience, very life-changing.

Then there was a former student who felt that Sudbury Valley prepared her for the kind of independence that enabled her to be open to extraordinary experiences through travel:

> I was at Sudbury Valley for fourteen years, so that was definitely an influence! I think a lot of that was learning how to be my own person, and being basically very grounded and independent, and kind of a problem-solver, because a lot of times you have to figure things out on your own at Sudbury Valley, so it makes you more proactive in addressing things that need to be done.
>
> Travel in general has been a huge influence on me. I think probably the most influential travel I did was when I was in Africa.

Up to that point most of my focus had been on environmental issues – at least my post-Sudbury Valley experience had been focused on environmental issues with my undergrad education and then also the work I did after that. Then I went to Africa and I started looking at things quite differently, from more of a human perspective. It wasn't the first developing place I'd ever been to, but it was certainly the most undeveloped place I'd been to, and that was in Eastern and Southern Africa in several different countries. In the U.S. it's very easy to talk about environmental preservation and conservation and stuff like that, but you go to Africa and people can't put food on the table or can barely get enough firewood for a cooking fire, and you can't talk about forest conservation. So that was a big paradigm shift for me which led me to go to grad school and to live overseas.

Another person was deeply affected by being in an environment where the love of learning was paramount:

Learning doesn't stop when you finish school; learning is part of life. At Sudbury Valley that's very evident – it's just part of life. I try to instill a love of learning in my children, and the ability to keep that desire for knowledge that you see in every three- and four-year-old, that sometimes gets pounded out of you in public school. It's something that I still have.

A musician recalled his early childhood experiences of hearing rock and roll, and the feeling that instilled in him:

I would say that without Sudbury Valley, I probably wouldn't have become a musician, because when I started going there, I was six, and it was the summer of 1968. Rock and roll was really kind of finding itself, and I was exposed to it at school. The first time I heard Jimi Hendrix, the first time I heard Led Zeppelin, the first time I heard Cream, Jeff Beck, the Beatles, the Stones – it made a huge impression on me as a kid, and pretty much led me to become a musician. It had a profound effect on me.

The overwhelming majority of the respondents – including most of those quoted above – pointed to their experience at Sudbury Valley as a major influence in their lives. The fact that they were aware that this study was being sponsored by the school may have brought their time at school to the forefront of their minds, but the intensity and clarity of their comments seem to reveal sincere, deep-seated feelings that go well beyond casual recollections. The following examples illustrate this:

> *I miss Sudbury Valley so much! I say this to everybody. That was the best time of my life. It had such a huge impact on how I developed and the person that I am now. It is really amazing.*

> *Well, I don't want to sound cliched – but the school was very important to me. My parents were divorced, my mom was depressed, things were screwed up in my life outside. The school was an opportunity to really think about life and it was an amazing influence. I spent 11 years of my life there, and I'm talking 8:00 in the morning until 5:00 at night. I hated when summer came around. I didn't want to not be at school.*

> *I had a lot of freedom to spend my time as I chose. I actually spent very large amounts of time wandering around in the forests behind Sudbury Valley School and around the pond. I had very meaningful times – either with other people or, often, by myself – just observing nature. It had a profound effect on me and generated a lot of the deep seated feelings I have about environmental protection.*

> *Had I gone through a traditional educational system, I think I would have turned out very differently. I think that my confidence in myself, and my ability to tackle whatever it is I want to tackle, in large part came from having been given the trust to shape my own education, and the trust that I would know what was best for myself from a young age. I never find myself in a situation where I feel like*

I don't have the tools to tackle it. Sometimes it takes a while, if it's something new, but I never feel like I don't have the inner strength and direction and ability to do whatever it is. That's a huge part of how I see myself.

Sudbury Valley School gave me a chance to really look inside myself and see what I was about. It also gave me a chance to learn about other people and how they act in situations when they're in control of their day, and they're in control of their life. I learned how to talk to people and how to communicate and in turn learned a lot from communicating with them.

Figure 60 displays the number of respondents who talked about being strongly influenced by various types of experiences. The Figure displays results only for those respondents who reported a particular experience as being a major influence in their lives.

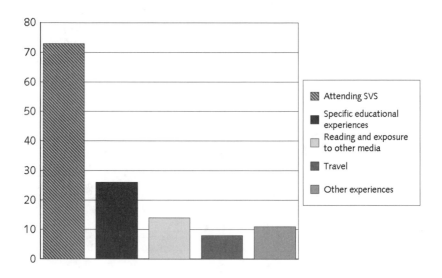

Figure 60 Experiences respondents felt were major influences. Some mentioned more than one category.

Domains of Influence

In the last two chapters we looked at what the alumni reported as having impacted their lives in a significant way. In this chapter we examine how the alumni felt their lives had been affected by the major influences they reported. We grouped their responses into several domains of influence, with results that are displayed in Figure 61.

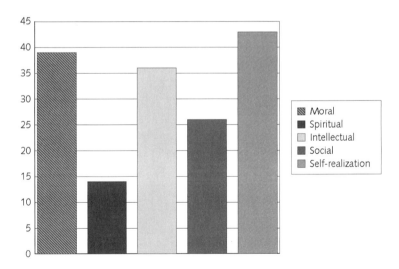

Figure 61 Domains of influence mentioned by the respondents. Several mentioned more than one domain.

We use the term "moral" here in its broadest sense; it refers to "judgment of the goodness or badness of human action and character," in the words of The American Heritage Dictionary. The following comments serve to illustrate the broad range this definition encompasses.

> *I probably drew most of my idealism from the early books and movies I saw and read – all the science fiction, fantasy, and heroism style stuff. So in terms of my attitude towards justice and ideals of fairness and so on, I drew a lot of it from reading* The Lord of the Rings, *and* Star Wars *and all of the books along those lines. I definitely believe in good aims and fairness when possible and all that other fun stuff.*

> *My parents and SVS definitely taught me to be independent, taught me how to think and how to be logical, think through things. Just that sort of thing. I think that's the most important thing there is: to be able to look at things in a clear way. Or at least do your best.*

> *A book by Helen and Scott Nearing made one of the biggest impressions on me. It is called* Living the Good Life: How to live Sanely and Simply in a Troubled World. *They're kind of the starters of the Back to the Land movement.*

> *One thing that was very influential was a phrase my dad used to say. It was just something he'd say sometimes about an employee. He would say he liked someone because this person looks around, sees what needs to be done and does it, and I've always wanted to be the person who looks around, sees what needs to be done and then does it. That has served me in good stead for about twenty-five years now. That was an influential phrase. Improve your situation.*

Quite a few people talked about the affect that certain experiences or people had on their religious and spiritual development. Here are a few examples:

I had a history teacher in eighth grade who introduced me to Taoism and Eastern philosophy; he was an excellent teacher. And then, when I was at Sudbury Valley, I started taking martial arts and Tai Chi. I continued taking classes and learning from the same teacher after Sudbury Valley. That was a really big part of my life too, such a big part I take it for granted.

My husband has been a major influence. I was pretty agnostic for a while and I always question things still. I'm not one particular religion. But he's very well-versed in all the world religions and he knows a lot about the other realm of things, the psychic realm, and he's kind of helped me to believe in a lot of other energies that I wasn't aware of before and to believe in my own ability to manifest.

There was a book that I read that really influenced me by Herman Wouk called This is My God. It was really the book that got me turned on to Judaism, so that was a big thing

In a curious turn of events, the very free-thinking atmosphere of Sudbury Valley led to a deep religious commitment for one respondent:

My religious faith is very important to me. I became much more Catholic than I ever would have been because I went to Sudbury Valley School. Everybody seemed to be Jewish or Unitarian, you know? At that time anyway, almost to a person. And I was Catholic. So when you're 15, 16 years old, there's a natural, pathological tendency to want to rebel. Becoming more and more Catholic was rebellion at Sudbury Valley School! I would read the Office during School Meeting. It was awkward. But yet, it was important because that immaturity actually led me to places of great depth and of maturity. And, who is to say how God works?

Alumni who talked about intellectual influences that they could identify made reference to books:

> *I always have read a lot, and I think that reading a lot has been a major influence. I like to read novels; for me, it is the closest you can get to being somebody else. That's one of the attractive things, that you can have some idea of what it is like to be somebody else;*

to the school:

> *At the school I developed a strong sense of focus that has worked well for me in terms of tackling new fields and being able to zero in on something and not be particularly intimidated if I didn't know anything;*

and to particular people:

> *There's a woman in New York City named Maggie Black, a famous teacher. I don't know if she's teaching anymore, but there are a lot of disciples of Maggie Black's techniques and philosophical approach, and I studied with some people in San Francisco who were offshoots from her. I think it's true of anything – when you're educating yourself in any sort of discipline you learn a lot from different people and at a certain point there's somebody that helps you make that whole thing gel and come together as a cohesive whole. Those were the people who helped me do it. I went through the San Francisco Ballet School and there were a million different styles going on and I remember going to auditions and just wondering, "Should I wrap my foot around my ankle when I do this move? Should I be in front of my ankle?" I just didn't know, because there are a bunch of different styles of ballet that you study, and I felt confused. Then when you're in an audition situation, you're trying to give them what they want and you're thinking, "I don't even know what it is, what they want." That whole Maggie Black thing helped me just put it together in one*

clean package and made me feel secure about how to do things. It really helped me take off as a dancer.

The area of influence most people talked about was that of self-knowledge, or self-realization. Given the centrality that this concept plays in the philosophy of Sudbury Valley and in the American system of beliefs, this should not be surprising. Some comments were brief: "Because there is so much freedom at Sudbury Valley, I had a real opportunity to have a look at who I am, my strengths, and to develop those for the first time in my life"; "I learned self-confidence at Sudbury Valley. I learned how to try different things and I learned my strengths and weaknesses"; "Sudbury Valley gave me the confidence to be comfortable in myself, and that's something I definitely lacked before coming to Sudbury Valley. I also became a fighter, or not so much a fighter but just an advocate for myself."

Others were more extensive:

Sudbury Valley was a major, major, influence. I really don't think I would be where I am now or who I am without it. I'd gone to private school before Sudbury Valley where there was such big age segregation. You know, the teachers were like Sir and Ma'am and I remember everyone laughing at me – nicely, but laughing – my whole first week at Sudbury Valley because I'd go up to Denise or Mimsy and say, "Excuse me, ma'am." And they'd be like, "My name's Mimsy." It was just mind-blowing to be able to relate, to have these adults talk to me like I was a human being, not that I was underneath them, but just like I was a regular equal. And then to have these little four year old girls coming up and talking to me so boldly, not bratty, but just, "Hey, I'm just like you. I deserve respect." It was just by being in that environment that I relaxed a lot and realized that in real life age is not important and it's who somebody is inside that matters.

We were all pretty well equal. There weren't very many of us at that point, but there really wasn't too much difference between us as far as any status was concerned. Everybody had their own say in any matter: I think this is one of the most delightful examples of something like that: A little girl got a complaint form and went to somebody – she couldn't write – to get that person to write out a complaint against Danny. And she won! Everybody was listening just as closely to the five-year old little girl as they were to Danny. It gave you a sense of belonging, equality. Your self-esteem was probably better. Mine certainly was a lot better.

Probably through my martial arts study, and somewhere else along the line, I got this peculiar feeling or belief that if I just try hard enough I can do better than everybody else at something. That's where I sort of get the drive to try and be the #1 student in philosophy, the #1 student at the university. I try and do as well as I can. I have the belief that if I just try hard enough I can probably do it.

I think the one thing I got out of Sudbury Valley was, ding! ding! ding! I got the clue – light – I am responsible for my own outcome! The day is good when I wake up. I can screw it up if I want, but I can do something good with it if I want. That was the main thing I learned at Sudbury Valley, I am responsible for myself. No one else is. That definitely stayed with me and will be imparted to my own kids.

As we have seen, references to SVS abound. We tried to isolate these references and to find out the areas of influence that the respondents specifically attributed to their experiences at school. Figure 62 displays what we found.

One student felt that SVS allowed him to get directly to what was important in his life:

When I was going through 6th grade, I was headed in the wrong direction. If you gave me a rule or an assignment, I would say, "Why?" and if it made sense, "Well, that's a cool rule. I like that. . . . I'll do it." But public school didn't have a lot of that. It was teaching me a lot of things that bored me greatly, and I've always been very poor at memorizing dates and numbers and things like that. I like learning concepts and ways to look things up. So whatever they wanted me to do, I wasn't going to do it. Sudbury Valley School came along and gave me absolutely nothing to rebel against, because every single rule was explained, made perfect sense, and I could understand that. There was a reason for it. It was logical. There was no point in rebelling against something that made sense. The laws of the school made sense. I stopped making that effort of rebelling. That probably saved me more than anything else, because I was able to channel into learning all that energy that I had been spending creatively rebelling against the system.

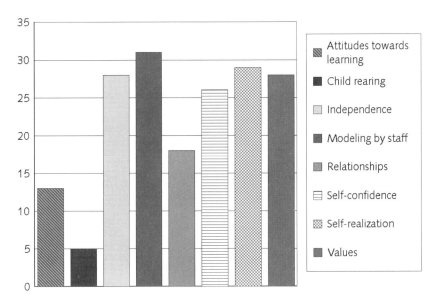

Figure 62 Domains of impact of Sudbury Valley School mentioned by the respondents. Several mentioned more than one domain.

The Pursuit of Happiness

"I think that I could sit back and be completely satisfied, but then I would feel kind of static and not be trying to do other things. In my center, I'm satisfied, but on the edges I'm always looking out for new things, and always trying to do all kinds of new and interesting things."

Do I Control my Destiny?

Students who attend Sudbury Valley are expected to be responsible for their lives and their community from the time they enroll until the time they leave. We were interested in finding out whether our former students had retained the feeling, nurtured during their time at school, that they are responsible for their life outcomes.

Figure 63 shows the answers given by the respondents to the question, "Do you feel in control of your life?"

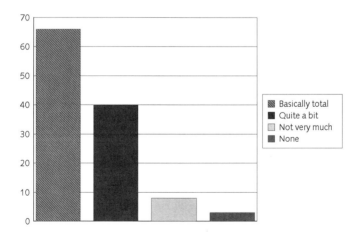

Figure 63 Amount of control respondents feel they have over their lives

Clearly, the vast majority felt very secure in the level of control they had over their destiny. Since this issue of empowerment is so central to people's sense that they can move their lives in a meaningful direction, and hence lead fulfilled lives, we thought it was appropriate to give a large sampling of their replies, which convey vividly the nuances of their attitudes.

A lot of people were concise, confident, and to the point. "I think I am in complete control," said one. "I definitely try hard not to blame external factors for problems I encounter, and I try to give myself credit for positive things that happen." Another said, "I have close to 100% control – at least 99%. I don't believe in fate so much. I feel like I control my own destiny." A third person, who had a great deal of exciting life experience behind him, found it hard not to knock on wood: "I feel pretty damn totally in control. But I do feel that there's a lucky charm here somewhere." A more recent graduate, struggling to make her way in theater, was emphatic: "I feel very in control. I feel like I'm doing exactly what I want to do. I know what I want to do, and I'm doing what I have to do to get there." This was echoed by another young woman, who is working full time as she completes her college education: "I think I can make any changes that I need to. I've changed my life to what I want it to be for now, and I feel that I can change it in whatever way I want to in the future."

Here are some fairly typical longer answers that fall in the category "basically total" control of one's life:

> I have every influence on where I go, what I do, and I've planned out every step of my career. I've set goals and reached those goals, and now I have to go through setting a whole bunch more goals because I reached my goals so fast. Everything that's happened in my life is the way it is because I made it that way. Obviously my wife has some part of it, because we're a team; but everything that I've done to this point has been my doing. It was even my choice to go to Sudbury

Valley. It wasn't like my parents said, "You have to go here." It was an option that was given to me.

I control pretty much all of my life, I guess. Usually, whenever there's something I haven't liked about my life, I've changed it myself. If I didn't like a job, I changed it. When we didn't like an apartment that we lived in, we changed it. I didn't like the friends that I was hanging out with, so I stopped hanging out with them. The only parts that you can't control are the instances that you have absolutely no control over – auto accidents, people dying, people getting sick, things of that nature – but not many of those things have happened to me in my life. So I feel like I'm driving the bus pretty well.

That's one of my problems – because I'd say almost 100% control, or very close to it. So any time anything goes wrong, I have nobody else to blame. I control where I'm going. You run into hurdles and stuff but, if you know what you're headed toward, you expect those. It's basically up to you. I take full responsibility for almost everything I do.

I think you are responsible for the way your life goes. You make your choices. I chose to leave public school. I chose to go to Sudbury Valley, and I chose to go to nursing school. I could have just hung out all day. I always have control of my life. This is why I had some conflict in my earlier years. I don't want anybody to tell me what I can or can't do. My mother hated Sudbury Valley from day one. But I was going there. I chose.

I feel I have the power to overcome any outside forces. There's no way that I feel like I have to be at a particular place and do a particular thing. There's always a way of changing things, so I feel totally in control of my life that way. I guess I'm fortunate that I have different talents and that I can always rely on them.

I feel like I can basically change anything at any point in time. The hard part is actually finding what it is that I want to change to, rather than actually changing it. For other people it's the other way around. I am not paranoid about change, and not about how I'm going to do it.

I control my life to a huge degree. That's what Sudbury Valley was all about. You could either take charge, or you could sit there, it was all up to you, and you were the only one who really influenced the way your life turned out, the shape your education took. The responsibility was all on your shoulders, and that certainly has paid off for me. Sometimes I want to give it up, sometimes I want to say, "Why me?" But you can't; you have to take responsibility for everything that happens to you that's not created by some unforeseeable outside force.

I have a lot of control. I'm really privileged. I went to a school that allowed me to be focused and aware of what interests me, and to be able to do something if I'm interested in it. I also have some economic freedom to do that, to actualize it, so I have probably more control over the course of my life than most people do.

I like the fact that I'm in control of my own destiny. I know that I pretty much can create my own path to fulfilment. I like what I do. I learned that philosophy early on. I don't know where, but somehow it just sort of came about long ago – figuring out, hey, if you want to do something, set your mind to it and think positively about it, and it can happen.

I found that anything I set out to do, I will do. This is one of the gifts from my mother and father, how they view people in their own healing work, and this is also how I view healing in the body: we create our world around us. The more time I spend with healing, the more I see it. In my opinion, there are no coincidences, there are no lucky breaks. You make opportunities for yourself. To me, anything is possible. The only limitation is me.

Over and over again, the same theme is struck: "I have a self-directed lifestyle with very consciously set goals and choices"; "I do think that there is such a thing as fate, but I think that I can influence it by listening to my own heart"; "The flow of my life is influenced by me all of the time. I am the flow! I influence my life, nobody else"; "I influence the flow of my life 100%, but then I give some of that flow away – to my family"; "I feel very in control of my life, because this is all by my design. I'm the only one who has made the decisions that have put me where I am"; and, in a nutshell, "Do I feel responsible for my overall fate? Yes, of course. Anybody who answers 'no' to that question is lying, aren't they?"

Many others, as the figure shows, felt they controlled their destiny "quite a bit." For example, one respondent said, "On a day-to-day basis I feel very in control. Existentially, I have no illusions that I have any control over anything." Others elaborated rather more on the theme:

> *I feel like when I decide I'm going to do something, I do it, but it never turns out exactly how you envision it. I had a vision when I was a child of what life was going to be like. I'm 39 now and it's completely different from that vision. You get to a certain point in your life when you realize that life's not going to turn out exactly the way that you planned it, and that's okay. You don't have complete control over your life and that's part of the fun. I just keep moving on, seeing where it takes me, and enjoying where I am.*

> *I feel in control of my life and in control of my destiny. I feel like if I want something to happen, if I want to make changes, I can do it. But I also feel like certain things are fate, or karma. I have a little bit of that thrown in. I can do my best at something and that's pretty much all I can do. If something's not going to change, then it's not*

going to change. If someone's not going to love me in a relationship, then I can do my best to make them love me, but if they're not going to love me, then I can't change that. But I feel happy and in control of my life.

It depends on the day. Sometimes I think I really take the bull by the horns and steer things in the directions I want to go in, and everything falls into place. But then I also sometimes think that there's a superior power that has been leading me. I honestly think that my mom, who passed away about eight years ago, has sort of been fueling my direction too. I will exhaust every aspect I possibly can to get what I want, but I'm also very open to the way things are. So I certainly can start in one direction and realize, through a process of being very direct and forceful, that's not where I should be.

I feel like I have a good handle on my life. But there are a lot of times where I feel like I'm not in control, and those are usually the most peaceful, languid times. I have an easier time making decisions when I'm not in control. I'm not religious, but I'm deeply spiritual. There are times when I feel insignificant, and those are the times that are peaceful and comforting. I find that they happen when I let them, really. Just as an example, I was so nervous about going out and applying for an architectural position, given my inexperience, that I was a wreck. And my dad gave me a Sufi prayer to meditate on. I had three interviews for my current job and every time I would go, I would say the prayer, and then I just had to go in and not let my fear or my nervousness affect my performance. I guess it worked. I can't really say that it was anything that I did.

Then there are the handful of respondents who replied that they really didn't think they had much of a say about their destinies in life, such as these:

A lot of people wind up getting along in life until they're 35, have had 3 kids, 2 marriages, a house they're putting up for sale, and they're looking for a third marriage. I mean, how the hell did they get there? We all just sort of stumble through life. A lot of things we do as human beings are things that our parents did, so the cycle continues.

If you don't take yourself out of the cycle, you wind up being where your parents are, through no fault of your own. It just happens. If you don't figure out how you got there, then you're screwed. That's as close as I can get to having inner resources.

I try to influence my own life. If you don't try to make a decision about something or do something, life's going to make a decision for you. Nobody has control. That's a complete illusion. I'm responsible for myself, and that's about as far as it goes.

I don't think that anybody actually can control their life, but I do think that it's possible to have a degree of control over the circumstance of your life so that you can increase the odds of an accident happening in your favor. I would say that at the moment I seem to be doing reasonably well in that regard, but not as spectacularly as I might like to.

When I do the dishes and when I do the laundry are the only two times that I can seem to have any control over my life. When I'm teaching martial arts I have some modicum of control as well. But outside of that I accept the fact that I just don't at all.

Amusingly enough, these last three respondents turn out to have lives that other people would consider to have been the outcome of a high degree of personal initiative and control. One is a business entrepreneur, one is establishing a dojo for martial arts, and one is a highly innovative artist!

Happiness

The overwhelming impression one gets from the lives of these former students is that they are, one and all, seeking happiness in their lives, in the classic meaning of the term: "a state of pleasurable content of mind which results from success or the attainment of what is considered good."[20]

Let's take one last look at the way the respondents carry on with their daily lives. They know the things that give them pleasure and fulfillment, and can articulate why they feel the way they do:

> I am very attached to the realm of activities which are usually classified as "academia". I always tell people that the main reason I went back to Sudbury Valley as a staff member is that I have never been in a more intellectual community in my life. I have never seen another place where people would talk about everything starting from first principles, and mean it – and not for grades. People are in the conversations because they want to be there. They're not trying to impress anyone with their knowledge, they're not trying to win praise, they're just talking about these things because they're so interested. I wanted an intellectual community, I wanted to be part of that kind of give-and-take, and I really have seen very little of it outside of Sudbury Valley, although I've been to a lot of universities.

---

[20] As defined in The Shorter Oxford English Dictionary.

For the last few years, I've had opportunities to do work solely because of intellectual curiosity – only to satisfy my own curiosity, whether or not other people read my papers. It's all motivated by intellectual curiosity. I'm not making a specific product. There's no product for lots of what I've done.

The most important things to me are the people I love, and the work that I do – being able to make things, actually. If you were going to torture me, you would say, "You can't make things!" Because that's what I do. I've always made things. Being able to be creative, being able to go into that space, that's the most important thing, because that's the way I communicate.

My family, my friends, and my art have always been most important to me. Artistic creation and the time that you spend with the people that you love are probably the two most important things in life. I'm much more cued in now to how creating the work that you need to create, creating some beauty, creating something interesting, is totally tied to the people that you love. I need to make stuff, I need to make interesting things happen. It's the thing that I do as an expression of my own humanity. Even if the only people I'm sharing it with are the people I love, those are the most important people to share anything with.

I've totally divorced it from outer ambition. I used to be, I think, more outerly ambitious. Now I've realized that my real ambition is to simply do really interesting work. The people who you actually know and care about are the people who see it anyway. If it spills onto a few other people, that's nice too, but you are fundamentally creating it out of your striving to break through your own barriers, to achieve your own excellence. You're never going to do more than a tiny slice of all the possible art that can be created. You do your own little slice as well as you can. You get out there and you share it with the community that you're in, which for me is now a pretty big community, because it includes a huge swath of the musicians in the area. So it's not just my family in the direct sense; I feel a kinship with a very large group of fellow musicians.

I'm passionate about work. I care a huge amount about my job; I'm always trying to make my job easier, and I'm always trying to do a better job. And I'm passionate about treating the people who work for me fairly.

I like being out in nature, walking. We live six miles from one of the Great Lakes, so I love going to the beach and hanging out and reading. I have a hard time separating what is leisure and what is work in my life. For example, yesterday, Sunday – we don't have anything that we have to do on Sunday, it's a day off – I was gardening, because it was really where I wanted to be, but that is also considered work. That also goes for my art. Sometimes leisure is just taking a few hours and going out and sketching plants.

I always like to be doing something interesting or engaging. I very much like to be engaged intellectually in what I'm doing, to one degree or another. Whenever I'm actually doing something, I like it to be something I can think about – aside from the occasional break for yard work, and even then I'll find myself tumbling numbers in my head or something.

I love the natural world and I really enjoy leading a simple and quiet life. I live among dozens and dozens of beautiful lakes in the foothills of the White Mountains, so I have access to almost limitless opportunities for hiking, canoeing, swimming, boating and fishing. The ocean is only forty-five minutes away, and if I want to be in a large mountain range, that's only a forty-five minute drive. Also, the quality of life here is wonderful. There's still a nice comforting sense of community, and yet if I want privacy I have that as well.

I value learning but not necessarily book learning. Book learning is really cool and it can be wonderfully useful and it also can be completely useless. For me, the process of learning is the thing that is valuable in itself.

I'm pursuing the study of Egypt, which is what I've wanted to do since I was a small child. When I was younger it was more of a recreational pursuit. It was an interest, and I would go to exhibits and watch TV shows, and I read some books, but it was more superficial. Now that I am focused in on it, I've gotten to know certain aspects much more in depth and started to define what it is within the field that I want to do. "Egyptology" sounds really specific, but within that you've got to specialize.

In most schools you have a track of language, a track of art, and a track of archeology. But religion is what interests me the most, which makes things a little more difficult because archeology and language and art all play into that, but there's no specific track dealing with religion. If I go to a place that's very heavy on philology, the language is really big – there are a lot of religious texts, so language is important. But so is archeology, because religious objects certainly matter. And the artistic aspect of religion is very important too.

I really love nature. I don't have any bumper stickers on my car; I don't fit into that kind of genre. I just really appreciate everything about being outside. My car broke down today and it was raining and it was just really nice to be outside! My wife is pretty much the same way. We are able to remind each other of that when one of us is faltering, when one of us is in a funk. It's a beautiful thing.

Overall, the alumni reveal in all their diversity a tremendous depth of satisfaction with their lives, together with a life-long striving for beauty and excellence. When the interviewers asked them to discuss how satisfied they were with their lives, many gave direct answers, which are displayed in Figure 64. Only a handful were not, and of those most were in the process of making changes to improve their situations.[21]

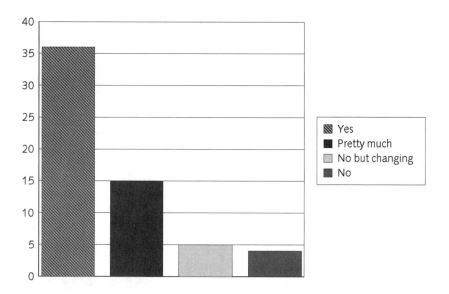

Figure 64 Respondents' satisfaction with current life

Let's close with what the interviewees had to say about their state of happiness:

> *I would say that I'm satisfied but I'm still seeking; I'm happy but it's not a done deal yet.*

> *I would say that I am satisfied to a point, but not completely. I think that I could sit back and be completely satisfied, but then I would feel kind of static and not be trying to do other things. In my center, I'm satisfied, but on the edges I'm always looking out for new things, and always trying to do all kinds of new and interesting things.*

---

[21] Of the nine who fell into these last two categories, one was a long-term former student.

I wouldn't say I feel fulfilled because I'm not really searching for that. But I'm as close to being fulfilled as I see I'm able to be. When I think of "fulfilled", I think of "done" – it's over, that's it. I feel like there's a lot more left. I feel like I need to stay hungry, you know what I mean?

I'm satisfied with where I am on the path. I wouldn't like to stop here – I'm not that satisfied – but I am satisfied with where I am at this time.

I think the greatest satisfaction is feeling that I'm living in the moment, that I'm not deferred, that I'm not thinking, "Oh well, things would be okay if this were different or that were different, or I wish I were doing this, or I wish I was like this, or I wish I had this", or whatever. I'm excited about the work I do and I have a great circle of friends.

Everybody has ups and downs. I mean, that's life. If it wasn't up and down, you wouldn't notice it.

For me, satisfaction is a very ephemeral thing. That's not bad, but if I actually remain satisfied for any length of time, I think it would impair my productivity. Having a certain level of dissatisfaction kind of keeps me moving.

How do I feel about life? I feel like I'm too busy and I want a break. But . . . I like my children, I like my friends, I like my job, I like where I live!

I feel great about my life. I'm a very optimistic person and I feel like we live in an amazing time and an amazing culture and it should be appreciated.

I feel life is very wonderful. I just kind of stop and look around and go, "Wow! How did I end up this lucky?" Sometimes I feel guilty, because I am so blessed when there are others who are miserable and sick and dying and stuff like that. Sometimes I have to stop and get over the fear that I don't deserve this and that it's going to just slip away.

I love everything about my life right now. I'm very happy. I like what I'm doing for a living, I love my husband, I love our house, I love where we're living.

I'm definitely very motivated and able to push through really hard stuff. So I would say my general outlook is quite good. It's a little strange right now being 23 and not having gone to college yet, sort of being in this limbo point of your life when everyone's looking at you and thinking, "What are you going to be when you grow up?" And you say, "I don't know but I'm having fun figuring it out." I'm living in a really interesting place. I've met a lot of really great people out here who are good souls and who like to do fun things and have interesting conversations.

It doesn't really get much better than this. I feel like this is the fun part of being 39. It is as if you have finally lived through the hard parts, and you're getting your stuff together, and you're doing things you actually want to be doing. That's the psychological picture. That is totally tied to the school; I feel it's a pretty natural outgrowth. In a very funny way, like for the particular place that I'm at in my life right now, the school was an oddly perfect education. I'm very oddly niched in my life vis-a-vis society. This isn't a job that there's a lot of. It's a little opportunity you make. It's exactly what, in theory, the school enables you to do. In my case, it just happened to enable me to do that very cleanly.

I would not go back and change anything, but I think that's what life is about. You move forward, you learn what works for you, and if it doesn't work for you, you change it.

I'm very excited about getting married. I'm with a lovely woman, so that makes the quality of life pretty good. And my job's pretty good, and I've got a house. I can't ask for much more.

I'm satisfied with my standard of living, my morals about living, how I live my life, and how I treat people.

And, to sum it up:

I'm extremely lucky. I'm one of the luckiest people I know. I fly by the seat of my pants, in a certain way, I guess because of my occupation, but I have lived in the same place for four years and I feel very stable and happy where I am. I've done a lot of traveling in the past and I travel with the work that I'm doing right now, so it's sort of up and down; but I also have a very set community in New York, where I live. There's this contrast between feeling very happy and stable about where I am, yet also excited about the future and kind of never knowing what's going to happen.

There are certain people who like to have a good hold on the future, have long term goals and really strive towards them. I feel I'm not like that. I don't need to know where I'm going. Maybe that's because I'm really in a happy, stable spot right now. I can picture myself doing this for a long time. It's always really interesting and growing and changing.

Over and over again, Sudbury Valley alumni reveal themselves to be a wonderful collection of human beings – contemplative, purposeful, clear, happy, and able to cope with change, challenge, and setbacks. More than anything, that is the message that kept impressing us throughout our involvement with this study.

Appendix 1. Additional Demographic Information

Family Situation While at School

Throughout the book we have been discussing the lives of alumni since they left school. In this appendix we have included some information about their backgrounds and their circumstances while they attended school.

Figure 65 shows the marital situation of their parents while they were at school.

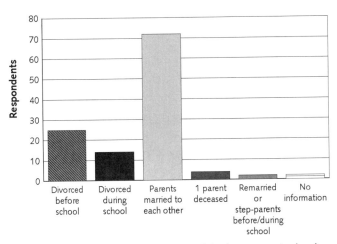

Figure 65 Status of parents of respondents while they were at school.

We also tried to find out from the respondents about their parents' level of education. Figure 66 shows the information available. Since many of the respondents were siblings, there were only 94 families represented in the survey.

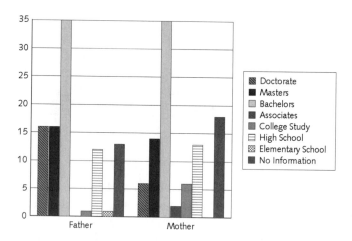

Figure 66 Educational level of parents of respondents.

In a similar vein, we asked about their parents' careers. Figure 67 displays the distribution of the responses we received.

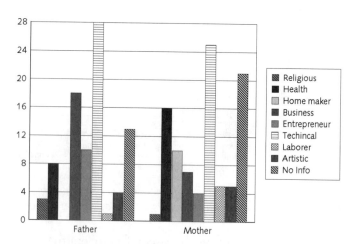

Figure 67 Career distribution of parents of respondents

Seventy-two of the respondents had siblings who also attended the school. Figure 68 shows the distribution of siblings for each of the 119 respondents.

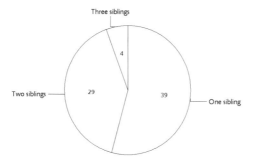

Figure 68 Number of respondents with siblings attending SVS.

Also of interest to us was the living situation of the respondents while they attended school. Figure 69 shows where they were living. Note that a person living with two parents was not necessarily living with his/her two biological parents.

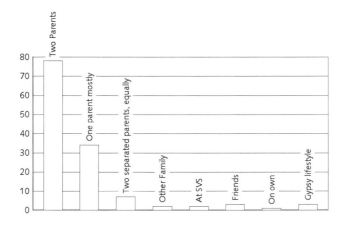

Figure 69 Living situations for respondents during enrollment at SVS

Does Having a Diploma Make a Difference?

The conventional wisdom is that a high school diploma is the sine qua non for a successful life, and absolutely necessary for entrance to an advanced education.

Of the 119 people in the study, eight did not receive diplomas from Sudbury Valley (or from another high school after Sudbury Valley). We thought we would relate the fates of these eight.

One went to college, left (voluntarily), and went on to a very successful career in computer programming.

One completed a Bachelor of Fine Arts degree and is a sculptor.

One is a musician and also successful in the business world as a manager and roving trouble shooter in a large chain of business service stores.

One went to college, went to Seminary, and is currently working on a Ph.D. He is also a writer of fiction.

One went to college, worked in the business world, and was at the time of the interview primarily a mother and a homemaker.

One, who was among the youngest respondents at the time of the interview, was attending college and had recently been married.

One left Sudbury Valley in order to continue her studies full time in a school of ballet, subsequently taught dance, and later became an event planner.

One went to college, graduated from medical school, and is a family practice physician.

The lack of a diploma did not seem to make the slightest difference for these eight respondents. In the course of these long, in-depth interviews, none of them mentioned any role that the lack of a diploma played in their lives. Indeed, it was clear that they think of themselves as leading satisfying, fulfilled lives. They considered their experiences at the school as being complete and positive to the same extent as those who received a diploma.

Having a diploma does not seem to be a necessary component of having faith in yourself and being as educated and successful as you wish to be.

Mobility

The respondents in our survey lived, while they attended Sudbury Valley, in 50 different towns. Their wide distribution reflected a pattern that has existed since the founding of the school, which has consistently drawn from a wide catchment area centered on Framingham.

It turns out that the respondents, after they left Sudbury Valley, have been a highly mobile group. Figure 70 shows the number of different towns the respondents lived in between the time they left school and the time of their interview.

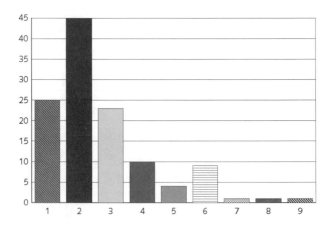

Figure 70 Number of towns respondents lived in after they left SVS

The alumni loved to travel, and made it a high priority in their lives. Figure 71 displays their travel experience around the world.

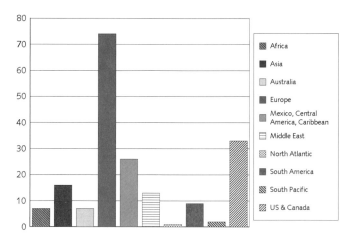

Figure 71 Regions of the world where respondents have traveled

Appendix 2.
Methodology

The interviews were conducted by three people, none of whom were affiliated with the school; most were done by one of the authors, Jason Lempka. They were conducted over the telephone, and tape recorded (with, of course, the knowledge and consent of the interviewees). The interviews lasted between 30 and 90 minutes, depending on the age of the respondent (and corresponding life experience), and on the extent to which the respondent wished to elaborate on their replies. The interviewers would, of course, follow up on the questions in the questionnaire (see below) as they felt appropriate.

The tapes were then transcribed, and mined for two types of information. Data of all sorts were extracted and entered into a database, with over 70 fields. This data formed the basis of all the Figures and Tables in the book. In addition, we chose segments of the answers given by the respondents to the various questions. We were eager to include as many verbatim formulations as possible, because more than anything we wanted the readers to experience directly the kinds of people alumni are, without the mediation of our interpretation.

The organization of the book itself reflected the organization of the questions, which, in turn, reflected the nature of the information that we were seeking. We were looking for a great deal of qualitative data that could flesh out pictures of the personality and character of the members of this varied group, in addition to the usual demographic information that describes the outlines of their lives.

This is the procedure we followed:

THE FIRST CALL

Purpose: To make an appointment for the interview, which will take from ½ to 1 hour; to introduce yourself

Will they do it at all?

If not, let us know; maybe we can find another approach to those particular people.

THE INTERVIEW: PHASE 1

DISCUSS TAPING

Is it OK to tape? Explain it's to help get the answer without delaying for writing, or paraphrasing.

If there are qualms or objections: we will be happy to send them the tape after it's transcribed or destroy it, and to send them a copy of the transcript to review and correct if they wish.

If they still don't want to be taped, say OK and apologize for it being a bit slower since the answers have to be written out.

PETTY DEMOGRAPHICS

Name
Address
Fax, email
Other phone number?

THE INTERVIEW: PHASE 2

PERSONAL DATA

Verify date of birth

Are you currently in a long-term relationship with someone? Have you been in the past?

[If yes:] How do you feel about your ability to form long-term relationships?

Do you have children? Specify. [If yes:] Do you feel you are a good parent? How did you go about learning to parent?
　　How have you chosen to educate your children?

How would you characterize your current lifestyle?

Where did you live when you were at SVS? Where have you lived for any significant length of time since you left? Where would you most like to live if you had the choice?

Have you traveled extensively? Tell us about it.

Media interests: What magazines, newspapers do you read regularly? What radio or TV shows do you like?

Do you go to/rent movies? What kind do you like?

Do you read books? What kind do you like?

Do you use computers at work? At home? How? Are you into email? Do you deal with the Internet?

How do you spend your leisure time?

Do you belong to any social, political or religious organizations? How active are you?

Tell us about your family background (e.g., what parents did, where from, what education they had, divorced or single parents, etc.)

THE INTERVIEW: PHASE 3

CAREER/ACTIVITIES

Did you have any formal schooling after SVS? Tell us about it (in detail, including length of time, names of schools, degrees if any). How did you get in? Was it worthwhile? How? If not, why not?

What important-to-you jobs have you had since you left school, or while you were pursuing your education? How did you get these jobs? (Get job titles if appropriate.)

Do you work now? What is/are your current jobs? Do you like it? Are you planning a change in the near future? Can you make a change now if you wanted to? (Why not, if not?)

How did you get your current job?

Are you preparing yourself for a major change in career down the road?

Can you live in a style satisfactory to you on your current income? If not, what do you want to do about it?

Do you have any other serious interests that you engage in, but not necessarily to earn money (although you might)?

[If they tell you they are academics, writers, musicians, ore artists, etc., find out whether they have published anything anywhere, written music, recorded, performed, exhibited, etc., - and follow up for details]

THE INTERVIEW: PHASE 4

THE WARMUP TO THE BIG QUESTIONS

SUBJECT MATTER: CONTACTS WITH SVS

Have you been in touch with SVS or they with you since you left?

Have you visited?

Have you received alumni newsletters or mailings (annual alumni questionnaires)?

Do you subscribe to the SVS Journal?

Were you ever part of a previous survey?

Have you ever gone to an event/picnic at SVS?

Are you in touch with other former students? Could you tell us who? Any of these recently, within the past year or two?

Are you in touch with current or former staff?

THE INTERVIEW: PHASE 5

THE HEART OF THE MATTER

WHO THIS PERSON IS (*WELTANSCHAUUNG*)

Fulfillment

Are you satisfied with your life these days? What do you like about it? What don't you like about it? Are you seeking a change?

How satisfied were you with your life during the various periods since you left school? What did you do when you weren't?

Reactions to changes and setbacks

Have you had major changes during your adult life? How did you feel about/handle them?

Have you had major setbacks during your adult life? [If this hasn't already obviously been addressed in the previous question.] How did you handle them? What would you have done differently if you had it to do over?

Are you satisfied with how you handle changes and setbacks?

What inner resources do you think you called upon in these situations?

Control over one's fate

To what degree do you feel that you influence the flow of you life (vs being at the mercy of powerful outside forces)? Are you satisfied with the level of control you now have?

Do you feel responsible for your overall fate?

Values

What is important to you in life? Do you feel your actual life reflects your values?

What kinds of things are you passionate about (both positively and negatively)?

Personal relationships (outside of family and significant others)

How comfortable are you communicating with other people?

Do you find it hard to get along with colleagues and acquaintances? Are you tolerant? Are you good at negotiating compromises?

Have you found yourself in personal conflict with others, and how have you handled such situations?

THE INTERVIEW: PHASE 6

MAJOR INFLUENCES

What do you feel the major influences have been in your life?

[If not included in the above answer:] Who have been the major influences on your life?

[If not included in the above answer:] What educational experiences, if any, have been important to your development?

Cover design by Christopher Bird
http://www.cbirdesign.com